RESEARCH METHODOLOGY

Theory and Techniques

RESEARCH METHODOLOGY

Theory and Techniques

(Including illustrative examples)

Jagadish R. Raiyani

Assistant Professor of Commerce,
Shree Maharshi Dayanand Saraswati MBA College,
Tankara, Rajkot, Gujarat.

New Century Publications
New Delhi, India

NEW CENTURY PUBLICATIONS
4852 / 24, 1st Floor,
Ansari Road, Daryaganj,
New Delhi – 110 002 (India)

Tel.: 011-4101 7798; 4358 7398; 98112 66355
E-mail: info@newcenturypublications.com

www.newcenturypublications.com

Editorial office:
4800 / 24, Bharat Ram Road,
Ansari Road, Daryaganj,
New Delhi – 110 002

Reprint: 2024

ISBN: **978-81-7708-294-4**

First Published: 2012

Published by New Century Publications and printed at Milan Enterprises, New Delhi.

Designs: Patch Creative Unit, New Delhi.

PRINTED IN INDIA

About the Book

Social research is an academic activity to explain, analyze, and understand a problem and find solution for it. A systematic approach of collecting, organizing and analyzing the information relating to a problem is adopted in a research.

Research aims at discovering new facts or verifying old ones to analyze their sequence, inter-relationship, and causal explanation to understand human behaviour. Therefore, the basic objective of social research is to understand and clarify the behaviour of man and the various forces or factors which influence him. Once the human behaviour is influenced, this affects the social institutions. In fact, in social research, the laboratory is the society and the objects are the human beings.

This book explains the methodology of social research. It is divided into two parts. Part I describes the various theoretical issues related to research, while Part II is devoted to quantitative and other techniques to reach meaningful conclusions to understand and solve social problems.

Author's Profile

Jagadish R. Raiyani is presently Assistant Professor of Commerce, Shree Maharshi Dayanand Saraswati MBA College, Tankara, Rajkot, Gujarat. He has published research papers in reputed journals including *Professional Banker* (ICFAI), *Yojana* (Planning Commission) and *Arthsankalan* (Kurukshetra). He has participated in many National and International level conferences. His research interests include accounting and finance, auditing and taxation.

Contents

Part II: Research Methodology: Useful Techniques

Preface

Research is a serious academic activity with a set of objectives to explain or analyze or understand a problem and find solution(s) for it. A systematic approach of collecting, organizing and analyzing the information relating to a problem is adopted in research.

Research should aid in understanding a problem and offering solution for the problem. While solutions for individual problems cannot be found out because of their heterogeneity, solutions for problems of groups of human beings could be attempted. With some homogeneity of members in a group, it would be relatively easier to analyze and offer solutions for the problems of the group. Again, these solutions may or may not be applicable to all the members in group. It is also an established fact that what is true of an individual need not be true of a society, but what is true of a society may be true and applicable to majority of individuals. Hence, while formulating policies for social problems, researchers always focus on group problems than individual problems. For example, instead of conducting research on the unemployment of one individual, it is worthwhile to explore the reasons for unemployment of a group of individuals. This approach to social problems is the crux of social research.

Research aims at discovering new facts or verifies old ones, to analyze their sequences, inter-relationships, causal explanations and natural laws governing human behaviour. Therefore, the basic aim is to understand and clarify the behaviour of man and the various forces or factors which influence him. Once the human behaviour is influenced, this affects the social institutions. For example, if sorry is considered as an evil in a society, then the outlook towards marriage undergoes a change. Similarly, when the joint family system is giving place to small family system, the number of old age homes and orphanages increases.

Therefore, social research helps to analyze and understand human behaviour which forms the basis for all decisions and policies. For example, research about unemployment, poverty, population explosion, etc., have far reaching effect on the behaviour of the human beings in a society. When these social problems are studied in depth then policies are evolved to minimize these social problems are studied in depth then policies are evolved to minimize these problems which in effect may improve the functioning of the social institutions.

In fact in social research, the laboratory is the society and the objects are the human beings. However, in spite of the complexity of human behaviour and a human relation, general pattern is always found which makes it possible to make a reasonable prediction possible. This is because the group behaviour can be predicted to some extent compared to individual behaviour. The social phenomenon is reflected to a large extent by the tradition, custom, values, etc, though they are all subjective. By using standardized techniques it is possible to measure even these subjective things in objective terms.

Rajkot, Gujarat
September 2011

Jagadish R. Raiyani

Part I

Research Methodology: Theoretical Settings

1

Meaning, Purpose and Approaches to Research

Introduction

Research is a serious academic activity with a set of objectives to explain or analyze or understand a problem or finding solution(s) for problem(s). A systematic approach: collecting, organizing and analyzing the information relating to a problem is adopted in research. A number of people question this meaning of research. But there is no formal definition of research available. This is because, one may be curious to know about something unknown adopting a highly informal method of collecting and processing the information. In other words, research need not always be considered as the area reserved for only academicians. There are instances when important facts are found even though no organized or systematic attempt is made to explore or investigate. Instances are also not infrequent, when findings which have no consequence or significance emerge out of serious and focused study. Therefore, it is very difficult to attempt a comprehensive definition of research. However, some of the following definitions may not be out of place.

Webster's new international dictionary defined research as, 'careful or critical inquiry or examination in seeking facts or principles; diligent investigation in order to ascertain something.' This definition simply states that research (i) is a purposive investigation or inquiry (that is, it has a set of objectives to collect and study about something) (ii) involves investigation or search.

According to Clifford, woody research comprises defining and redefining problems, formulating hypothesis or suggested solutions; collecting, organizing and evaluating data; making deductions and reaching conclusions; and at last carefully testing the conclusions to determine whether they fit the formulating hyper thesis. This definition simply lists out the research process and does not exactly state what research is.

The driving condition, driver's experience, traffic on the highway, advertisement hoarding kept on the sides, sand deposit on the road, reflector signs on the road, cinema posters on the side walls, etc. suppose the reflector paint used on the advertisement hoarding causes glare, affecting the vision of the driver, there is every possibility for an accident. Alternatively, the speed at which the van is trying to negotiate the curve might cause a drag resulting in an accident. Or maybe the sand deposit on the road makes it more slippery for a van moving at high speed. Hence, while ascertaining the causes for the accident, the traffic police would take into account all the factors and link them together. Similarly in the case of a doctor, while diagnosing a patient, he would take into account various factors and establish link between them. Hence, research is a disciplined exercise to establish or question the link between various factors and explain the unexplained phenomenon.

It is relevant to refer here how the philosophers of science connect these two stages as P–domain and C–domain. P–Domain is also called domain of protocol and the C–domain is called as domain of concepts. The P–domain consists of unconnected concepts, facts, etc., which remain isolated. These isolated facts or concepts are linked using logical interpretations. In other words some order is established among these isolated facts or concepts using logical deductions or derivations. Then all these concepts or facts gain some meaning, thereby a framework of inter-relationships among them emerges. Hence, in this task of establishing links among the various concepts and facts, one makes use of his own imagination, past experience, logical reasoning, etc to construct subjective mental images. Therefore, the characteristic nature of theory (C–domain) is to link various facts and concepts to explain a phenomenon (P–domain) which requires explanation and understanding.

Meaning of Social Research

Research should aid in understanding a problem and offering solution for the problem. While solutions for individual problems cannot be found out because of their heterogeneity, solutions for problems of groups of human beings could be attempted. With some homogeneity of members in a group, it would be relatively easier to analyze and offer solutions for the problems of the group. Again, these solutions may or may not be applicable to all the members in group. It is also an established fact that what is true of an individual need not be true of a society, but what is true of a society may be true and applicable to majority of individuals. Hence, while formulating policies for social problems, researchers always focus on group problems than individual problems. For example, instead of conducting research on the unemployment of one individual, it is worthwhile to explore the reasons for unemployment of a group of individuals. This approach to social problems is the crux of social research.

P.V. Young defined social research as "a method of studying, analyzing and conceptualizing social life in order to extend, modify, correct or verify knowledge whether that knowledge aids in construction of a theory or in practice of an art". According to this definition, social research involves application of scientific procedures of observation, analysis and synthesis to the social-human phenomena with a view to test, modify and enlarge the systematic knowledge about social facts and social life.

Therefore, such a type of research aims at discovering new facts or verifies old ones, to analyze their sequences, inter-relationships, causal explanations and natural laws governing human behaviour. Therefore, the basic aim is to understand and clarify the behaviour of man and the various forces or factors which influence him. Once the human behaviour is influenced, this affects the social institutions. For example, if sorry is considered as an evil in a society, then the outlook towards marriage undergoes a change. Similarly, when the joint family system is giving place to small family system, the number of old age homes and orphanages increases.

Therefore, social research helps to analyze and understand human behaviour which forms the basis for all decisions and policies. For example, research about unemployment, poverty, population explosion, etc., have far reaching effect on the behaviour of the human beings in a society. When these social problems are studied in depth then policies are evolved to minimize these social problems are studied in depth then policies are evolved to minimize these problems which in effect may improve the functioning of the social institutions.

In fact in social research, the laboratory is the society and the objects are the human beings. However, inspite of the complexity of human behaviour and a human relation, general pattern is always found which makes it possible to make a reasonable prediction possible. This is because the group behaviour can be predicted to some extent compared to individual behaviour. The social phenomenon is reflected to a large extent by the tradition, custom, values, etc, though they are all subjective. By using standardized techniques, it is possible to measure even these subjective things in objective terms.

However, even with these measurements, it is very difficult to establish causal relationship among social activities. It is in this context that social theories are useful to some extent as they help to arrive at generalization for broader application. It is to be also noted that the dynamic nature of human behaviour and human relations warrant a regular and repeated study of social problems and social activities. For example, in the past, there was little concern about the conservation of forests, water or environment, because people by nature were leading a life which was consistent with the demands of the nature. They considered all types of preservation and conservation as part of their duties. For example, a number of tanks and lakes used to be de-silted periodically to keep the water potable.

Use of plastics or non-biodegradable items was little known. Forests were preserved that seasonal rainfall rarely failed. At that time, there was no need for conducting social research on all these aspects. But today the situation is completely different, and serious research studies are undertaken by several organizations as well as governments to prevent any further misuse or deterioration in the natural resources like forests, water, etc. and pollution control norms are determined based on intensive research.

Similarly, the approach to social problems like unemployment, poverty, etc. has changed and continuous research is undertaken to identify solutions to these social problems. Hence, it may be said that social research is a continuous process as findings at one point of time will not be applicable at all points of time.

Importance of Social Research

1. Social research helps in formulating and guiding social planning. For example, by understanding the causes of rural unemployment, it is possible to create employment opportunities in the rural areas using the resource potential in rural areas.
2. As knowledge about working of the society and the institutions is acquired through social research, it helps to have greater control over the social phenomena. With increasing awareness of evils of dowry, public are now encouraged to report to the authorities concerned whenever there is any atrocity committed on women.
3. With social research better understanding and social cohesion can be achieved. Consequent to the understanding of ills of communal riots, peace committees, 'samathuvapuram' [where people belonging to different communities and beliefs live in an area], etc., were

attempted.

4. As social research analyses the problem in the 'total context' it is able to explain better the relationship among various complex variables. This helps in finding solutions for majority of the social problems. For example, by making people more aware of the consequences of polio type of diseases, it is possible to make people vaccinate their children against such diseases.
5. To limited extent, social research is able to bring some order among facts and thus provides the base for making reasonable predictions which in turn helps in social planning and control. Through wide publicity on the impact of population explosion, it has been possible to control the birth rate to a great extent and the objects of family planning projects are better understood.
6. Over a period of time, as the social phenomena undergoes changes the social research comes out with new solutions or modified solutions to solve the social problems, through improvements in the tools and techniques of research. For example, the approach to the acts of dreaded criminals is different these days. Instead of punishing them for their acts, efforts are taken to study the reasons for themselves turning out to be criminals and give them opportunities to change them and become useful to the society.

Purpose of Research

Research is a conscious approach to find out the truth which is hidden and which has not been discovered by applying scientific procedure. Therefore, each research has its own focus. This is stated in terms of objectives or purposes of conducting research. Objectives are like guide points in research so that the researcher does not lose his focus. As research is widely accepted as an activity with a view to find out something hidden or new, the researcher is like a person moving along an unchartered path. In such a case, the researcher should at least maintain his direction. This is made possible by clearly set objectives.

It is also believed that the objectives determine the nature of data to be compiled, the scope of collection, target group, sample size and several other crucial aspects which ultimately decide the success or failure, adequacy or inadequacy of research. Another view point is that anyone going through the theses or any writing would be able to place things in proper perspective in the light of objectives set by researcher.

For example, when a researcher specifically states though objectives that his study is about households in a society, any one reading the theses will not expect anything relevant to corporate sector or government. Though it may not be possible to generalize on the objectives of different types of research, broadly the following may be the purposes of any research study:

1. The research may be to understand or become familiar with some phenomena or to get to know more in depth about it. For example, since the days of steam engine, the research continued to come up with more powerful locomotive which could be operated with alternative sources of energy like diesel, electricity, etc. Similarly, the continued research to understand different aspects of the human physiology is another example to show how objectives are important to develop a focus.
2. To clearly reveal the characteristics of an individual or a situation or a group like a society is another type of research objective. For example, in these days, before a criminal is sentenced, efforts are taken to study why he had turned a criminal. This helps to develop an approach to create opportunities for criminals to change themselves and join the main stream of life.
3. To determine the frequency with which something occurs or with which it is associated with something else. Only recently, scientific researchers have come up with explanation for depletion of ozone in the air and how it is caused. Such studies have also indicated how the world

would become unsafe to live if the rate of environmental pollution is not controlled and stopped. Similarly, in social research one of the major areas of repeated and continuous research is analysis of poverty and unemployment.

4. To test a hypothesis about the causal relationship between variables being studied. This type of research is undertaken mainly to determine the relationship between various factors so that necessary policy options could be framed. For example, the reasons for several malpractices adopted in public distribution outlets include low salary and absence of regularization of service of the staff in such outlets. This in turn, makes them feel insecure and they resort to malpractices. Having found this, the government had taken a policy to improve the salary structure of these staff and regularize their services. Hence, the study of causal relationship might help in formulation of policies.

Approaches to Research

Approaches to research may be broadly classified in to the following four types: (a) historical approach, (b) descriptive approach, (c) case study approach, and (d) experimental approach. These approaches are adopted depending upon the nature and scope of research. Before discussing the selection of the approach, each approach is explained below.

Historical Approach: As the name of this approach suggests, in this approach historical data is given importance to undertake analysis and interpret the results. Following this approach, a researcher would collect past data for his research. This is accurate reproduction of historical events or achievements cannot be repeated, as is possible in the case of a scientific experiment. For example, one can only collect information about First World War and cannot recreate the First World War. But it is possible to produce oxygen in a laboratory any number of times repeating the experiments conducted in the past. A scholar using this approach has to depend on libraries for referring to the magazines or periodicals for collecting data. This process requires enormous patience on the part of the researcher. That is, he has to locate the sources of data, then study the data available, then select the data that he requires and then record the data available. Each one of these stages is time consuming. However, this approach enables a researcher to develop his understanding of the topic by analyzing the historical data.

A. Merits of Historical Approach:

1. Historical approach alone is relevant in certain types of research work. For example, to understand the trend in India's exports, one has to collect the export data for a period of say 20 years and then analyze it. Similarly to study the impact of the liberalization policy, one has to collect information from 1991 till date.
2. Historical approach makes research possible, as it is firmly believed that once we understand the past, our understanding of the present and expectations of the future could be predicted to some extent. Hence, historical approach provides the insight into the past and facilitates looking into the future.
3. Research problems which depend on historical observations can be studied only with this approach.
4. Under certain circumstances, the historical approach provides the background for solutions of some of the social problems. Unless the effectiveness of these solutions is known, they cannot be evaluated. On such occasions, the historical approach is the choice of the researchers.
5. A very important merit of this approach is the historical data are provided along with a number of related incidents or events. This helps the researchers to understand and interpret these data with reference to the situation prevailing in the past. Further, the historical recordings are made as seen or experienced by the researcher of those days. This is very valuable for evaluating the usefulness of the historical data.

6. Research activity involves continuity. To maintain this continuity, one has to depend only on historical research for example, India's struggle for Independence could be understood better only by studying the history from 1600 A.D.

B. Limitations of Historical Approach:

1. Personal bias of the people who had written about historical events or incidents cannot be ruled out. This would certainly distort the fact. Any use of such historical records would only mislead.
2. It is not possible for anyone to know whatever is happening at different parts of the world. So the relations explained through historical data are questionable.
3. Persons using this approach should be conscious of the fact that historical data can be taken to give any indication about the past, but formulation of solutions on that basis and applying them in the current period is not correct. This is because, the economic, social, cultural and other changes take place over a period of time. So what was applicable at one point of time need not be relevant at another point of time. Hence, comparison of the present with the past using historical approach is not correct.
4. Researchers tend to over-generalize their results using historical approach.
5. Subjective interpretation based on historical data cannot be ruled out. While objectivity in research is desired, subjective conclusions or derivations and inferences cannot hold good. But the subjectivity in social science cannot be ruled out because of the fact that the socio-economic variables are very complex and interpreted in different ways.

Descriptive Approach: This approach is one of the most popular approaches in these days. In this approach, a problem is described by the researcher using questionnaire or schedule. This approach enables a researcher to explore new areas of investigation. Normally, empirical problems are investigated adopting this approach. A researcher develops his hypothesis based on his knowledge about the subject matter of study. This helps him to define clearly the scope of his enquiry, the target audience from whom the information is to be gathered, and the time span available for conducting the enquiry, etc. When this approach is adopted, the researcher should be intelligent and alert to elicit the information required from the respondents as accurately as possible. He takes care to design his questionnaire.

As he goes into the field to collect the information, the researcher will develop insights into other aspects of the problem on hand and thereby he will be able to widen the scope of his study. For example, suppose a researcher wants to study the consumption behaviour of people in a village, then he collects information regarding the factors or variables that influence consumption behaviour. Based on this, he designs the questionnaire, determines the size of his enquiry, pre-tests the questionnaire, conducts the survey and collects the information. In the course of collecting the information, the researcher is able to observe a number of other aspects which influences the consumption behaviour of the people. This is used by him to widen the scope of his work.

A. Merits of Descriptive Approach:

1. This approach helps to test the conclusions and findings arrived at on the basis of laboratory studies. By using this approach, it is possible to substantiate existing theories and conclusions or modifying them.
2. Direct contact between the researcher and the respondent is brought about in this approach. This is very significant because, the researcher would be able to understand himself clearly the problem being studied.
3. With the possibility of direct contact with the respondent, the researcher is able to elicit all the relevant information and eliminate irrelevant facts.

B. Limitations of Descriptive Approach:

1. Unless a researcher is experienced, there is every

possibility of this approach being misused. Hurried conclusions and generalizations may be formed based on the inaccurate field data.

2. As this approach involves collection of field data, enormous time and efforts are required to plan and execute the field survey.
3. This approach also involves incurring heavy cost on data collection.
4. Unless the respondents are cooperative, it is not possible to collect data through this approach.
5. Since this approach requires considerable time for data collection, by the time the data collection is complete and analysis are undertaken, conclusions arrived at may not have any relevance.

Case Study Approach: Case study approach to research is a recent development. In this approach, the focus is on a single organization or unit or an institution or a district or a community. As the focus is on a single unit, it is possible to undertake an indepth analysis of the single unit. It is basically a problem solving approach. Therefore in this approach, a unit or an institution is taken for a comprehensive study. The finding may be used to address not only the problems being analyzed but also other issues of the single unit.

Suppose a researcher is interested in studying the problems of a two wheeler manufacturing companies, he might select one company which has a sizeable market share, say for instance, Bajaj Auto. Bajaj is manufacturing different categories of vehicles and suppose the research is notably about 100 cc four stroke motor cycle segment. Then the scholar studies the unit manufacturing different 100 cc four stroke motor cycles. He would not consider the other divisions of Bajaj Auto. He will collect information about the unit manufacturing the particular motor cycle.

He will study every aspect of this unit, viz., design, planning, marketing, finance, human, resources, training, training, purchase, orations, after sales service, spare parts, etc.

After studying all these, he will explain the reasons for the problems of this unit and also suggest solutions to solve these problems. In this sense, the case study is an intensive probing of a single unit or institution. The researcher has the independence to approach the problem on hand from any angle of his choice. This is no restriction as in the case of historical approach.

A. Merits of Case Study Approach:

1. As this approach involves a focused study, there is lot of scope for generating new ideas and suggestions.
2. It may provide the basis for developing a sound hypothesis.
3. New areas of research, hitherto unexplored, could be studied adopting this approach.
4. This approach provides scope for objective analysis.
5. As the researcher studies the problem from his own point of view, very useful and reliable findings may be obtained.
6. If the researcher is unbiased, thin this approach will bring to light the crux of the problems with which practical solutions may be developed.

B. Limitations of Case Study Approach:

1. A significant limitation of this approach is that unless the researcher is experienced, he might ignore very important aspects.
2. This approach also depends on the information furnished by the respondents. Unless the information is accurate, the conclusions are bound to be irrelevant.
3. This approach does not give importance to the past history or achievements of failures. But these are also very important in analyzing the problems of a single unit or organization.
4. It is often said that case studies are based on the observations of the researcher conducting it. So unless the researcher is well trained in applying observational technique, this approach may fail to bring reliable findings and conclusions.

1.5.4 Experimental Approach: This is a very scientific approach. In this approach the researcher first of all determines the problem to be explored or studied. Then he identifies the factors that cause the problem. He calls these factors as independent factors or variables. The problem to be probed is quantified and taken as the dependent variable. Then the researcher studies the causal relationship between the dependent and independent variable. Based on the findings, the researcher is able to specify the extent to which the independent variables included in the study explain the changes taking place in the dependent variable. He is also able to specify to what extent the dependent variable is influenced by each independent variable.

For example, food production is taken as the problem for a research study. Then the scholar would determine the factors that will affect food production, viz., size of land cultivated [X], rainfall [Y], quantity of fertilizer applied [Z], etc. These factors X, Y and Z are called independent variables. Food production [A] is called a dependent variable. Then by collecting data regarding all the four [A, X, Y and Z], the researcher is able to state what percentage change in the final food production [A] is explained by X, Y and Z. The effect of X on A, Y on A and Z on A is also studied. In this manner, the researcher is able to successfully indicate to what extent various factors included in the study are important.

This approach is very widely used in social sciences, because the causal relationships between various factors keep changing from time to time. Further, there is no scope for conducting experiment in social sciences. So by adopting the experimental approach, the relationship between variables is explained. The essence of this approach is for observing the effect on a dependent variable of the manipulation of an independent variable. This practice is often referred to as model building. Social scientists analyze under various circumstances, the relationship between variables by building models. These models may be either mathematical or econometric.

A. Merits of Experimental Approach:

1. This approach provides the social scientists a reliable method to observe under given conditions, to evaluate various social programmers.
2. This is one of the best methods of measuring accurately relationship between variables.
3. This approach is more logical and consistent. The conclusions drawn out of research based on this approach is well received.
4. This approach helps to determine the cause-effect relationship very precisely and clearly.
5. Following this approach, researchers could indicate clearly the areas of future research.

B. Limitations of Experimental Approach:

1. Unless a researcher is well experienced and trained in model building, this approach cannot be easily followed.
2. By relying more on models, this approach may not add anything significant to knowledge, except restating the same old truths substantiating them with analysis.
3. A serious limitation of this approach is that it relies on sampling and collection of data. Unless these are properly planned and executed, the outcome of analysis will not be accurate.

Review Questions

1. Write about the significance and scope of social science research.
2. Define 'research.' Why is it necessary?
3. Examine the limits and uses of scientific method in good research.
4. Explain what do you understand by a 'theory' and how [if at all] it is different from a law? Give one example from economics to illustrate.
5. What is the need for theoretical frame in research?
6. Explain the aims and objectives of social research.

7. Explain the role of concepts and operational definitions in scientific investigation.
8. Explain the importance and scope of social surveys.
9. Write a short note on 'fact and theory'.
10. Evaluate the importance of concepts in social research.
11. Discuss the purpose of research.
12. Explain the significance of analytical research in social science.
13. Explain the basic elements of the scientific method in social science research.
14. Do you think that empiricism is a viable method for social science research? What are its shortcomings?
15. What are the aims of social research?
16. Explain the aims and objectives of social research.
17. Explain the role of concepts and operations' definitions in scientific investigation.
18. Discuss the usefulness of social research.
19. Distinguish between experimental approach and case study approach to research.
20. Examine the merits and limitations of experimental approach to research.
21. Discuss the historical approach to research. What are the limitations in using it?
22. Explain the meaning of case study approach with an example? How is it different from historical approach to research?
23. Discuss various approaches to research.
24. Explain the factors that determine the selection of approach in research.

2

Steps Sequencing in Research

Research is a process. That is, it involves a number of activities which are carried out either sequentially or simultaneously. It is difficult to design an ideal research process as it would depend on various factors, like, the researcher and his ability, topic research, time available, budget allocation, etc. However, we can broadly indicate the various stages through which most of the research work would progress. The various stages are briefly discussed below.

Identification of Research Problem

It is said that research is an activity with a focus on something. This focus is the topic or the problem about which the research is conducted. Therefore, what is to be researched about is more important than research itself. In other words, unless a researcher has a problem to study about, he cannot conduct research. Therefore, identifying the research problem is one of the basic steps in research. Any researcher who has succeeded in identifying the research problem is half-successful. It is often felt that any problem is fit enough to research about, but unless a problem is systematically derived and identified, there is little prospect of conducting research on it.

Experience of researchers have clearly indicated how the entire process of research suffers if there is no systematic attempt to identify the research problem. For example, a research scholar approached a knowledgeable person and requested for a research problem. Based on the suggestion, the researcher worked only to end up with the finding that the problem ceases to be relevant. To cite another example, it is certainly not in tune to work on branch expansion of commercial banks, when the attempt is to identify the non-performing banks and merge them. Therefore, problem identification in research alone can decide whether a researcher is conducting research or not.

There is rarely any literature available regarding the procedure for identifying a research problem, while there is no dearth of literature on how to conduct research on a problem identifies. This is mainly because; there is no specific or formal methodology available to help in the process of identifying a research problem. It is in this stage that 'vision' plays an important part. But this is helpful only to those who have research experience and not to any person who enters the field of research. Unfortunately, the curriculum prescribed at the graduate and post-graduate levels in India also does not lend much in this connection.

Students are expected to mechanically learn something and reproduce them in the examination without even knowing the relevance of what they read. Therefore, when a person after his post-graduation studies, enters research, he finds a sudden big discontinuity in the academic process. There are instances when such students fling themselves ill prepared for research. On the other hand, in several western countries, before a person takes to research, he is made to work on a few term papers, prepare a number of seminar papers, etc. All these give a person the necessary training before embarking on research. Though a few institutions in India do insist on such publications before accepting a person for research programme, yet students do not have sufficient exposure or experience in identifying researchable problems. At the maximum, they only succeed in indicating a broad area of research like green revolution, self-reliance, poverty, unemployment, inflation, etc.

In this context, a pertinent question to be answered is that whether a researcher himself should identify the research problem or the guide should suggest the problem. Both these alternatives have their own merits and limitations. But it should be noted that the role of the guide is only to train the researcher in the methodological aspects of research instead of becoming a subordinate to the researcher and attend to every aspect of research. Further, a problem suggested by guide may not at all be familiar to the researcher. But when it is accepted, the researcher will be conducting research without any devotion or involvement. Sometimes, the researcher may feel that the guide imposes the research problem on him.

He develops an attitude that the guide will attend to all the stages of research and help the researcher earn the degree without much difficulty. In short, the researcher becomes dependent on the guide right from the first stage. To cite an example, a guide suggested a problem, which warrants application of quantitative tools. The scholar is completely ignorant of such tools or their application. But he accepted the problem suggested by the guide, thinking that the guide would do all the necessary analysis and interpretation. The guide was under the impression that the scholar would develop his analytical skill and carry out the research. After some period, when the guide reviewed the progress made by the scholar, he found that the scholar had nothing to report. The reason the scholar quoted was that he thought that the guide would do the analysis and interpretation! Such experiences are very common in the field of research.

Sometimes, the guide is so fond of certain areas that he would suggest only research problems relating to his areas of liking, whether they are current or out of date. A dependent scholar in such situation remains a mute witness and does not make any worthy contribution. Another problem in this approach is that it is ultimately the scholar who is answerable for anything contained in his research findings. So, depending on the guide, he would only make the scholar less original. Therefore, the response to this question: who should identify the research problem, is, that at the maximum the guide can suggest a topic for research, and it is the basic responsibility of the researcher to convert it into a research problem. This is because, a guide being fully aware of all the developments that have taken place in the topic suggested for research, could effectively discourage the researcher from taking up the beaten track or the uncharted path. Further, the guide would be able to make the researcher do a more focused work instead of straying into irrelevant areas.

Identifying the Research Topic

Therefore, the problem identification in research involves multiple steps. They are explained hereunder.

In the first stage, the researcher has to identify the broad area in which he would like to do research. This he can identify based on his interest and competence. Interest or inclination should be matched by his competence. For example, a person may be very keen to take a completely theoretical area or a highly quantitative area and if he has the necessary skills to manage with the theoretical area of research or possess the requisite quantitative base to undertake the research. One should be honest to evaluate himself to decide whether he has the required competence to manage such research.

Similarly, another tendency often noticed among the researchers is that they feel that their research work should end up with something which is celebrated as an extraordinary finding. They may feel that their work should become comparable with that of Milton Friedman, Keynes, and other notable economists. While there is nothing wrong in having such a view, the researchers should note that the recognition for several great economists did not come for their doctoral theses. Further, by being so ambitious, a researcher might ignore manageable research problem and end up with something, which is really complicated. It should also be noted at the same time, these days a research work is evaluated with reference to the methodology and the approach to conclusions rather than the revolutionary findings or original discoveries.

This is not to discourage the researcher from being

original. But for the sake of being original if the researcher is selecting an area beyond his capability; his research will not be completed. In this context, it should also be noted that the researcher should not feel that his work should turn out something useful to solve a social problem or economic problem. While the research should be valuable, and the researcher should have commendable motive, yet it is not important what a researcher says but how he says that and how he reaches the conclusion. That is, the ultimate suggestions are not important but the methodology of reaching such suggestions is important.

Assuming that a research area is identified, in the next step, the researcher should now narrow down to a topic. In this stage, he might take the help of the guide. A guide with a good grasp of the subject and experience can easily help the scholar. Further, the scholar should also read books, dissertations, journals, reports, seminar papers, etc., relevant to his area of research to zero in on a topic. During this process, the scholar would be able to understand the research work already done in a particular area and avoid any duplication. This will also help the scholar to understand the approach of the earlier researcher in identifying a research problem and the methodology followed by them.

Reading though all these sources of information would help the scholar to identify bibliography and footnotes. While the bibliography would give an indication about the sources available on a particular research topic, footnotes are the real source from which major researchable problems could emerge. Well researched articles or papers focus on a particular problem and by reading them, the researcher would be able to cultivate the habit of focusing on a problem and then blow it into major researchable area. Several research articles in professional journals are blown up at a later stage into books.

Instead of the scholar laying hands on whatever is available, the guide can put the scholar on the right track by making him select and read books and journals relevant to the research areas identified. It is also very useful to read though the surveys of research published by several agencies like Indian Council of Social Science Research. Several professional journals also carry research abstracts, commentaries on research, etc. which would also be a very useful source for narrowing down a broad area into a research topic.

So far, we have understood the procedure for identifying a research area. But the researcher should have the ability to convert the area of interest into a research topic and then identify the research problem. The ability to succeed at this depends on the grasp of the subject by the researcher. He has to be highly intuitive and use his technical competence to go through this stage of research. Hence, in this stage, the researcher will be alone characterized by his inability to communicate with his guide. He feels that his guide is becoming less helpful. It is at this stage that the researcher should intensively read books and periodicals.

Articles or papers which are relevant to his field of work should be read again and again so as to be familiar with the logical sequence, approach of the earlier researchers, etc. The researcher has to carefully digest these and then he would realize that he is reacting to what he read and understood. At this stage, reference to the past literature on the subject or the problem, would be of some help. It is advisable that the researcher lays hands on all the connected materials–right from the original article, to rejoinders, critical comments, remarks, evaluation, improvements, methodological issues, etc. This would give the researcher an idea about the possible developments that he can achieve in his work.

At this stage it is crucial that, unless the researcher is serious enough, he would be lost. This is like a person running with the moving train for some distance before getting into it. Hence, the researcher should read the relevant articles and papers and then note down his reactions, whether they are relevant or not, correct or wrong. In this process, he would be able to identify the gap in arguments, logical arguments, etc. Then he might work on these to develop his own research problem. He should give special attention to footnotes, bibliographical notes, etc. From this, he might be able to (i) reconcile conflicting views, (ii) substantiate some arguments for a theory, (iii) amend the earlier conclusions in the light of new facts, and (iv) carry out empirical examination of earlier conclusions, etc.

Based on all these efforts, the researcher would be able to narrow down his topic to a research problem. This process of moving from a broad area to specific problem is compared to two funnels that are joined together at the tips of their spouts, as opined by Dr. Kurien. From a broad framework, the researcher narrows down and then spends lonely period focusing on a specific issue. Then once he has crystallized the problem, he seeks evidences and supports to validate his conclusions. Then he attempts to apply his findings where he once again crosses the spots to enter into the broad area. What happens within the spouts of the funnels is a process of contraction and finally resulting in expansion.

It should be noted that the process of identifying research problem explained above, need not be taken as the only way to identify a research problem. This process would undergo change at different points of time and at different places. For instance, in the 60's and 70's in India, research used to be a challenging task with very little availability of data. But now, not only authentic and relevant data are available from various sources, a detailed analytical work is possible with the help of computers. The revolution in information technology has made the job of researchers more interesting and challenging. Attempts are being made to simplify complex areas of research. Access to authentic information is no longer impossibility. Transfer of information through electronic media or satellite technology has reduced the time required for compilation of facts.

Having identified a research problem, the next task is to

state the problem clearly. It is often said that half the research work is complete, when the research problem is clearly stated. It is at this stage where the researchers fumble and they need support. Possibly, the guide or colleagues of the researcher may be of some help. It is advisable first to state the problem in a very general way. Then the researcher should deeply study it to understand its nature. At this stage, surveying the available literature on the specific problem would be of great help. Then through a process of useful interactions, discussions, evaluation, etc. the problem could be rephrased and given its final shape. It should be noted that the statement of the problem would go on changing with every additional remarks and information, but at a stage, further filtering may not be useful. Then we could say that the research problem has reached its final form. Other important points to be considered at this stage are:

1. The problem should be stated in as precise a manner as possible. Avoiding ambiguous terms, complicated and uncertain expressions are advisable. It is better to state the problem in a quantitative form if it is possible. All the terms and concepts associated with the problem should be fully explained.
2. The assumptions required for the study of the problem should be listed out clearly.
3. The justification for the study of the problem should be spelt out detailing the importance and the usefulness of the study.
4. The period of study and the sources of data should be considered and indicated.

Once all these stages are completed, then the research problem is well identified and the researcher can pursue his efforts to intensively study the problem.

To explain the above process of problem identification let us consider the following example. Suppose a scholar is interested in taking up a research problem on unemployment. This is a very broad area. Now in a study on unemployment, there are several aspects that could be considered: rural unemployment or urban unemployment, voluntary unemployment or involuntary employment, unemployment among men or women, unemployment among educated persons or illiterates, unemployment among generalists or technicians, unemployment of persons below 30 years or above 30 years, seasonal unemployment or cyclical unemployment, causes for unemployment or effects of unemployment or solutions for unemployment, and so on. Suppose the scholar selects rural unemployment as his area. Then he should consider whether he should study this on an all- India basis or only for a particular state. If the focus is only on a State then whether he should consider all the districts or only one district. Suppose he decides to study the rural unemployment in a district, then how should he identify the geographical region where he could undertake his study.

Suppose he decides to take a few villages in the selected district, he should identify the types of unemployment prevailing in these villages. He cannot take all the types of unemployment, but select only one type. Suppose if he selects unemployment among artisans, again it may be necessary to specify the category of artisans about whom the study will be made. Accordingly, the scholar chooses the unemployment among the potters as his research problem.

The above example clearly indicates how from a very broad area the scholar narrows down to finally identify his research problem. It is not necessary that he should stop with this, he may still continue his efforts to identify a specific aspect of unemployment among the potters and choose that aspect as his research problem. From example, it would be clear that unless a scholar spends considerable time on reading about unemployment, he would not succeed in narrowing down, leave alone the identification of his research problem.

Extensive Literature Survey

This is a very crucial stage in research. It is in this stage that the researcher makes himself/herself familiar with all the previous studies and their findings relevant to his field of work. He learns the methodology and approach developed by these past studies. He evaluates the conclusions of the precious studies in the light of the data he has collected. He questions these conclusions and tries to develop the alternative, possibly better conclusions. At this stage, the researcher understands the latest developments in his field of work. This would help him to avoid duplicating the past works. He would also be able to take necessary precautions for proceeding with his work.

He would get information about the sources wherefrom he can get the relevant data, facts, etc. in a nutshell; the researcher at this stage develops an insight into the research problem.

Review of literature means the scholar presenting the review of all the previous studies, articles published, books published, etc. The scholar would normally classify this chapter into three or four parts viz. (i) review of journal articles, (ii) review of books, (iii) review of thesis, and (iv) review of reports. The purpose of presenting the details of the previous studies is to prepare the relevant background. Through this, the scholar would be able to state the findings of the previous study on the topic being researched by the scholar. While reviewing the previous study the scholar should focus on the objectives of such studies, concepts used, methodology adopted and the conclusions arrived at.

These conclusions may corroborate or contradict or contradict the ones arrived at by the scholar. The scholar should present the reviews starting from the earliest and ending with the current ones. This will give a clear picture about how the conclusion or the concepts have evolved over a period of time. The scholar should also take care to avoid any duplication and irrelevant literature. The scholar should not reproduce the article or the text, unless otherwise necessary for the context. Normally, such reproductions are presented through endnotes or footnotes. Always every article reviewed should be backed by the source.

While indicating the source, the scholar should follow the sequence: the name of the author, title of the article, name of the journal, volume number, issue number and page number, while reviewing an article from a periodical. The sequence will be different in the case of a book, viz. name of the author, title of the book, name of publisher, place of publication, year of publication, edition and page number. He should follow the rules with regard to name of the author, page number, etc. These are discussed in the topic on bibliography in this book.

Often the researchers used to dispute about the number of reviews to be made. While no specific number can be spelt out, it is always recommended that the researcher should review as many articles and books as possible. At the same time for the sake of achieving the number, the researcher should not be hasty to include all the irrelevant reviews. In this task the guide/supervisor's role is very important.

Developing the Hypothesis

Hypotheses are a statement developed on the basis of suspected or anticipated relationship among various factors studied. Normally at the beginning of the research, the scholar would formulate a working hypothesis with which he would progress with his work. Working hypothesis is a provisional statement which guides the researcher in limiting the scope of his study. It enables him to avoid collecting irrelevant data and facts. It helps him in focusing his attention on a particular aspect thereby eliminating wastage of time and resources. The working hypothesis can be formulated either in discussion with the experts in the fields of work, or on the basis of data and facts collected or review of similar past studied, or by making an initial investigation into the field of work.

Need for a Hypothesis: A question frequently raised by every researcher is whether hypothesis is necessary for every research. A broad answer for this question is 'NO.' Depending upon the nature of the research study, the need for a hypothesis will be explained. For instance, in studies concerned with the basic objective of finding out or explaining the relationship between two or more variables, hitherto unexplained or to be tested to prove, a hypothesis is certainly required. But research studies undertaken mainly in the form of an inquiry into the happening of an incident or an event or submission of report to the government or any other organization, etc., hypothesis is felt not necessary.

Because, in such cases, the focus or the objectives are well defined and so the researcher knows that he has to only report his findings. There is little scope for interpretation or denying what had happened. For example, if an inquiry is ordered about a communal riot or a firing, no hypothesis is necessary. Similarly, if Reserve Bank of India is organizing a study to examine the prospects of a new type of financial service offered by the commercial banks in the country, no hypothesis is needed. In all such instances, only the facts found are reported and no formal cause-effect relationship is questioned or examined.

However, even in such instances, hypothesis formulation may help to pin point the investigation or clearly define the scope of inquiry. Though the terms of reference are usually mentioned for an inquiry, the effort may be to spell out these terms of reference in terms of hypotheses. Hence, though hypothesis formulation is not a pre-condition for all types of research, yet considering the usefulness of hypothesis it is advisable to formulate it. The basic function of hypothesis is to provide a useful direction to the researcher. Similarly, it serves as a basis for future knowledge. As Goode and Hat stated, "every worthwhile theory permits the formulation of additional hypotheses. These when tested are either proved or disproved and in turn constitute further tests of the original theory". Hence, hypothesis is useful in the process of research though formulating it need not be a pre-condition for conducting the research.

Formulation of Hypothesis: Hypothesis formulation is one of the difficult exercises undergone by every researcher.

As hypothesis provides the necessary direction to the researcher it assumes significance. A researcher may form hypothesis based on the assumptions, observation, shrewd guess or profound hunch. After this stage, when the hypothesis has to be tested, it becomes difficult for the researcher. Based on his observation, a researcher develops an opinion and due to his interest he may collect data and analyze the same to draw conclusions.

After testing, if the conclusions are accepted, then they constitute a body of knowledge. If rejected, even then it is valuable. It is often said that if a researcher succeeds in formulating hypothesis, he succeeds in his research. In order to develop the ability to formulate hypothesis, a researcher should understand the characteristics of a good and usable hypothesis which are explained below:

1. The hypothesis must be conceptually clear. As Urine stated, "when the researcher attempts to establish relationship among various facts [domain of protocol] and translate these relationships in to concepts [Domain of concepts], he succeeds in formulating the hypothesis". Hence, when a hypothesis is conceptually clear, it provides a clear direction to the researcher. For example, suppose a researcher wants to find whether sex and industrial accidents are related. Then the researcher first studies the industrial accidents in an industry or a region or a country in terms of data collected. Based on the data behaviour, he might formulate a hypothesis about the relationship between sex and industrial accidents. Then he studies the relationship between sex and number of industrial accidents to confirm or reject the hypothesis. In this way, the researcher would be clear of his hypothesis.
2. Hypothesis should be amenable for verification and empirical analysis. Though hypotheses can be verified in terms of moral judgments, yet such verification process would be questionable. In simple terms, any hypothesis which lends itself for rigorous test with related data, could

be considered as a usable hypothesis. For example, hypotheses like 'educated people are more quarrelsome' cannot be so easily tested or proved. Similarly, a hypothesis likes 'increase in social crimes is a reflection of erosion in values' cannot be tested satisfactorily.

3. The hypothesis should be very specific and not a general statement. It should not be ambiguous and it should be clearly stated. It is wiser to construct a hypothesis in simple language than resorting to flowery and confusing terminology. Technical jargons should be preferably avoided in the construction of hypothesis. As is said, 'well begun is half done', unless the hypothesis formulated is in easily understandable form, progressing further in research on that basis would only cause confusion. Suppose, the hypothesis is 'sex and industrial accidents are not related'. It is very clearly stated and can be rested with relevant data. On the other hand, it is very difficult to test the hypothesis 'student indiscipline is due to syllabi which is out of date'.
4. Hypothesis formulated should be testable with the available technique of analysis. Even while formulating a hypothesis, a researcher should ascertain the relevant techniques with which it could be tested. Unless the researcher is familiar with such techniques, the hypothesis formed may remain untested. For this purpose, the researcher should review the literature to be familiar with the analytical tools and techniques related to the hypothesis formulated. There are a number of parametric and non-parametric tests of hypothesis available. For example, suppose a researcher is using small samples to test his hypothesis, he should apply only relevant tests like the 't' test. On the other hand, suppose the hypothesis is about the effectiveness of a medicine, then X^2 test may be used to test the hypothesis.

Hypothesis should facilitate establishing relationship with a body of theory. Guided by likes and dislikes, researchers often formulate hypothesis without examining whether the inquiry will help to oppose or support the existing theoretical basis. Therefore, when the hypothesis is formulated, the researcher should confirm whether it is related to any existing theory or not. This will help him to relate his finding to an existing body of knowledge. However, it is not unusual to come across researches which initially remain virtually separate pieces of knowledge and are subsequently linked with other theories.

Testing Hypothesis: In the course of developing the research work, the researcher may develop hypothesis and for this he has to test with the data available. He may use various statistical tools for the test of hypothesis. It is not to imply that every research work should have a hypothesis to work with. When a research work is completed and generalizations are arrived, they can be taken as hypotheses for subsequent research work. However, the researcher should know that statistical evidence is not conclusive evidence.

Preparation of a Research Design

This is a stage in which the researcher clearly spells out how his work is carried out. In other words, a research design is a description of conceptual structure within which the research will be conducted. Here, the researcher indicates the method of data collection, the skills at the command of the researcher, the execution plan for collection of data, the time and other resources available, the financial implications, etc. It may be noticed that the research design would undergo changes with every step of progress. It has to be kept flexible so that it can be modified as necessitated by changes. The researcher would indicate through the design whether he adopts experimental design or formal design. He would also state the purpose of his research work viz., descriptive, diagnostic, explorative or experimental.

Research involves a planned approach to unravel the mastery or unexplained. A researcher has to plan his work in advance so as to anticipate any obstacles in the course of research. Such a plan would also help the researcher to take decision relating to sample size, the type of data to be collected; the analytical tools to be applied, etc. Hence, a research design could be defined as the blue print specifying every stage of action in the course of research. Such a design would indicate whether the course of action planned will minimize the use of resources and maximize the outcome. Research design is the arrangement of conditions for collection and analysis of data in a manner that aims to combine relevance to the research purpose with economy in procedure.

Research design would answer the following questions:

1. What is the study about?
2. Why is the study being made?
3. Where will the study be carried out?
4. What type of data and where would it be collected?
5. What is the period of study?
6. Whether any sample would be used and if so, what type of sample will be used?
7. What type of analytical tools would be used?

Broadly, there could be four different types of research design, namely,

1. Sampling design–all the details connected with the sampling process, from the determination of sample size down to the collection of data, would be spelt out.
2. Observational design–if the study makes use of observational technique, then what type of observation technique would be used, conditions under which the observation will be made, would be indicated.
3. Statistical design–this part of the research design would spell out the type of analysis that would be carried out.
4. Operational design–this design would lay down the steps that would be taken at each stage as the design is executed.

Research design is necessary for every type of research as it helps to:

1. Make the research efforts fruitful.

2. Utilize the available resources in the best possible way.
3. Bring out the deficiencies in the proposed plan of action so as to correct it even before the action commences.
4. Determine the type of resources, like time, money, manpower, etc.
5. Prepare the researcher in advance for undertaking the complicated analysis.
6. Ascertain whether the course of action planned is in conformity with the objectives set for the study.

A good research design should possess the following features. However, the qualities of a good research design would differ from study to study. Broadly, the following may be stated as the features of a good research design:

1. It is flexible. As and when it is called for, the research design should be amenable for accommodating any change.
2. It should help to minimize bias at every stage.
3. It should facilitate collection and analysis of maximum information.
4. The design should be closely linked with the objectives of the study.

Types of Research Design: Research design may be broadly classified as:

A. Exploratory Research Design: This is also called as formulative research design. It aims at formulating a problem for more precise idea or hypothesis. Based on this, the subsequent stages of research could be planned. As this design is only of formulate type, it should be highly flexible. While applying this design, three different methods are followed.

Survey of related literature–by studying intensively the past studies and contributions relating to the field of study, the research problem could be easily formulated.

Conducting experience survey–this refers to undertaking collection of details and discussion with the experienced people in the chosen field of research. This would help the researcher to determine the extent to which he is original and can avoid duplication.

Analysis of insight stimulating examples is yet another method, in which depending upon the study on hand. In this method, the experience of people would be used as a guide to develop or formulate a hypothesis.

B. Descriptive and Diagnostic Research Design: Descriptive research design is concerned with the research studies with a focus on the portrayal of the characteristics of a group or individual or a situation. The main objective of such studies is to acquire knowledge. For example, to identify the use of a product to various groups, a research study may be undertaken to question whether the use varies with income, age, sex or any other characteristic of population. Similarly, such studies are used to examine the characteristics of the corporate sector or consumer behaviour etc.

On the other hand, the diagnostic studies aim at identifying the relationship of any existing problem. Based on the diagnosis, it would also help to suggest methods to solve the problem. In this process, it may also evaluate the effectiveness of the suggestions already implemented.

In this type of research studies, two methods are alternatively used, viz. case study method and statistical method. The former is a type of study in which the entire focus of the research is on an organization or a problem.

C. Experimental Research Design: The experimental research studies are mainly focused on finding out the cause and effect relationship of the phenomenon under study. Actually, when observation is arranged and controlled, it becomes an experimental study. An experiment is a test or trial or an act or operation for the purpose of discovering something unknown or of testing a principle, supposition, etc. It is a process in which one or more variables are manipulated under conditions that permit the collection of data that show the effects of any of such variables in an unconfused fashion. There are different types of experiments, such as: methodological, pilot study, heuristic, fact finding, boundary, simulation, theoretical, illustrative, etc.

The experimental design is broadly classified as (a) an informal experimental design, and (b) a formal experimental design. The former includes, after only design, after only with control design, before and after without control design, before and after with control design and exposit facto design. The formal experimental design would include completely randomized design, randomized block design, Latin squares design and factorial design.

Factors Affecting Research Design: Several factors play a key role in the process of constructing a research design. They are:

1. Non-availability of sufficient data: This is one of the basic factors affecting research design. A design developed at one stage may undergo change in the process of research, as data may not be available. Then the design would be suitably modified. To overcome this, usually researchers conduct a pilot study to ascertain whether the required data would be available or not.
2. Availability of time: In the research process, various stages are time consuming. For example, problem identification, data collection, analysis and interpretation, etc. require a lot of time. The research design would be depending upon the availability of sufficient time to carry out all these processes rigorously.
3. Availability of resources: Certainly the availability of human and financial resources will influence the research design. A study which requires highly specialized skill or experience, identifying such personalities would itself consume a lot of time. Similarly, the level of accuracy aimed at, would also call for liberal funding of the research process. Therefore, researches with ambitious objectives are usually undertaken only by organizations or with sponsors or by the government, considering the volume of funds required.
4. Ability of the researcher: Not every researcher is gifted

with all the qualities required for conducting a good research. A study which is highly analytical would call for knowledge about the analytical tools and the interpretation ability. Similarly, an experimental research would require a special temperament. Hence, depending upon the potential and ability of the researcher, the research design would be prepared. Several external factors like co-operation of the informants, literacy level of respondents, the social and economic conditions of the informants, the places or documents to be pursued, etc also play a crucial role in formulating a research design.

An ideal research design would contain the following details:

Clear statement of objectives of research;

Explicit statement of the problem to be studied;

Specific definition of concepts used in the process of research;

The method to be adopted being spelt out clearly;

The tools and techniques of analyses stated clearly;

Method of quantification, if required, is explained;

Clear cut description of the population included for the study;

The details of the sampling process–right from sample size to sample selection;

The data processing methodology being explained in detail;

If any pilot study or test is conducted, the result of it should be stated; and

A scheme of research report should also be stated.

Every researcher understands the term hypothesis in his own way. For some, it is the starting point of research. For some, it is the guide point in research. For some, it is an integral part of the research. For some, it is a mere statement to be tested or examined. Whatever way the term is understood, the term is invariably tested or examined. Whatever way the term is understood, the term is invariably mixed up with every stage of research, every person reads and experiences so many things in life, but only a few are bent upon probing such experiences to understand the relationship among various factors or variables.

There are also persons who go by their gut feeling about the relationship between various factors or variables. In the case of a few, they guess the relationship between various factors. For example, from his experience, an elderly person would be able to state that reason for more number of divorces is due to an increasing desire to be independent. Similarly, the small family concept has given place to an increasing number of old age homes. Increase in absenteeism in colleges is due to increasing unemployment among educated young men.

When such understanding is stated before being confirmed, it is called hypothesis. Once the understanding is examined and explained, proved or disproved, it becomes an accepted theory or a body of knowledge. Hence, hypothesis may be said to be a statement made in the process of an attempt to probe the content of the statement. We may refer to some of the following definitions on hypothesis to get different viewpoints about its meaning and content.

For Lundberg, a hypothesis is a tentative generalization, the validity of which remains to be tested. At the elementary level, it may be a mere hunch, guess, and imaginative data, which becomes the basis for action or investigation.

For Emory, when propositions are formulated or empirically tested, they are called hypotheses. Propositions are combinations of concepts designated by statements that may be judged true of false, if they refer to observable phenomena.

According to Goode and Hatt, hypothesis is a proposition, which can be put to test to determine the validity.

Karlinger stated that a conjectural statement of the relationship between two or more variables is called hypothesis. They are always a declarative sentence form and they relate either generally or specially from variables to variables.

Gopal defined hypothesis as a tentative solution posed on a cursory observation of known and available data and adopted provisionally to explain certain events and to guide in the investigation of others. It is, in fact, a possible solution to a problem.

It may be noted that in all the above definitions of hypothesis, the emphasis is on the above definitions of hypothesis and on the tentativeness or the suspected nature of the statement made. So any statement can be treated as a hypothesis. Once the statement is confirmed, it may become theory. At the same time, it should be noted that the theory accepted at one point of time becomes irrelevant at some other time. In such a case, a new hypothesis is born, tested and if accepted, becomes a theory.

For example, third degree treatment of criminals was an accepted practice in olden days to bring out the truth. But today, human rights commission condemns that approach. Similarly, the days of promoting senior persons to the higher position are gone and now a days, it is the performance and not the seniority, which determines the elevation in an organization. Similarly, the benefit principle of taxation has given place to ability to pay principle and indirect taxes have emerged significant than direct taxes. Indian government's approach to rapid economic development has shifted from administered and controlled system to liberalization. All these examples prove that in research, hypothesis is formed to question and determine relationship among various factors.

Determining the Sample Design

This is an important stage in research. Not every research can be a complete study of population. The researcher has to make a careful selection of a few elements from the population and then study them intensely and reach conclusions which can be safely applied to the population. The selection of sample is a very important task. The researcher should determine the size of sample, the method of sample, the tests of sample, etc. While a large sample would always be preferred, it is not mandatory. Among the various methods of sampling broadly classified as random and non-random sampling, the researcher should make a judicious choice. Then, among the different techniques of sampling, (viz. simple random sampling, restricted random sampling like stratified random sampling, cluster sampling, systematic random sampling, non-random sampling like convenience sampling, judgment sampling, quota sampling, multistage sampling, and sequential sampling), an appropriate technique should be selected and justified. If the choice of the size and technique of sampling is wrong then the study would only invite serious criticisms.

Collecting the Data

The researcher at this stage should clearly spell out the sources of data for his work. He could use both primary as well as secondary data. While the former refers to the data collected for the first time by the researcher himself from the informants or the sample respondents specifically for his work. The latter means the data already collected, published or unpublished and available for use. When the selection is for primary data, then it involves taking the following decisions:

The researcher should first decide whether to use observation or interview, or questionnaire or schedule to collect the data.

He should collect the data personally himself or appoint a few investigators. If investigators are used, then they should be trained before being inducted into the field.

He should design the questionnaire or schedule, pre-test it and then adopt it.

He should arrange for classifying, tabulating and analyzing the data after ensuring the quality of the field data collected.

If the choice is for using secondary data, then the researcher should always identify the authentic sources and then collect data from them. Whatever be the source of data, the researcher should plan the collection of data and then execute the plan properly. The quality of data collected will ultimately decide the findings of the research work and so the researcher should arrange for surprise checks and controls over the collection of field data. He should cross check the data collected and take steps to rectify any defects in the data.

Analysis of the Data

Once the data are collected, they should be classified and tabulated. Then the analysis of the data should be undertaken.

At this stage, the researcher should select the tools of analysis which are consistent with the objectives of the study. The tendency to carry out irrelevant analysis should be avoided. For example, just because the researcher is familiar with correlation does not mean he should apply it wherever possible. Similarly, he should be fully aware of the limitations of the various measures of analysis applied, so that when the results are carefully interpreted, he may select either statistical or mathematical tools. He may use the computer aided research analysis also.

Preparation of Thesis

With all the stages complete, the researcher should now attempt preparing the draft of his thesis. He should be familiar with the format of thesis and strictly adhere to it. The thesis should clearly indicate the justification of the study, period of study, sample size, sources of data, tools of analyses, bibliography, review of past studied, etc. It should also have a separate chapter on results and discussion where the researcher would report all his findings and give his interpretations. This should be followed by a chapter on summary of findings of the research work and the policy implications. Care should be taken to incorporate relevant tables, diagrams, etc. at the appropriate places.

The stages explained above constitute the detailed research

process. It should be noted that this process may vary from study to study but generally the research should be carried out in a systematic and scientific manner.

Review Questions

1. Briefly examine the stages involved in formulation of a research project.
2. Account for the major steps followed in planning a research project.
3. Explain the meaning and need for literature survey in research.
4. The selection of a topic for research is only half a step forward. Discuss.
5. How is research problem selected? Illustrate your answer with suitable examples.
6. Illustrate the issues involved in identifying a research problem.
7. Explain the points to be considered in the process of identifying a research problem.
8. Who should identify the research problem–the guide or the scholar? Explain the strengths and weaknesses of each source of research problem.
9. List the sources that should be referred in the process of identifying a research topic.
10. How does a researcher narrow down from the identification of a research topic to a research problem?
11. Discuss the components of a good research design.
12. What is a research design and what steps would you envisage in preparing a research design?
13. What is a research design? Explain the basic difference between formulative and descriptive research design.
14. List and explain the factors that influence a research design.
15. Discuss various types of research design.
16. Discuss the features of an experimental research design.
17. Explain an evaluative research design.

18. What is a diagnostic research design?
19. Discuss the components of a good research design.
20. What do you understand by hypothesis? How is it formulated and tested?
21. What do you mean by a hypothesis? Examine their nature and role in social research.
22. Enumerate the sources of hypothesis.
23. Discuss the need for review of literature in research.
24. Explain the purposes for which review of literature is made.

3

Sampling Techniques

Introduction

Statistics requires volume of data to analyze and interpret the results to arrive at a meaningful conclusion. Data may be collected though secondary source or primary source. When the secondary data cannot be collected, primary data should be collected. Primary data could be collected either by following the census method or the sampling method. The former refers to the collection of data from all the elements constituting the universe while sampling method refers to the collection of data from a few elements of the universe.

Population or universe refers to the aggregate of data source. For example, the number of trees in a forest is the population of trees, the number of cars manufactured by Maruti Udyog is the population of Maruti cars, the number of schools in Chennai city is the population of schools in Chennai city, etc. Hence, population need not be taken to refer only to human beings. Any aggregate from which data is collected is called a population or a universe.

Sampling is not anything, which is followed only in statistics. It is used in every day life. When rice is purchased in a provision store, a small quantity is initially purchased and tested. Sometimes, the small quantity is cooked and if it is found good, then the bulk is purchased. Similarly, when a patient has to undergo a blood test, the clinical laboratory takes a few drops, tests it and then gives the report. Imagine if the entire blood from a patient is taken out for testing, what will be the result! Sampling as a method is also used in research.

Suppose a researcher has to collect data regarding consumption behaviour of the people in Chennai city. It is obvious that he cannot collect the data from every person living in Chennai city. First he divides the Chennai city into different areas and then collects the number of people living in each of these areas. Then he decides to collect the information from about 10 percent of the people living in each area. This 10 percent of the people from each area will constitute the sample. By analyzing the sample data, the researcher gets some findings, which he uses for arriving at the conclusions. These conclusions are based on sample elements, which are drawn from the population. So if the sampling process is correctly followed, the conclusions based on sample would be applicable to the entire Chennai city. In an export-import business, a sample is used as the basis for deciding the business.

There is always difference of opinion in using sampling as the basis for data collection and conclusions. Those who argue against sampling state, that whatever care is taken in selection of sample, cent percent representation of population cannot be achieved. Further, there is always a possibility for exceptions in any population and how will the sample take care of these exceptions. There is also a danger of relying more on the judgment of one or few persons selecting the sample. Inspite of all these arguments, sampling has come to stay as a scientific way of analyzing the population. The operational problems of sampling can easily be solved and these problems need not discourage any one from using it.

Laws of Sampling

The following are the two laws of sampling:

1. Law of statistical regularity.
2. Law of inertia of large numbers.

Law of Statistical Regularity: According to the law of statistical regularity, when a moderately large number of items are chosen at random from a large group, the sample would almost on an average possess the characteristics of a large group. That is larger the sample, greater is the representativeness of the sample. In other words, a large sample selected from population would certainly represent better features of the population than a small sample. For example, suppose a researcher has to collect sample data regarding consumption behaviour of people in the Chennai city and the total population of the Chennai city is 5 lakh. Here, a sample of 500 people would certainly not represent the population. However, if the sample size is 10,000, it might represent a sizeable population than a sample of 500 people. Further, if the sample size is increased to 50,000, a better representativeness of the population could be achieved.

Law of Inertia of Large Numbers: According to the law of inertia of large numbers, other things remaining the same, larger the sample size, greater is the accuracy of the results obtained. In other words, large size of sample would be more stable than the small size of a sample. Though this law is a corollary of the first law, yet, it emphasizes the fact that to get accurate results, the sample size should be increased. For example, the accuracy of results from a sample of 500 people in Chennai city out of 5 lakhs would be certainly less, compared to a sample size of 50,000.

Essentials of Sampling

Usefulness and reliability of sampling depends on the following features of sample.

Representativeness: The sample selected should fully represent the population from which it is drawn. This means, all the characteristics or features of the population should be reflected by the sample. If not, sample conclusions will not be fully applicable to the population. Suppose by talking to five boys in a college of 2000 boys, one cannot come to any conclusion about the college.

Adequacy: The size of the sample should be large enough so as to provide accurate results. Though it is difficult to state what the ideal size of sample should be, statistically it can be determined. In a research, such an approach is used to determine the sample size so that the results obtained will be accurate and applicable to the population.

Randomness: Samples should be selected at random. There should be no bias in the selection of sample elements and each item in the population should have an equal chance of being selected. Only when the sample is selected at random, its reliability and representativeness would be achieved.

Homogeneity: Any number of samples could be drawn from a population. But all these samples should have similarity in every respect. Suppose a researcher selects 200 students from a college out of 2,000 students in day section, the sample elements [i.e, students selected] should be from the day section of the college alone. No student from evening section should be included in the sample. Similarly, suppose a researcher selects 5,000 people from Chennai city as a sample to study consumption behaviour of the people, then the sample elements should all be people living in the Chennai city. It should not include people who have come to Chennai city as tourists.

Methods of Sampling

Sampling method can be broadly classified as: (1) Random or probability sampling, and (2) Non-random or non-probability sampling. Under the former, every element of the population enjoys an equal chance of being selected, while the under the latter, the elements constituting the sample are selected on some basis and hence not all elements would get an equal chance of getting selected. For example, suppose from 2,000 students in a college, 200 are selected on random basis. Then each one of these 2,000 students have an equal chance of getting selected.

On the other hand, in the case of non-random sampling, 200 students out of 2,000 may be selected in such a way that there are 50 pure science students, 50 arts students, 50 commerce students and 50 life science students. In this case, the sample is purposely selected. So it is not a random sample.

Types of Random/Probability Sampling

Random sampling can be classified into two types: (a) simple or unrestricted random sampling, and (b) restricted random sampling.

Simple or unrestricted random sampling is of the following types.

Lottery Method: In this method, all the items in the population are given numbers and these are written on chits of uniform size. Then these chits are placed in a bowl or a bag and the required number of chits is selected. Even here, when the chit selected first is replaced before picking the next one, it is called a 'lottery method with replacement'. Suppose, the chit selected in the first pick is not selected and then the second pick is made, we call it a 'lottery method without replacement'. Of these two, the first one is preferred as the probability of the second and the subsequent chit selected will remain the same. In the second method, the probability of selecting the second or third and subsequent chits will be different, as there is no replacement of chits already picked.

Table of Random Numbers: In this method, first the size of sample is determined and then using the random number table, the required number of items is selected from the sample. In these tables, random numbers are printed in columns and rows. Random number tables are available with two digits, three digits and more number of digits. Let us presume the sample size is 25 out of a total of 200 items. First, a serial number [two or three or four digits] is assigned to each item. Then using a random number table, row-wise or column-wise, 25 numbers that match with the serial number are selected which will constitute the sample. For example, whenever a new car is introduced in the market, people who are booking for the new car are assigned a serial number after the last date for booking is over. The company will generate those who would be given the allotment for the month, going by the random numbers. Once the required numbers are selected, the customers who are assigned that number are intimated about the allotment.

Restricted Random Sampling: In this method, a specific principle or basis is followed while selecting the sample elements. There are three different methods of restricted random sampling.

Stratified Random Sampling: Stratum means a layer. Population from which samples are to be selected may contain a number of layers. From each layer, a few samples are selected. Hence, this method is called stratified random sampling.

In this method, first the population is divided into different strata (i.e. segments). The items in each segment are homogeneous. That is, each stratum will contain elements, which are similar in every respect. Then from each stratum, a few elements are selected to constitute a sample. While making this selection from each stratum, either same number of items could be selected from each strata or the number of items selected may not be the same for each stratum. If same numbers of items are selected from each stratum, it is called proportionate stratified random sampling. If the number of items selected is not the same for all the strata, it is called disproportionate stratified random sampling.

Suppose for a research work on the literacy level in Tamil Nadu, data is collected from all places in Tamil Nadu. Adopting stratified random sampling method, first the state is divided into different districts. A few districts are selected at random. Then these selected districts are divided into panchayat unions. From this second stratum, a few panchayat unions are selected.

Each selected panchayat union is divided into panchayats and a few panchayats are selected at random in the next stage. Then with each panchayat containing a number of villages, a few villages are selected at random. In this manner, the state is divided into different strata and from each stratum random selection is made. Suppose we select at random, 100 families from each village, then it would be called proportionate stratified random sampling. Suppose the number of families selected at random from each village is not the same, it is called disproportionate stratified random sampling.

A. Merits:

1. Stratified random sampling has better representativeness.
2. It also gives more accurate information and there would be a better coverage of the population.

B. Limitations:

1. This method requires lot of care and pre-planning. Unless the different strata existing in the population is known with certainty, using this method is not possible.
2. Further the basis of segmenting the population should be scientific. In the example given above, the revenue division of Tamil Nadu state is used as the basis. Suppose a person wants to select the number of schools in a place as the basis, then he should first collect the details of different types of schools in number of unrecognized schools existing in so many places. Therefore, stratified random sampling method is time consuming.
3. Care should be taken to make selection from each stratum random, which may not be practically possible. Any bias in selection from each stratum will affect the accuracy of the results.

Systematic Random Sampling: In this method, the sample is formed by selecting the first unit at random and then selecting the remaining items at evenly spaced intervals. For example, suppose from 2,000 college students we have to select a sample of 50 students. Each of these 2000 students are given a serial number.

First we determine the sampling interval [k]. This is obtained by dividing the size of population by sample size (2000/50). We get the sampling interval (k), of 40, and then from serial number 0001 to 0040 we select at random, a serial number. Suppose we have selected the student with the serial number 15, then to this we add the size of k, (here it is 50), to select the second student, i.e. 15+50=65.

So the second student selected bears the serial number 115 and the next one selected will have the serial number 165 and so on. In this manner, we select 50 students who constitute the sample.

A. Merits:

1. It is very convenient and simple to adopt.
2. The time and cost involved are relatively less.
3. With a large population, this method of sampling is easy to use.
4. Random selection of items is ensured, once the sampling interval is determined.
5. Sampling interval is determined scientifically depending upon the size of sample desired.

B. Limitations:

1. It is less representative, as once the first item is selected at random, subsequent items are all lying at uniform interval. So the selected items may lack complete representativeness.
2. This method requires correct understanding of the methodology or otherwise, the sample selected will not be correct.
3. The first item selected should be strictly at random. If there is any bias in the first stage, it will influence the items selected at subsequent stages.

Multi-stage or Cluster Sampling: As the name of the sampling method suggests, the samples are selected at different stages. In this method, the population is first divided into different stages. Then from the first stage, a few items are selected at random based on a specific feature or characteristic. From these, in the second stage, a few elements are selected at random possessing the characteristic, from which, in the third stage a few items are selected at random satisfying the characteristic, and so on, to finally make the necessary selection of samples. The entire sample selected at random at different stages will possess the common characteristic or will be homogeneous on some basis.

For example, suppose we have to select 1,000 farmers from Tamil Nadu. Then in the first stage, we will divide the state into district, from among which we will select two or three districts at random in which agricultural operations are predominant. Then in the second stage, each selected district will be divided into different *talukas* from which a few *talukas* from each selected district will be selected at random. Only *talukas* where agricultural occupation/operations are predominant, are selected. Then from each *taluka* selected, a few panchayat unions consisting of a number of panchayats and so, will be selected, based on the predominance of the agricultural operations. From each panchayat consisting of a number of villages, a few will be selected where agricultural operations are performed at large scale. Then from these villages, the required number of farmers (1,000) is selected. Since the sampling is done at various stages, it is called multi-stage. It is also called cluster sampling because in each stage the attempt is to locate only those items which have the desired characteristic. In the above example, since the object is to select 1,000 farmers, in each stage, units with predominant agricultural operations alone are considered. In this manner, the focus is only on items which possess the desired characteristics.

A. Merits:

1. It is highly flexible.
2. It ensures better representativeness.
3. Results and conclusions based on the sample will hold good for the population.
4. This type of sampling is very useful either for formulating policy or evaluating an implemented policy.

B. Limitations:

1. In practice, this method is found to be less accurate compared to other methods because any bias at any stage will get accumulated.
2. Unless a person is fully aware of the various stages into which the population can be divided, he cannot be

effective in selecting the required number of samples.

3. The characteristic of feature to be present with samples at all stages may not be fulfilled in all cases. Suppose if a study is about the effectiveness of pollution control policy, it should be decided at the first stage that which type of pollution is to be studied [viz. air, water, noise, etc]. These types of pollution is very common in all the places and selecting a few samples at random from each stage will be cumbersome.
4. The bias of the person selecting the sample will get reflected in the process. For example, in the case of a study on pollution, the degree of pollution will differ from place to place. Then the places above a certain level of pollution alone may have to be selected. That means, data regarding the level of pollution of various types, should be available. In the absence of this, selection will not be strictly random.

Non-random Sampling or Non-probability Sampling

Non-random or non-probability sampling refers to the sampling process in which the samples are selected for a specific purpose with a pre-determined basis of selection. This type of sampling is also required at times when random selection may not be possible. Therefore, the reliability of conclusions based on this type of sampling is less. Whenever a researcher uses this type of sampling, he would make a specific mention of it in the thesis, so that the conclusions would be evaluated accordingly. There are different types of non-random sampling and some of the important ones are explained below.

Judgment Sampling: In this method, the sample selection is purely based on the judgment of the investigator or the researcher. This is because the researcher may lack information regarding the population from which he has to collect the sample. Population characteristics or qualities may not be known, but sample has to be selected. In such instances, judgement sampling method is used. The investigator on the field is allowed to select any item of his choice to constitute the sample.

Once the sample size is determined, the investigator is free to select any item on the field. For example, suppose 100 boys are to be selected from a college with 1,000 boys. If nothing is known about the students in this college, then the investigator may visit the college and choose the first 100 boys he meets. Or he may select 100 boys all belonging to III year. Or he might select 25 boys from commerce course, 25 from science courses, 25 boys from arts courses and 25 from fine arts courses. Hence, when only the sample size is known, the investigator uses his discretion and selects the sample.

The strength of this method is that the sample elements are selected by the investigator on the spot using his understanding of the population. So the samples may fairly represent the population. But if the investigator may be biased, this type of sampling may not be fully representative of the population. Further, there is a need to train investigator to do this job correctly.

Convenience Sampling: This method of sampling involves selecting the sample elements using some convenient method without going through the rigour of sampling method. The researcher may make use of any convenient base to select the required number of samples.

For example, suppose 100 car owners are to be selected. Then we may collect from the RTO's office the list of car owners and then make a selection of 100 from that to form the sample. But unless the list at the RTO's office is up to date, the sample selected will be wrong. Further, if an investigator is biased, the sample selected may not be random.

Quota Sampling: In this method, the sample size is determined first and then quota is fixed for various categories of population, which is followed while selecting the sample. Suppose we want to select 100 students, then we might say that the sample should be according to the quota given below: boys 50 percent and girls 50 percent. Then among the boys, 20 percent college students, 40 percent plus two students, 30 percent high school students and 10 percent elementary school students. A different or the same quota may be fixed for the girls.

In this method, the quota has to be determined in advance and intimated to the investigator. The quota for each segment of the population may be fixed at random or with a specific basis. Normally, such a sampling method does not ensure representativeness of the population.

Sampling and Non-Sampling Errors

While using sampling, errors are committed. These errors are broadly classified as sampling errors and non-sampling errors.

Sampling errors arise due to drawing inferences about the population on the basis of a few observations. That is when the same size is not a true representative of the population, any conclusion drawn on the basis of sample will not be applicable to the population. Such errors are caused due to several factors. Basically, such errors may be due to the bias of the investigator or due to wrong operational aspects of sampling process. These are discussed below.

Biased Errors: Biased errors are understood as the interference of the investigator's likes and dislikes in the process of sampling. For example, if an investigator has to collect data from a specific group of people, on the field he might collect the data from unrelated group also. This may be because of the investigator's urge to complete the work early or failure to understand the purpose of the survey or difficulty in distinguishing between the target group and the other group. Such a mistake may result in collection of wrong data, which eventually will result only in wrong conclusions or inferences about the population. Before discussing the methods of eliminating the biased errors, it would be worthwhile to study the reasons for biased errors.

Faulty Process of Selection: This refers to a situation

when the investigator does not apply the randomness in his choice or selection of the sample elements from the population. For example, suppose a college student is asked to select 50 students from his college. Though he is explained the purpose of the survey, yet it is most likely that he would select his own close friends, not worrying about randomness of the selection. Sometimes, while adopting a particular method of sampling, say cluster sampling, the investigator may violate the basic rule of selection. For example, suppose 1,000 farmers are to be selected from a district. After dividing the district into *talukas*, panchayat unions, panchayats and finally villages, instead of selecting farmers in the villages, he might select self-employed persons who were farmers in the past. This may be because he can collect data from the self-employed persons easily than from the farmers. This type of wrong inclusion of sample elements will affect the accuracy of the data collected.

Sometimes, response from all the sample elements included in the sample might not have been collected. That is there may be non-response by some sample elements. In such circumstances, the investigator would gather data, which will not be complete. This may be experienced while adopting interview or questionnaire method to collect data. Similarly, the type of questions raised may also elicit responses not truly reflecting the opinion of the respondents. For example, questions like “don’t you like this?” is bound to get response in the affirmative [i.e. yes]. Such suggestive questions may result in biased replies which would fail to bring out the facts. All these may be due to the faulty process of selection.

Faulty Collection of Information: Adoption of faulty method of collecting information may cause errors. For example, suppose the population or the scope of the survey is not clear. This might lead to collection of information from sample elements not relevant to the survey. For example, while data regarding the performance of students in studies in college is collected, the scope may not be clearly defined. That is, whether to treat the students undergoing correspondence courses are included or not, may not be clear. As a result, information may be collected even from such students. This results in wrong collection of information. Similarly, while collecting information, the investigator should be careful to edit the information received, before recording them.

Often the respondents state additional information for a question. This additional information has to be edited before being recorded. For example, suppose in response to a question "how many children you have", respondents might say 'three children, and two died'. Whether the three children are alive or only one is alive has to be ascertained before recording the data regarding the three living children.

Mostly, such errors are caused either because of untrained field staff or improperly structured questionnaire or interview by untrained investigator.

Faulty Method of Analysis: This is the most frequently committed mistake on the part of the researcher. When the data collection is completed, the researcher embarks on data analysis. Before this, the data has to be properly classified and tabulated. If any mistake is committed in this stage, then the subsequent analysis will yield only wrong results. Similarly, in the selection of tools of analysis, the researcher should be very careful. First of all, depending upon the method of analysis used, the data should be arranged. Without that if the analysis is carried out, results will be misleading. In the urge to use advanced method of analysis, a researcher should not use improper data.

Minimizing the Sampling Errors

It is necessary that efforts should be taken to eliminate or at least minimize the sampling errors. This could be achieved by ensuring randomness in the sample selection process. The investigators should be properly trained and oriented for the purposes of the survey. Appropriate methods of data analysis should be selected. For this purpose, the analysis undertaken by earlier researchers could be studied or consulting experts or specialists in the field of analysis may be useful. Most important method of minimizing the sampling errors is to increase the sample size. It is well established that with large size sample, the accuracy will increase and the sampling errors would come down.

Unbiased Errors: These errors are caused due to chances not strictly due to any bias on the part of the investigator. Sometimes the findings from the selected sample may be different from other elements not included in the sample. Such errors could be avoided only by specifying the sample elements clearly.

Non-sampling Errors: Non-sampling errors are those errors, which are not due to any sampling process. It is due to several other causes. However, even if much care is taken to plan and execute a survey for data collection, errors may creep in due to various reasons. Such errors are more due to the following reasons:

1. Investigators may collect data without using the complete schedules, or proper definitions or proper measurement. As a result data collected may not be relevant at all.
2. Faulty method of interview or observation may also contribute to non sampling errors. The investigator may approach the informants without any pre-planned questionnaire or structuring of the questions to be raised at the time of interview. Or he may not be familiar or well versed with the process of observation that he might fail to observe for the relevant facts.
3. Use of untrained and unskilled investigators only causes more confusion rather than carrying out the work properly. Such investigators would often report incomplete or irrelevant data.
4. There are instances when the organizer of the survey does not plan for close supervision and control over investigators in the field. As a result, coverage of respondents may not be complete, questionnaire or schedules may be filled up by the investigators based on

the response given by a few informants, etc.

5. Mistakes committed in data processing are also a source of non-sampling errors. Data processing requires adequate pre-planning and preparations. In the absence of this, processing might be taken up in haste or inefficiently.
6. Selection of wrong presentation of data also adds to the non-sampling errors. This could be avoided only by training and educating the analyst on the representation techniques. For example, a person not familiar with the difference between a graph and diagram may represent the data making a wrong choice.
7. Interpretation of data requires enormous experience and skill. Not everyone can handle interpretation easily. Wrong interpretation of the analysis results will lead to wrong understanding of the outcome.

It may be noted that the total sampling error consists of both sampling errors and non-sampling errors. To minimize the sampling errors if we increase the sample size, the non-sampling errors are bound to increase. For this purpose, effective steps should be taken to bring down the non-sampling errors. As the causes for non-sampling errors could be identified easily, appropriate steps should be taken to eliminate them.

Sample Size

One of the most important issues to be settled while using sampling method is to determine the size of sample. More often than not, researchers commit mistakes in deciding their sample size. There is a thumb rule, which says that to satisfy statistical requirement, the size of the sample should be a minimum of 30 and above. In statistics any sample with 30 and more elements is considered a large sample. Less than 30 elements in a sample constitute only a small sample. By definition this might appear to be an easy way out to determine the sample size. But it should be noted that there are several other considerations of factors which influence the sample size. These are discussed hereunder.

1. *The size of the population*: Depending upon the size of population, the size of sample has to be decided. If the population is very small [say for example only 50], then the sample size could also be small. But, it should be remembered that larger the size of population, larger should be the sample size to achieve representativeness and accuracy.
2. *The resources available*: What amount of time and financial resources are available to the researcher will determine the size of sample. With sufficient time and large volume of funds available, the sample size could be large, otherwise it should be small.
3. *The extent of accuracy desired*: One of the requirements of data analysis is the accuracy level. There is no choice about the level of accuracy that one wants to achieve or maintain. But while dealing with large population, due to constraints on resources, sampling has to be adopted. In that case, the level of accuracy that is desired must be spelt out. Suppose, the choice is for achieving cent percent accuracy, then sampling itself cannot be thought of, alternatively, if the accuracy desired is 95 percent then sample size should be large. Any level of accuracy less than this [95 percent] may require only small sample size.
4. *Nature of population*: The similarities and dissimilarities identified with population itself may affect the sample size. If the population contains a lot of heterogeneous sub-population [i.e. small segments of population with different features or characteristics], then a large sample size is required. For example, if in a computer training institute, sample is to be selected drawing from students undergoing different courses, then the sample size should be large. Alternatively, suppose from a commerce college a sample is to be selected, a small size is sufficient as there is no dissimilarity in the population.
5. *Method of sampling adopted*: Several sampling methods

have been elaborated in the previous section of this topic. Depending upon the method of sampling used, the size of sample will be decided.

6. *Nature of respondents*: Success or failure of a sample survey depends ultimately on the response of the informants. So the nature of respondents will influence the sample size. Suppose in a survey on the opinion of a policy of liberalization, introduced by the government, if the respondents are literate, the size of sample could be smaller. If the respondents are illiterate or less literate, the size of sample should be large. Sometimes, mathematical formula is used to determine the sample size. The formula is given below:

   $n = (Z\,\sigma / d)$

   Where **n** is the sample size, **Z** is the degree of accuracy desired [specified level of confidence], **σ** - is the standard deviation of the population and **d** is the difference between the population mean and sample mean.

Merits of Sampling

1. Sampling method requires lesser time as only a part of the universe is included for data collection.
2. Since only a part of the universe is included for the data collection, the cost incurred on data collection will also be less.
3. With suitable method of sample selection, the results could be more reliable.
4. There are certain occasions, when only sampling method is possible. For example, when a parent has to undergo blood test, it has to be a test of blood sample.
5. Sampling method is more frequently used for testing the accuracy of information collected through census method.
6. Properly constituted sample always yield results, which concur well with the results obtained through population.
7. In research, unless sample is used, there is every possibility for the findings to become outdated. For

example, suppose metro water in Chennai city is mixed up with sewerage water and it is insisted that water from every tap or pump should be collected and tested before any action is taken. By the time this process is completed, some disease would have affected the entire city. Instead, suppose water sample is collected and tested and based on the results, action is taken, it would solve the problem quickly.

8. In research it is not possible to collect the data from the universe always. Suppose the consumption behaviour of people in Tamil Nadu has to be studied. Then collecting data from every person in every place is not possible and practical. Moreover, for an individual researcher, it is impossible. So sampling is the best alternative.
9. In research, sample data based analysis is not accepted only after conducting rigorous tests. Hence, conclusions arrived at on the basis of sample data are applicable to population.
10. One more advantage of sampling method is there are different types of sampling and depending upon the need and relevance, appropriate type could be selected. This would enable adherence to scientific method of data collection.

Limitations of Sampling

1. Unless sampling method is carefully applied, it may result in misguided findings.
2. Sampling requires perfect and elaborate planning and execution.
3. Use of sampling method requires the services of experts and specialists. This in turn will reflect on cost.
4. Sometimes when the sample size itself is very large, then sampling method would also be time consuming and costly.
5. Sampling method can never be a substitute for census method.

6. Apart from a detailed process to be followed, sampling also calls for application of a number of tests to verify the findings and results. This makes the sampling method more complex.
7. While using sampling, the investigators have to be fully trained. This will add to the cost.
8. Personal likes and dislikes of the investigators affect the quality of sampling data.

Review Questions

1. What is meant by sample and sampling? Explain the need for sampling in social research.
2. Examine the factors which determine the sample size.
3. Define random sampling and explain the usefulness.
4. State and explain the importance of random sampling.
5. Explain the technique and usefulness of multistage sampling.
6. Write the merits and demerits of sampling.
7. Distinguish between systematic sampling and stratified random sampling.
8. Explain the different methods of sampling. What are the sampling errors and how do you eliminate them?
9. How do you establish the unrepresentativeness and adequacy of sampling?
10. What do you mean by stratified sampling and what is its importance in research?
11. Explain the different methods of sampling.
12. Explain the system of cluster sampling with suitable examples.
13. Distinguish between systematic sampling and stratified random sampling.
14. State and explain the importance of random sampling.

4

Data for Research

Nature of Data

Data refers to information or facts. Often, researcher understands by data as only the numerical figures. However, it also includes descriptive facts, non-numerical information, and qualitative and quantitative information. In a research, if the data is available, the research is half-complete. Very few scholars are blessed with such experience. Others are always in search of the data. In this search, the scholar should understand clearly what data he/she has to collect. Clarity in this respect itself would help them to locate the sources for the data required. Clarity would be there only when the scholar has confirmed objectives of his/her research topic.

Supposedly, if a research study is about unemployment problem in India, the topic is understood but not clear, because, unemployment is of different varieties. What type of unemployment problem is focused in the research should be clear. Suppose, the study is about urban unemployment, then related to the topic, specific objectives should be laid. If not, every type of data on unemployment would be collected and the scholar really may not know what he wants to do with that data. To avoid this, the scholar may choose from the following objectives: the pattern of urban unemployment or the nature of urban unemployment or the causes for urban unemployment or the magnitude of urban unemployment or solution for urban unemployment, etc. Suppose all these are set as objectives of the research, then the sources of information for studying these objectives could easily be determined.

Data could be broadly classified as:

Primary data, and

Secondary data.

Primary data is known as the data collected for the first time through field survey. Such data are collected with specific set of objectives to assess the current status of any variable studied. Primary data always reveal the cross-section picture of anything studied. This is needed in research to study the effect or impact of any policy. For example, suppose the transport department wants to study whether introduction of one way regulation in a main road has helped to ease the traffic congestion. This can be studied only by collecting information on the spot for a few days from the common public, vehicle using population, shop keepers, policemen on duty and others who are directly affected by such one way regulation. Such information is called the primary data. Similarly, suppose the government wants to study the impact of the policy regarding prevention of pollution by a tannery in a village. This is possible only by collecting information from people residing around the tannery at periodic intervals. Data collected at one point of time will reflect only the status of pollution at that time. It may not be relevant at different point of time.

Secondary data refers to the information or facts already available. Such data is collected with the objective of understanding the past status of any variable or the data collected and reported by some source is accessed and used in the objective of a study. Normally in research, the scholars collect published data and analyze them to explain the relationship between variables, which may not have been studied or the relationship might be explained in a new way. For example, data relating to production and productivity of rice in Gujarat may be analyzed by different scholars for different purposes. One scholar may just study the pattern of change in production and productivity over a period of time, another may be interested in studying the impact of the introduction of a new variety of paddy or new fertilizer on production and productivity of rice.

The new variety of paddy or the new fertilizer might have been introduced three years back. Then only by studying the production and productivity of rice before the introduction of the new variety of paddy or the new fertilizer and comparing it with the period after the introduction of them, he would be able to explain the impact of the new variety or the new fertilizer on production and productivity of rice. Similarly, comparing the performance of economics graduates of the current year in the university examinations with that of the other batches in the previous years, one can understand whether the performance has improved or not. Studies of such comparative nature require only secondary data.

Sources of Data/Information

Primary Data: As the primary data is the information collected for the first time, there are several methods in which the data is compiled. Some of these methods are very popular while the others are rarely used depending upon the need or circumstance. Various sources of primary data are discussed below.

Observation: It is a method which requires familiarity and experience. In this method, the observer applies his sense organs to note down whatever that he could observe in the field and relate these data to explain some phenomena.

Interview: This is a method in which the investigator and the respondent meet and questions raised are answered and recorded. This method is adopted when personal opinion or view point are to be gathered as a part of the data.

Questionnaire or Schedule: In this method, a pre-printed list of questions arranged in sequence is used to elicit response from the informant.

Feedback Form: In the case of some of the consumer goods, the supplier or the manufacturer sends the product and its usage is explained and the customer is requested to fill it up and send the feedback form. Based on this, the first hand information about the product from the consuming public is obtained.

Sales Force Opinion: On several occasions, the

manufacturers or distributors collect information about the movement of the product or market size, market share, purchasing pattern, etc. through the sales force on the field. The salesmen or representatives visit the distributor or the retailer's shop to note down the details of stock movement, availability of items, etc., which gives valuable information.

Party Audit: In this method, the investigators stay at the consuming point and observe the purchasing behaviour of the people. From this, valuable information like the price response, quality consciousness, response to prize and incentive schemes, who takes buying decision, credit facility required, etc. is obtained. All this information influences the marketing strategy of the organization concerned.

Consumer Panels: The consumer panels refer to an arrangement with select consumers to maintain details of their consumption behaviour in their diaries. Based on these recorded information, useful first hand information is collected about the product and behaviour of the consuming public.

Collection through Mechanical Devices: There are several shopping establishments where hidden video cameras are positioned at vantage points. This is used for observing the public inside the shop. Apart from helping to eliminate pilferage and theft, they provide very useful information on the consumers and their preferences for products.

Projective Techniques: This technique is adopted to study the consumers through various methods like recalling advertisement theme, story completion tests, quizzes, thematic apperception tests, etc. Through this technique, it is possible to compile information to be used as the basis for projecting the demand for the product at different points of time.

Content Analysis: In this method, the investigator would listen through various audio visual records to obtain the required information. Of course, in this process, what is already recorded by somebody for some purpose is used to cull out useful information.

Observation Technique

Observation as a method of data collection is used very frequently, whenever collection of data through other methods is difficult. For example, it is not always possible to conduct interviews with every person to collect required information. Similarly, using questionnaire or schedule for data collection is not free from limitations, especially when the response to questionnaire is very poor. On such occasions, observation is more useful for collecting the data. There are occasions when no other method can be adopted for data collection. For instance, suppose a scholar wants to study the lifestyle of a hill tribe. It is certainly not possible to use a questionnaire or schedule or conduct interview. Only alternative available is observation; as the respondents would not reply to any question orally or in written. There are also instances when apart from the data collected through questionnaire/schedule or interview one has to have a clear understanding of the surroundings or environment. This is possible only by adopting observation technique.

Formal Definition of Observation: Observation may be defined as, "sensible application of sense organs in understanding less explained or unexplained phenomena." Using the sense organs, one could see and understand things. One could listen to what is being explained to understand anything. It may also be possible by interacting with people to understand anything. Whenever a researcher is unable to compile information through any other method, then he has to effectively apply his sense organs to observe and explain. So it may be said that observation involves recording of information by applying visual understanding backed by alert sense organs.

A few more examples will make clear the meaning and usefulness of observation. Suppose the reaction of people to a day light robbery committed is to be studied. A person who is present on the spot when the robbery takes place would be able to notice and feel several things, which even a video recording may fail to bring out. Similarly, a very popular film star is visiting a place. The reaction of the people to his visit cannot be completely brought out in any other manner except observation. The sharing of joy or sorrow, way of living, habits, practices, etc. can be understood better through observation.

Types of Observation: Types of observation could be broadly classified as: structured observation, unstructured observation, participant observation, non-participant observation, controlled observation and uncontrolled observation. Each one of these types is explained below.

1. *Structured observation*: When observation takes place strictly in accordance with a plan or a design prepared in advance, it is called structured observation. In such a type, the observer decides what to observe, what to focus on, what type of information or activity should be given importance, who are all to be observed, what conditions are to be fulfilled to carry out observation, etc. in advance. He sticks to these decisions when he observes. This has the advantages like: (a) filtering what is relevant and focusing on it, (b) avoiding waste of time, (c) studying only the target group, (d) minimizing the bias of the observer, and (e) elimination of any scope for vagueness. However, the disadvantages are: (i) unless a person is well trained he cannot be effective in undertaking structured observation, (ii) it is possible that vital aspects are missed, as they were not conceived at the time of designing the observation, and (iii) by limiting the independence of the observer, crucial things might be left out from being observed.
2. *Unstructured observation*: In this type of observation, there is no advance designing of what, how, when, who, etc. of observation. The observer is given the freedom to decide on the spot, to observe everything that is relevant. For example, while observing the lifestyle of a hill tribe in their place, the observer may be able to observe several interesting things like how they discuss their plans, how they settle quarrels, who takes decision, etc. Some of these

may not be observed if structured observation is adopted. The main strength of the unstructured observation is that at the time of observation everything is taken note of and the researcher then segregates the related and relevant details. Of course, one important quality required of the observer is that he should be well trained and experienced.

3. *Participant observation*: In this method, the observer is very much present in the midst of what is observed. For example, suppose a researcher is studying the lifestyle of a hill tribe, then he might understand the lifestyle of the tribe better, only when he stays with them. By being present on the spot, he would be able to continuously observe and note everything that is happening around him. But he may not interfere with anything that is happening. He is a participant in the sense; he is physically present on the spot to observe and not influence the activities. Similarly, a journalist may be present at the site where an earthquake had happened. He might only take photograph or shoot what he sees apart from noting several other sections of people on the spot, but not directly or indirectly participate in anything. The significant merits of this type of observation are: (1) the observer will not miss anything which is relevant, (2) there is every scope for him to clarify things which he cannot understand, (3) he can interact with people to get more information, and (4) there is no need to depend upon hearsay or reported information. But this method of observation also has the following demerits: (a) an inexperienced observer may not know what is relevant and what is not relevant, (b) He tends to focus more on things of interest to him, than what is relevant, (c) there is lot of scope for his bias to intervene in his interpretation of what is observed, and (d) the conduct or behaviour or reaction of the target audience may be influenced by his presence.
4. *Non-participant observation*: This is a method in which the observer remains detached from whatever is happening

around and does not involve himself in any activities taking place. He is present only to observe and not to take part in the activities. Sometimes, he may even remain anonymous. That is, the target audience does not know his presence at all. For example, the plain clothe men [policemen not in uniform] are deputed on observation duty whenever a procession takes place or whenever any important political personality participates in the public meeting or a place where a murder is committed. The object of such action is only to notice what is happening and not to be involved in what is happening. The most important strength of this method of observation is that the observer would collect first hand information without being noticed or influenced by anyone.

5. *Controlled observation*: This is a slightly modified version of unstructured observation. In this case, the observer performs his work in an environment or situation, which is very much planned or designed or set. For example, sometimes to test the effectiveness and alertness of airport security system, a mock event [like hijacking or fire accident] is carried out. Resultantly, how the security staff reacts to such mock event is observed and based on this, the weaknesses in the system are noticed and steps taken to eliminate them.
6. *Uncontrolled observation*: This method is a modified version of unstructured observation. No attempt is made to intervene the naturalness of the environment or situation. The observer is at freedom to observe whatever is taking place around him in the natural set up. For example, an animal lover may like to watch the conduct and behaviour of the animals in their natural habitat. Their behaviour is controlled in a zoo or a sanctuary but they are free in a forest. Some of the serials shown in discovery channel are filmed in the natural setting where animals live. This helps to understand the natural behaviour of animals.

Merits of Observation:

1. If observation is done correctly, the scope for bias is very much minimized.
2. Through observation, the current scenario in which anything is happening is noticed and explained. There is no interpretation of how things would have happened in the past or will happen in future, etc.
3. As there is no need to get any reply or details from the respondents, observation does not require any co-operation of the respondents.
4. This is a fairly reliable method, provided the observer is well experienced, trained and sincere.
5. Whenever respondents are illiterate or incapable of answering any question, [due to language barrier or cultural background, etc.], observation is the only method of data collection available.

Limitations of Observation:

1. This is a relatively costly method of data collection, because the observer has to be present on the spot to observe whatever is happening. Further training an observer is the additional cost to be incurred.
2. The scope for the bias of the observer interfering in what is observed and understood is high.
3. It could be noticed that what is observed may bring out only part of the facts, while data collected through questionnaire or interview ensures better coverage.
4. Sometimes, it may not be possible to observe what is targeted. This may be due to the difficulty in reaching such people or spot.
5. There is a lot of scope for the observer to get distracted or influenced by unexpected factors which would affect the accuracy of information collected.
6. A very important limitation is that only the observer can effectively establish link among whatever he has observed to give a meaningful interpretation. Based on his report nobody else can give satisfactory interpretation. Therefore,

the ability to relate things and interpret them intelligently is a quality expected of an observer.

How to Make an Observation Successful?

1. First the researcher should have a clear grasp of what he should observe and the purpose or objectives of such observation.
2. The person should be trained in adopting observation method of data collection.
3. The person should avoid any of his personal likes and dislikes, intervene in the process of observation.
4. Unless the observer is alert and intelligent, he might ignore important things.
5. The observer should be able to convince his target audience the need and importance of what is observed.
6. Unless an observer is able to relate various things seen or heard or felt, he may not be able to give a satisfactory explanation for what is observed. So he should be a person of analytical and critical nature.

Before concluding, it should be noted that observation alone may not be useful in collecting the data. If it is combined with other methods of data collection like questionnaire/schedule method or interview method, it would help to make data collection comprehensive.

Interview

One of the very old methods of compiling data [facts] is the interview method. Interview method involves direct or indirect meeting of the respondent by the researcher. The researcher determines the questions to be raised at the time of interview and then elicit the response for them. The reply given is either written down in a notebook or recorded in an audio or video cassette. This method has to be necessarily adopted whenever details regarding any confidential matter are to be collected or when authentic information about anything is to be obtained or the research requires data collection directly from the respondents or there is no other way of collecting data.

It should be noted that the interview conducted for employment is different from that of the research interviews. While the former is meant to examine a candidate's ability to communicate, manners, suitability for the position, etc., the later type of interview has purposes depending upon the scope of the research. It is also noticed that in employment interviews, the interviewer may touch upon various aspects like general knowledge, sports, music, subject, personality, etc. The research interview normally focuses on specific issues relating to the topic of research. In the case of employment interview, it is the candidate who tries to prove himself in every aspect, whereas in research interview, it is the researcher who should be more purposeful, oriented and persuasive to obtain the required information.

Types of Interview: Interview may be broadly classified as:

1. Direct interviews, and
2. Indirect interviews.

In both these types, different approaches may be followed like: structured interview, unstructured interview, focused interview, non-directive interview and telephonic interview. These types of interview are discussed hereunder.

Direct Interview: In this type of interview, the interviewer and the interviewee meet personally either with prior appointment or not. This type of interview may further be classified as: structured interview, unstructured interview, focused interview, clinical interview and non-directive interview. Usually when this technique is adopted, the interviewer may brief the respondent about the purpose of interview and its scope in advance. This enables the respondents to be ready with necessary details or data. For example, suppose the chairman of ISRO is to be interviewed. Then an appointment must be obtained and the subject matter of interview or the purpose of the interview should be stated in advance. This will enable the chairman to collect the necessary data in advance so as to give authentic information at the time of interview. But there are occasions when the respondent is contacted and his opinion collected. In such cases, there is no possibility for briefing him about the interview. For example, television crews [like Sun TV] meet the people coming out a theatre screening a new film and ask them about the film. The response is simply the opinion of the audience and there is no advance intimation given.

Structured Interview: In this type of interview, the person collecting the information decides in advance, the nature and scope, questions to be asked, the persons to be contacted, etc. At the time of interview, no deviation is made from the questions to be asked or scope or the persons. For example, it is usual for a journalist to interview the finance minister after the presentation of budget. On such occasions, the journalist should be well prepared and decide in advance the questions to be asked, the details to be quoted, the instances to be recalled, etc. Sometimes even the questions to be asked and other details have to be submitted to the authorities concerned, before conducting the interview. Similarly, during the college re-opening season, the principals of various colleges are interviewed regarding the demand for admission, number of applications received, popularity of various courses among the students, etc. Unless the interviewer decides the questions in advance, the principals may not have time to reply to the questions raised off-hand by the interviewer.

The most important advantages of such structured interview are:

1. The interviewer is well prepared and so the interview is conducted in a focused manner.
2. As much details as possible could be collected about the subject matter of interview, as the interviewer decides in advance the depth of the interview.
3. Time of both the interviewer and the respondents could be saved.

4. This is the only type of interview possible when the respondents are VIPs.
5. There is no scope for irrelevant matter to find a place in the course of interview.
6. If the respondent is informed in advance, he could prepare necessary details so that the outcome is reliable.

But this method of interview has the following limitations: (1) since the subject matter is decided in advance there is no scope for elaborating or extending the interview; (2) sometimes the respondents may manage to give well rehearsed replies which would fail to bring out the real information; (3) there is a need for the interviewer to plan the interview properly and so if the plan is not perfect, the interview findings may not be complete; (4) there is some scope for the interviewer to be biased while preparing the questions to be raised; and (5) there is also little scope for exercising the creative nature of the interviewer.

Unstructured Interview: In this type of interview, interview is conducted on the spot without any preparations or advance information to the respondent. For example, suppose an organization producing a new health drink wants to know the opinion of the people directly. Then it might send trained field investigators who meet people at random and offer them a cup of that new drink. After they drink, their opinion is asked and the responses are noted down or recorded. As such interviews take place with people not informed in advance except the location nothing can be decided by the organization conducting such type of interviews. So the investigators raise questions with the respondents and records the answers. Such interviews are used when an opinion poll is conducted. For example, during election time, the TV channels would meet people moving around and ask them about their opinion about different parties and the one to which they would vote. Similarly, after the budget is presented in the Parliament, public opinion is collected on the announcements in the budget through unstructured interview.

The unstructured interview has the following merits: (1) the interviewer could plan his interview depending upon the response of the informant and possibly collect additional information; (2) the scope for bias on the part of the interviewer or the respondents is less; (3) the real opinion of the respondent could be obtained through such interview; and (4) such interviews will be usually very short and specific and hence not much of time is wasted.

The demerits of the unstructured interview are: (a) the interviewer has to be very much alert to obtain the specific response; (b) sometimes the respondent may answer the questions without understanding them, as there is no time available for explaining the questions; (c) it is possible that irrelevant respondents are contacted and irrelevant responses are obtained; (d) the interviewer may intelligently ask the questions suggestive to obtain the desired response. [For example: an interviewer collecting the opinion about a film may ask: Don't you think that the hero could have done better? Don't you feel that the music in this film is bad? Don't you think that this film will flop?]

Focused Interview: This type of interview is unstructured by nature. In this type of interview, the object of the interviewer is to focus the attention of the respondent on a specific issue or point. The interviewer has the freedom to plan the interview and conduct it the way he wants it. The question sequence, wording of questions, etc. are all decided by the interviewer on the spot. For example, suppose a detective is questioning a person regarding a crime committed in an area. The detective has to be very much experienced to make the person interview to answer only about the crime and nothing else.

Non-Directive Interview: This is again an unstructured type of interview. In this type, the interviewer encourages the respondents to say whatever he likes and feels on a subject matter. There may not be much of questioning taking place. The respondent is free to express his views or opinions without any direction from the interviewer. For example, in a college, students are on strike. Then an interviewer may encourage different students to say whatever they feel about the reasons for the strike. He may not intervene when the students are stating the reasons. Through such a process, more facts may come to light and that is when the interviewer guides the respondents.

Telephonic Interview: This is basically a type of direct interview but there is no scope for physical presence of both the parties to the interview. Such interviews are used when the informant and the interviewer are geographically separated [i.e. a person in India interviewing a person in the US]. Since the interview has to be very much focused, the interviewer should prepare in advance the questions to be raised. A well prepared interview will bring to light a lot of information. But the problems in this type of interview are: a] the respondent should be accessible by phone, b] there is not much time available for giving any clarification, c] if there is disturbance in the telephone line, then the information given may not be clear, and d] it is also costly.

Merits of Interview as a Method of Data Collection:

1. Interview enables personal contact with which factual information could be obtained.
2. The interviewee can guide the respondents to understand the questions and suitably rephrase or modify the questions.
3. The non-response in this category of data collection is low.
4. Spontaneous reply of the respondents can be obtained which would truly deflect their opinion.
5. Interviewer has the flexibility to handle the interview to collect relevant information.
6. The interviewer can combine observation with interview so that a lot of additional information about the environment, nature, behaviour and attitude of the respondent could be noted.
7. The interviewee can be persuasive to obtain the response

of the respondent while this may not be possible in the case of questionnaire method of data collection.

8. The interviewee can adapt himself better by using the language with which he can reach to the respondents better and understand the educational level of the respondent.
9. It is also possible to obtain personal information which will not be revealed through questionnaire.

Demerits of Interview as a Method of Data Collection:

1. This method presupposes the existence of rapport between the respondent and the interviewer. In case there is no rapport, the interview cannot be held at all.
2. It is a costly method of data collection, as the interviewers are more than what it is under questionnaire method.
3. The time taken for covering a large sample of respondents is more than what it is under questionnaire method.
4. It is possible for a respondent to conceal his real opinion or views and so genuine data may not be available.
5. The interviewer may also be biased and thereby his bias may influence the interview outcome.
6. Interview method requires an elaborate organizational arrangement.
7. Sometimes this method cannot be followed as it would require fixing up appointment, specifying the questions that are to be answered, duration of interview, the person interviewing, the organizational background, the purpose of interview, etc. Inspite of providing all these information, it may not be possible to get an appointment to conduct the interview.

How to Make an Interview Successful? If the interview has to be successfully conducted, the following points should be taken into account:

1. The interviewer should be carefully selected.
2. The interviewer should be trained properly.
3. Different methods of obtaining the response from the informants have to be explored and the interviewee should be trained in all these aspects.

4. Unless the interviewer is experienced he would not be able to conduct the interview properly. But without conducting interviews he cannot be experienced. So care should be taken while selecting this method of data collection.
5. Honesty and integrity of the interviewer determines the outcome of the interview. So the qualities of the interviewer should be objectively studied.
6. The interview must first create a rapport with the respondent and ensure presence of cordial atmosphere to conduct the interview.
7. The interviewer should be fully equipped to clarify any questions raised by the informant.
8. Qualities like courteousness, politeness, conversational, unbiasedness are all necessary to make the interview successful.
9. The interviewer should avoid showing his reaction to the response of the respondent as otherwise the replies given may be biased.
10. The interviewer should be alert and intelligent with presence of mind to keep the interview focused on the subject matter.

Questionnaire Method

Collection of data is an important stage in research. In fact, the quality of data collected determines the quality of research. While secondary data is collected, several methods could be adopted. Of these, the most popular and widely adopted method is the use of questionnaire. A questionnaire is a sheet(s) of paper containing questions relating to certain specific aspect, regarding which the researcher collects the data. The questionnaire is given to the informant or respondent to be filled up. Sometimes the questionnaire is also in the form of files generated through computer. This is usually called the soft copy of questionnaire.

Often there is confusion among researchers regarding the usage of questionnaire and schedule. It is better to understand the difference between them, before adopting any of them in the process of data collection. Questionnaire is already defined. Schedule is also a sheet(s) of paper containing questions relating to certain specific aspect, about which the scholar is collecting data. But the schedule is not sent to the informant. It is taken by the researcher, used by him while eliciting the information. The reply is recorded by the researcher himself against each question. Hence, the schedules are different from questionnaires only in respect of usage.

Pre-requisites for using Questionnaire in the Process of Data Collection: Every researcher should keep in consideration the following points while using questionnaire for data collection.

1. The scope of the survey should be clearly determined in advance. This will help to determine the segment of informants or respondents from whom the information should be collected.
2. The purpose of the survey must be established and stated in the questionnaire.
3. The researcher should prepare the draft questionnaire and revise it until it is fit for the purpose of enquiry.
4. Follow-up arrangement after dispatching the questionnaire should be planned in advance.
5. Maintenance of list of respondents, to whom the questionnaire is sent, is necessary.
6. Whether to use structured or unstructured questionnaire is an important decision to be taken.
7. Time frame for different activities connected with the questionnaire like, preparation of questionnaire, its finalization, printing, collecting list of respondents and their addresses, dispatch and follow up, etc is important.

Structured and Unstructured Questionnaire: A structured questionnaire is one in which every aspect of the questionnaire is determined and there is no scope of any modification or alteration after the final draft is adopted. The questions are final in their form and structure. Even the responses are indicated and the respondent has to only indicate his choice. For example, a question with four alternative possible answers may be given and the respondent has to select the closest answer within the four alternatives given. Suppose the question is:

How would you rate the quality of service extended by the reception staff in this office?

a. Excellent; b. Very good; c. Good; d. Bad.

The respondent has to mark [or] tick only one of the four alternatives given as response to the question.

In an unstructured questionnaire, there is no such rigidity with regard to the answer for questions. There is scope for the respondent to give more information on any question.

Usually structured questionnaire is used when the researcher wants only a specific answer to questions or when the respondents are known to be less educated or when the researcher wants to help the respondent in answering the questions by taking minimum time. Further, a researcher will be able to make necessary arrangements in advance for classification and tabulation of data as the responses are to be only within the given alternatives for each question, by using structured questionnaire. However, this type of questionnaire limits the scope for giving additional information on any question by the respondent.

Mechanics of Questionnaire Construction: The following are the points to be given importance while designing a questionnaire:

1. Questionnaire should be printed/cyclostyled/Xeroxed.
2. The first part of the questionnaire should specify the object or purpose for which the information is required.
3. An assurance to the respondent that the information furnished would be kept confidentially must be given.
4. Some introduction about the person/organization which is collecting the information is to be given. Sometimes, this is given as a letter enclosed with the questionnaire.
5. Questions should be constructed using simple language

and technical jargons, terms, concepts should be avoided.

6. Questions should never be lengthy. It is wiser not to combine a number of questions in one question itself.
7. Each question should be specific and clear.
8. Personal questions on wealth, habits, etc. should be avoided.
9. Questions should be given in a sequence. [For example, question relating to marital status should precede the question about the number of children].
10. Questions should not require any referencing before replying.
11. Questions should not force the respondent to recall from his memory anything to answer.
12. Questions needing computation or calculation or consultation should be avoided.
13. Questions on sentiments/belief/faith should be avoided.
14. Repetition of question should be eliminated.
15. In case of any instruction required for filling up the questionnaire, such instructions should be given separately specifying the question number and the related instructions. For example, the application form for university examination is given with instructions sheet regarding fees to be paid, mode of payment, subject code, etc.
16. Sufficient space should be given for answering questions.
17. The questionnaire should be made attractive; as otherwise, the respondents may not be motivated to answer.
18. If any diagram or map is used, then it should be printed clearly.
19. Questions, which cross-checks the response, could be built into the questionnaire.
20. Instructions regarding how to return the filled up questionnaire must be given. It is desirable that a self-addressed sufficiently stamped envelope is sent along with the questionnaire to enable the respondents to send back the filled one.

Pre-testing a Questionnaire [or] Pilot Study: It is often suggested that before a questionnaire is finalized, it should be field-tested. That is, after the questionnaire is drafted, to decide whether it is comprehensive or not, it is used with a few respondents. Their responses are studied to determine the need for restructuring the questionnaire, re-sequencing the questions, addition or deletion of questions, giving more instructions for filling up, etc. Further, the pilot study will bring to light the weaknesses of the questionnaire. Based on the pre-test, necessary modifications in the questionnaire can be made and then it could be released for use.

Use of Schedules: Whenever a researcher uses schedule to collect the data, the following steps should be taken.

1. The researcher should prepare the list of respondents to be contacted or the area where they can be contacted.
2. Depending on the requirement, investigators should be selected.
3. The investigators should be explained the purpose of the survey, their job, responsibilities, accuracy desired, and importance of answers recorded, the need to be clear in recording details, etc.
4. The investigators should be trained with the schedule.
5. Necessary instructions to the investigators to deal with different types of problems [like non-availability of respondent, non-cooperative respondent, etc.] on the field should be given.
6. Sufficient arrangement for field control, monitoring and supervision should be made.
7. Method of follow up of non-response should be determined in advance.
8. The investigators selected should be honest, sincere, hard working and patient and take all efforts to collect the details.
9. Time frame for completing the data collection should be clearly spelt out.
10. Periodical review of the filled up schedules would help to

reframe the questions or change the sequence or initiate corrective action.

Merits of Questionnaire:

1. It involves lesser cost as questionnaire could be sent by post to a wide area.
2. It does not interfere with the respondent while answering the question.
3. The bias of the investigator is completely eliminated.
4. Respondents are given sufficient time to fill up the questionnaire.
5. If respondents cannot be reached personally, questionnaire is the alternative method available.
6. This method is useful when the sample size is very large.
7. If the questionnaire is designed properly with instructions, then the time and cost of recruiting, training, supervising and controlling the investigators is saved.
8. Confidentiality is ensured as the respondents directly send the filled up questionnaire to the researcher.

Demerits of Questionnaire:

1. It is always found that the response rate in questionnaire is very poor compared to using schedules.
2. Bias of the respondent cannot be determined easily.
3. Only if the respondents are educated, questionnaire only adds to the cost and time.
4. There is no scope for giving any clarification to the respondents in case of need.
5. Accuracy of response cannot be ensured.
6. A lot of care is required to design and structure a questionnaire. Hence, unless a scholar is good at drafting a questionnaire, this method cannot be adopted for data collection.

Secondary Data

It has been already explained that secondary data refers to use of information already collected and published or unpublished. Such a source is used to save time and cost in compiling the data of the past for the first time. So this source is used for collecting the historical data. There are several methods of collecting the data and these are discussed below.

Books: This refers to the published documents like books. The data contained in standard books published in the past give very valuable information. But there are occasions when data published by different books differ, causing confusion among the people compiling data.

Periodicals or Journals: This is one of the very valuable sources of information. While books may deal with historical information, periodicals contain articles and abstracts which provide the latest information. The current thinking on any aspect is brought out through such publications.

Research Thesis and Dissertations: This is another useful source of secondary data. But while using this source, the scholar should be careful to study the objectives of the thesis being referred. It should also be remembered that thesis submitted in the distant past may be used only for understanding the relationship but not for replication.

Bibliographies: These are alphabetically arranged list of useful publications with details about the year of publication, author, title, etc. This may serve as a source of information to locate and access the information relevant to the work being done.

Foot Notes: At the end of each page of any published material, foot notes are given. These notes would throw light on the source of information. By tracing this source, original information and additional facts may be available.

Encyclopaedia: This is a publication where every useful information is presented with authority, supported by diagrams and facts. This will give an authentic base for any fact being used in the research study. Several standard encyclopaedias are available and the scholar may refer them for reliable information.

Statistical Data Source: Several organizations publish at regular interval, compiled statistical data on various aspects.

For example, United Nations Statistical Year Book, Demographic Year Book, Census publications, etc. compile, classify and present codified statistical information on various aspects. Use of authentic source of statistical data would add to the quality of the research work.

Directories and Year Books: This is another source of secondary data in which specific and focused information is available. For example, Kothari's Directory of Industries provides reliable data industry-wise in India every year. Year books are published by various agencies giving details about the current status of various sectors.

But the problems in using the secondary data source are the following:

1. *Data reliability*: This is one of the basic problems. The reliability or authenticity of the data published has to be checked. Unfortunately, even among the official sources, differences are found in data provided. So while using secondary data, the following questions relating to reliability are to be raised: Who publishes the data? What is the source of information for the publisher? Is the data up to date? How was the data compiled–using scientific method or not? What is the level of accuracy claimed by the publisher and what is the accuracy level desired?
2. *Suitability of the data*: Sometimes the data may be available, but it may not suit the purpose of the study on hand. For example, RBI Bulletin publishes data regarding the foreign investment. Before 1997, no break-up of the foreign investment used to be given. But after 1997, the portfolio component and the direct investment component of the foreign investment is provided. A scholar working on the foreign direct investment will feel handicapped in the absence of specific data. Though data are available, sometimes they are not suitable for the study.
3. *Adequacy of data*: Sometimes, a researcher may require weekly data on foreign direct investment. Though data regarding foreign direct investment is available, it is

certainly not available week-wise. So data adequacy is not met. On the other hand, price quoted in Indian stock exchanges for various scraps are available on a daily basis. This could be used for undertaking any study requiring daily data.

4. *Continuity of data*: This is another problem in using secondary data. For example, the format used for providing some data may not be consistently followed by the source. Depending upon the page constraints or availability of material, the data presentation in a format is decided. So frequent change in the format would only add to confusion to the people using the data from such sources.

Selection of Appropriate Method of Data Collection

Having discussed various aspects about compilation of data for research, the question to be answered is 'which method of data collection should be adopted'? There is no standard answer to this question. The answer depends on a number of factors, which are discussed below.

1. *Nature, scope and object of the data collection*: Elsewhere it was pointed out that if the objectives of the study are clear, the type of data to be collected could be easily determined. If the research topic is of current nature like impact of earthquake in Gujarat, then primary data is the automatic choice. Suppose the topic is the pattern of foreign trade in India. To get a clear picture over the past few decades, historical data [i.e. secondary data] should be used.
2. *Budget constraints*: With liberal availability of funds, primary data could be the choice. Otherwise, secondary data is to be collected.
3. *Availability of time*: The time frame fixed for the research work will directly influence the choice between primary and secondary data. If sufficient time is available, the researcher could probe into the past with secondary data

and capture the present using the primary data.

4. *Degree of accuracy desired*: A very important condition is the level of accuracy of the data collected. In case of compilation of data regarding the deviation from the standard measurements in a workshop, the data should be cent percent accurate. Similarly, the data regarding the patient condition explained thorough various parameters, should be very accurate. On the other hand, for data required for a social research on poverty, even 95 percent accuracy is acceptable. Hence for greater level of accuracy, primary data should be selected.
5. *Period of study*: A study based on historical data, requires secondary data source while the study on the patient status in a hospital requires primary data.

Review Questions

1. Briefly examine the various techniques involved in data collection.
2. Discuss the merits and imitations of primary data.
3. Explain the strengths and weaknesses of secondary data.
4. Examine the importance of primary and secondary data in social science research.
5. Distinguish between primary and secondary data.
6. Examine the availability of secondary data for social science research in India.
7. How do you construct a questionnaire?
8. What are the precautions to be observed in the preparation of a questionnaire?
9. What are the criteria for a good questionnaire?
10. What are limitations in using questionnaire for data collection?
11. Distinguish between a questionnaire and a schedule.
12. Explain the use of questionnaire in economic research.
13. Explain the importance of secondary data in social science research.
14. Discuss the questionnaire method as a source of data

collection.

15. What are the considerations in constructing a questionnaire?
16. Explain the mechanics of constructing a questionnaire?
17. Distinguish between questionnaire and schedule.
18. What are the pre-requisites in the use of questionnaire as a method of data collection?
19. Distinguish between structured and unstructured questionnaire.
20. What is meant by pre-testing of a questionnaire? What are the purposes behind it? Explain how you would conduct a pre-test.
21. Explain the steps you would take while using schedules for data collection.
22. How do you construct an interview schedule?
23. Illustrate the use of 'interview' as a tool for collection of data.
24. Describe the pre-requisites that ensure a successful interviewing.
25. Distinguish between structured and unstructured interview.
26. What are the difficulties involved in collecting data through interview method?
27. Explain the preparations required to use interview as a method of data collection.
28. Comment on the relative strengths of direct interview over telephonic interview
29. What are the qualities of a good interviewer?
30. What are the merits and limitations of interview as a method of data collection?
31. Explains the steps that you would adopt to make interview a success.
32. Describe the usefulness and limits of observation as a method of scientific enquiry.
33. What are the distinct advantages of observation as compared to other methods of data collection?
34. Distinguish between overt and covert observation with

examples.

35. Distinguish between participant and non-participant observation.
36. Distinguish between structured and unstructured observation.
37. What is meant by an observation technique? What are the qualities of good observation?
38. Discuss the pre-requisites for using observation as a method of data collection.
39. Discuss the merits and limitations of observation method.
40. How do you consider observation and interview methods should go together to facilitate comprehensive data collection?
41. Explain participant observation.
42. What are the distinct advantages of observations as compared to other methods of data collection?
43. How would you make observation successful?

5

Data Processing

Processing of Data

Processing refers to subjecting the data collected to a process in which, the accuracy, completeness, uniformity of entries and consistency of information gathered are examined. It is a very important stage before the data is analyzed. Most commonly, processing is understood as editing, coding, classification and tabulation of the data collected. It should be noted that except editing, all the other activities are determined before the actual data collection process starts. Editing on the other hand is carried out after the data is collected. Though in terms of operations, editing comes after data collection, yet even at the time of planning the data collection specific guidelines for editing are laid down. The processing of data is necessary because, the data collected should be examined and errors and mistakes rectified so that at the stage of analysis of data, no difficulty is experienced. Various activities involved in processing of data are explained below.

Editing: Editing means to rectify or to set to order or to correct or to establish a sequence. Once the data collection is complete, it is examined carefully to eliminate any errors or mistakes. Whether the data collected is in tune with what should be collected i.e. whether the data content meets the data requirement, has to be examined. It is better if the data collected is verified even before the data analysis is carried out. So in the editing stage, mistakes and errors in the data are removed. Data entered in the questionnaire/schedule is carefully scrutinized. Persons with the editing responsibility should be trained and experienced for in this job. For example, if we get a newspaper unedited, how will the news appear. Similarly, an unedited film will have no sequence of events, which means the story cannot be understood at all. Editing is performed at two stages and depending on that it could be of two types: field editing and centralized editing.

Field Editing: Field editing refers to the performance of the editing immediately in the field where data is collected. The advantage of this is to correct the data at the stage when it is collected. The nature of editing will depend upon the method of data collection.

Suppose the data is collected through questionnaire/schedule, then verifying whether all the questions are answered or not, whether the recording of answers for the questions is correct, whether the coding for answers is correctly followed, whether the writing on the questionnaire is legible or not, whether the number of respondents to be contacted have been met or not or the extent of non-response, etc becomes important.

This type of editing is also carried out immediately after the notes on interview conducted or observation is complete. In these methods of data collection, often, the bias of the investigator would influence the notes on information gathered. Some of the questions may not have been answered by the respondents. The investigator records the answers for such questions based on his own impression of how the respondents would have replied. For example, suppose in an interview of common public about their opinion on the adequacy of buses in a particular route, the investigator does not raise this question. But he writes down the notes stating that the people are not satisfied with the number of buses. This response is only based on the investigators own opinion and not truly reflecting the public opinion. Such type of interview notes may be misleading. Similarly, after the observation is made, when the observer develops his notes, it is quite likely that he allows his personal bias to influence the data. These inaccuracies are rectified in the field itself. Therefore, field editing is undertaken within one or two days of recording the information or collecting the data.

Centralized Editing: In this type of editing, editing is done by a person or a team after all the recorded questionnaires/schedules are collected. So clearly, it is not carried out on the field itself or immediately after the data is collected. In such editing, normally the instructions regarding editing are printed and circulated to the person or the team doing the editing. This is only to ensure that there is uniformity in editing. For example, the unit of data collection may indicate that monthly income should be collected and recorded, but in the field the investigators would have annual income. Or sometimes, the answer for a particular question would remain unfilled. Or the code letters given for specifying the answer would have been ignored. All these corrections are carried out at one stretch in all the questionnaires or schedules. Sometimes, the respondents may have to be contacted for clarifying certain points. The editor must score off all the wrong answers, if he identifies some bias in such answers. Such answers should not be taken up for analysis and so the editor should mark them clearly.

Sometimes, depending upon the nature of editing done, it is classified as subject editing, language editing and document editing.

In general, editing is governed by certain guidelines. Some of the important guidelines are: (i) editor should follow the instructions for editing accurately; (ii) editing process should be free from any personal bias; (iii) editor's knowledge of the subject matter will help to perform the job better and so the background information about the data should be practiced to him; (iv) wrong entries must be marked and scored off, but not defaced; (v) editorial notes on the work done is important as it would indicate the basis of rectifying wrong entries; (vi) colour pencil or pen should be used for editing; (vii) editor's signature and date of editing should be clearly noted.

Coding: Coding is a practice which simplifies recording of answers. When standard answers for a question could be indicated, each answer is assigned a code. So instead of writing the answers in full, the investigator simply writes the code. This not only saves time but also helps to avoid confusing answers. For example, suppose a computer hardware engineer is attending a fault in a computer. The system may be out of order due to several reasons, say, booting failure, software corruption, improper cable link, low voltage, memory failure, mother board failure, etc. The engineer cannot write down each time the reasons for the failure of the machine. Each one of the above causes may be coded like A-for booting failure, B-for software corruption, C-improper cable link, etc. Hence, in his service report if the engineer writes code B against the reason for the failure, it is clearly understood. Otherwise, some service engineer would simply write system not working, which may mean several things. Another advantage in using coding is that each coded answer is specific and exclusive, i.e. there is no scope for mixing up two different answers. Usually in research surveys, coding is widely used. This helps the scholar at the time of tabulation of the data collected. Further at the time of data entry and classification as well as counting the frequency, it is easy to note the coded letter, count and write the frequency.

Coding will be effective only if sufficient thinking goes before the questionnaire or schedule is finalized and printed. It is advisable to use alphabets or numbers for coding, as these would be immediately recognized by the investigator. Care should be taken to avoid mixing alphabets and number for the same answer. Each answer should have a distinct code. The meaning of each code should be stated clearly nearby the answers for each question.

Classification: Classification of data means grouping the data on the basis of some common characteristics. In other words, when some homogeneity could be established in the data collected, then each group with similar characteristics should be segregated. Such arrangement of data in groups or class is called classification. Classified data can be used for specified purposes with ease. Further, classification adds to clarity and helps to maintain consistency. Data analysis becomes easy with classified data. Classification can be made on the basis of: (a) common characteristics or attributes like sex, literacy, colour, height, weight, age, etc., (b) geographical regions like north, south, east, wheat, etc., (c) time-oriented classification like monthly data, weekly data, yearly data, etc., (d) value-based classification, in which the collected data are grouped. For example, data regarding marks scored by students, the data could be classified as students between 0-10 marks, 10-20 marks, 20-30 marks and so on, and (e) reply-based classification like number of people who have answered 'yes' to a question, 'no' to a question, 'no opinion' to a question, etc.

Once the data is classified, then the frequency of each class is computed and entered. In this process, tally bars or tally marks are used. Tally bars refer to small vertical lines each representing an occurrence. The tally bars erected for each class is then counted and the number is recorded against each class.

Tabulation: Tabulation is the arrangement of classified data in an orderly manner. This involves creating tables for recording the data. The process of presenting in an orderly manner the classified data in a table is called tabulation. In other words, it is a method of presenting the summarized data. Tabulation is very important because (i) it helps to conserve space; (ii) it avoids any need for explanation; (iii) computation of the data is made easier; (iv) comparison of data becomes very simple; and (v) adequacy or inadequacy of the data is clearly visible.

A table contains columns and rows. These columns and rows create small boxes which are called cells. Entries made in each cell or box is understood with the title of the column and the row. Tables are classified as (a) one-way table, (b) two-way table and (c) multi-way table. Depending upon the purpose of the table and type of analysis to be undertaken, and also depending upon the purpose of the table and type of analysis to be undertaken, choice among the three types of tables could be made.

Tabulation has several rules and the most important ones are listed below.

1. Every table should be numbered. Numbering could be in alphabet, aerobic or roman or alpha numeric.
2. Each table should have a distinct title. The title should be short and clearly indicate what the contents of the table indicate.
3. Unit of measurement of the values in the table must be specified like crores, millions, tones, etc.
4. Each column should be titled.
5. Each row must be titled.
6. Columns and rows are to be numbered.
7. Any additional information about a cell [i.e. box] may be indicated using a symbol and giving the explanation of the symbol under the table.
8. Foot notes of the table should indicate the explanatory notes on the data in the table and the foot notes must be positioned below the table.
9. Data to be compared must be placed in adjacent columns.
10. In case of numbers loaded in the cells, these numbers should be arranged as per the digits.
11. The table should be simple and easily understandable.
12. Abbreviations should be avoided and if used, must be elaborated through foot notes.

Data Analysis

Quantitative Analysis: In research, a scholar explains the tools that he has adopted for analyzing the data. The scholar should select the tools of analysis by considering the objectives set for the study. He should examine the type of analysis required for accomplishing each objective set. Based on this, he must explain the features of the tool and how is it applied. Suppose the scholar wants to select functional form for some variables, he should first study the relationship between these variables. This is easily done through scatter diagram. Depending upon the nature of scatter obtained, the scholar should select the type of functional form. If the scatter indicates linear relationship, then the selection is for linear function, if not, non-linear form. Based on this, he should select the linear straight line function or a quadratic function. Similarly, if he selects multivariate analysis, then he should first determine what are the relevant variables by working out correlation among them.

Those with a high degree of positive or negative correlation have to be dropped and the remaining are to be included in the multivariate analysis. No scholar should attempt such analysis if he is not familiar with it. Suppose such an analysis is adopted for the study, then what is the general form of the function, what each letter in the function represents, why each of the variables was selected, the type of test statistics like [F test, test, R2 etc.] and the limitations of the function, should all be stated clearly. It is advisable to explain these tools in the order in which the objectives are studied through the analysis.

Qualitative Data: One of the important problems that researchers in social science experience is the accurate measurement of qualitative and subjective variables. In the absence of measuring possibilities, the inferences and conclusions drawn in several studies in social science are subjected to criticism. Therefore, the interpretation of the social scientists, however much important, goes unnoticed and command no values, as they are not quantified. It is true that every variable cannot be quantified and analyzed, but if there is a methodology with which the qualitative variables are also analyzed and interpreted with reasonable level of accuracy, it should be adopted.

The behavioural and social scientists have developed tools and instruments to overcome the difficulties in quantifying subjective and qualitative information. These tools and instruments are widely known as 'scaling techniques'. As a result of the scaling technique, the social scientists are able to now quantify any variable and conduct rigorous statistical analysis. Further, the use of scaling technique enables them to rank the variables they deal with.

For example, while compiling data regarding the performance of a public service like general hospital, the social scientists may develop a number of indicators like courteousness of the staff, effective treatment by doctors, availability of medicines, cleanliness in the hospital, etc. All these cannot be accurately measured. But by suggestion, different degrees of status of these variables, a researcher should be able to come to some conclusion. For this purpose, he may suggest the following degrees of status: excellent, very good, good, fair, poor. When questions on the above indicators are raised to the patients in the hospital, they are asked to indicate their choice using the above degrees of status. The researcher also would assign some weight to each one of these degrees of status like 5 points for excellent, 4 points for very good, 3 points for good, 2 points for fair and 1 point for poor. After collecting the responses of the patients in the hospital, he uses the weight associated with each indicator and concludes. Hence, by using scaling technique, it is possible to quantify the subjective and qualitative variables.

Review Questions

1. What do you understand by processing of data?
2. Define editing and list out its purpose?
3. What are the different types of editing? Explain each of these types with examples.
4. Discuss the guidelines for editing.
5. What is coding?
6. Distinguish between classification and tabulation.
7. Explain the rules of tabulation.
8. Distinguish between quantitative and qualitative analysis.

6

Methodological Approach to Action Research

Introduction

"If you want it done right, you may as well do it yourself." This aphorism may seem appropriate if you are a picky housekeeper, but more and more people are beginning to realize it can also apply to large corporations, community development projects, and even national governments. Such entities exist increasingly in an interdependent world, and are relying on action research as a means of coming to grips with their constantly changing and turbulent environments.

This paper will answer the question "What is Action Research"? giving an overview of its processes and principles, stating when it is appropriate to use, and situating it within a praxis research paradigm. The evolution of the approach will be described, including the various kinds of action research being used today. The role of the action researcher will be briefly mentioned, and some ethical considerations discussed. The tools of the action researcher particularly that of the use of search conferences will be explained. Finally, three case studies will be briefly described, two of which pertain to action research projects involving information technology, a promising area needing further research.

What is Action Research?

Definition: Action research is known by many other names, including participatory research, collaborative inquiry, emancipatory research, action learning, and contextual action research, but all are variations on a theme. Put simply, action research is "learning by doing"—a group of people identify a problem, do something to resolve it, see how successful their efforts were, and if not satisfied, try again. While this is the essence of the approach, there are other key attributes of action research that differentiates it from common problem-solving activities that we all engage in every day. A more succinct definition is, "Action research...aims to contribute both to the practical concerns of people in an immediate problematic situation and to further the goals of social science simultaneously. Thus, there is a dual commitment in action research to study a system and concurrently to collaborate with members of the system in changing it in what is together regarded as a desirable direction. Accomplishing this twin goal requires the active collaboration of researcher and client, and thus it stresses the importance of co-learning as a primary aspect of the research process".

What separates this type of research from general professional practices, consulting, or daily problem-solving is the emphasis on scientific study, which is to say the researcher studies the problem systematically and ensures that the intervention is informed by theoretical considerations. Much of the researcher's time is spent on refining the methodological tools to suit the exigencies of the situation, and on collecting, analyzing, and presenting data on an ongoing, cyclical basis.

Several attributes separate action research from other types of research. Primary is its focus on turning the people involved into researchers, too—people learn best, and more willingly apply what they have learnt, when they do it themselves. It also has a social dimension—the research takes place in real-world situations, and aims to solve real problems. Finally, the initiating researcher, unlike in other disciplines, makes no attempt to remain objective, but openly acknowledges their bias to the other participants.

Action Research Process: Stephen Kemmis has developed a simple model of the cyclical nature of the typical action research process (Figure 6.1). Each cycle has four steps: plan, act, observe, and reflect.

CYCLE 1

CYCLE 2

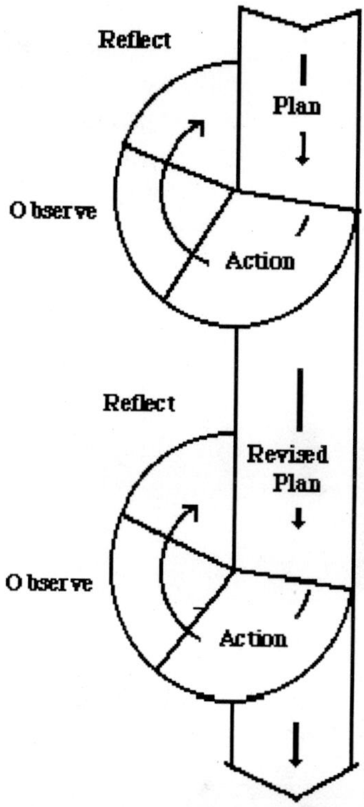

Figure 6.1: Simple Action Research Model (from MacIsaac, 1995).

Gerald Susman (1983) gives a somewhat more elaborate listing. He distinguishes five phases to be conducted within each research cycle (Figure 6.2). Initially, a problem is identified and data is collected for a more detailed diagnosis. This is followed by a collective postulation of several possible solutions, from which a single plan of action emerges and is implemented. Data on the results of the intervention are collected and analyzed, and the findings are interpreted in light of how successful the action has been. At this point, the problem is re-assessed and the process begins another cycle. This process continues until the problem is resolved.

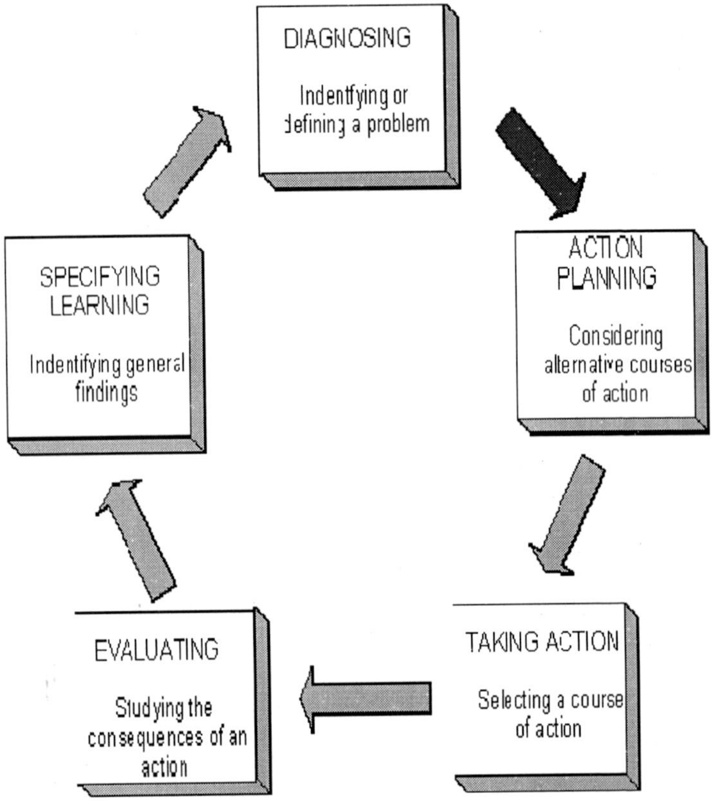

Figure 6.2: Detailed Action Research Model (adapted from Susman 1983).

Principles of Action Research: What gives action research its unique flavour is the set of principles that guide the research. Winter (1989) provides a comprehensive overview of the six key principles.

Reflexive Critique: An account of a situation, such as notes, transcripts or official documents, will make implicit claims to be authoritative, i.e., it implies that it is factual and true. Truth in a social setting, however, is relative to the teller. The principle of reflective critique ensures people reflect on issues and processes and make explicit the interpretations, biases, assumptions and concerns upon which judgments are made. In this way, practical accounts can give rise to theoretical considerations.

Dialectical Critique: Reality, particularly social reality, is consensually validated, which is to say it is shared through language. Phenomena are conceptualized in dialogue, therefore, a dialectical critique is required to understand the set of relationships both between the phenomenon and its context, and between the elements constituting the phenomenon. The key elements to focus attention on are those constituent elements that are unstable, or in opposition to one another. These are the ones that are most likely to create changes.

Collaborative Resource: Participants in an action research project are co-researchers. The principle of collaborative resource presupposes that each person's ideas are equally significant as potential resources for creating interpretive categories of analysis, negotiated among the participants. It strives to avoid the skewing of credibility stemming from the prior status of an idea-holder. It especially makes possible the insights gleaned from noting the contradictions both between many viewpoints and within a single viewpoint

Risk: The change process potentially threatens all previously established ways of doing things, thus creating psychic fears among the practitioners. One of the more prominent fears comes from the risk to ego stemming from open discussion of one's interpretations, ideas, and judgments. Initiators of action research will use this principle to allay others' fears and invite participation by pointing out that they, too, will be subject to the same process, and that whatever the outcome, learning will take place.

Plural Structure: The nature of the research embodies a multiplicity of views, commentaries and critiques, leading to multiple possible actions and interpretations. This plural structure of inquiry requires a plural text for reporting. This means that there will be many accounts made explicit, with commentaries on their contradictions, and a range of options for action presented. A report, therefore, acts as a support for ongoing discussion among collaborators, rather than a final conclusion of fact.

Theory, Practice and Transformation: For action researchers, theory informs practice and practice refines theory, in a continuous transformation. In any setting, people's actions are based on implicitly held assumptions, theories and hypotheses, and with every observed result, theoretical knowledge is enhanced. The two are intertwined aspects of a single change process. It is up to the researchers to make explicit the theoretical justifications for the actions, and to question the bases of those justifications. The ensuing practical applications that follow are subjected to further analysis, in a transformative cycle that continuously alternates emphasis between theory and practice.

When is Action Research Used?

Action research is used in real situations, rather than in contrived, experimental studies, since its primary focus is on solving real problems. It can, however, be used by social scientists for preliminary or pilot research, especially when the situation is too ambiguous to frame a precise research question.

Mostly, though, in accordance with its principles, it is chosen when circumstances require flexibility, the involvement of the people in the research, or change must take place quickly or holistically.

It is often the case that those who apply this approach are practitioners who wish to improve understanding of their practice, social change activists trying to mount an action campaign, or, more likely, academics who have been invited into an organization (or other domain) by decision-makers aware of a problem requiring action research, but lacking the requisite methodological knowledge to deal with it.

Situating Action Research in a Research Paradigm:

A. Positivist Paradigm: The main research paradigm for the past several centuries has been that of Logical Positivism. This paradigm is based on a number of principles, including: a belief in an objective reality, knowledge of which is only gained from sense data that can be directly experienced and verified between independent observers.

Phenomena are subject to natural laws that humans discover in a logical manner through empirical testing, using inductive and deductive hypotheses derived from a body of scientific theory. Its methods rely heavily on quantitative measures, with relationships among variables commonly shown by mathematical means. Positivism, used in scientific and applied research, has been considered by many to be the antithesis of the principles of action research (Susman and Evered 1978, Winter 1989).

B. Interpretive Paradigm: Over the last half century, a new research paradigm has emerged in the social sciences to break out of the constraints imposed by positivism. With its emphasis on the relationship between socially-engendered concept formation and language, it can be referred to as the interpretive paradigm.

Containing such qualitative methodological approaches as phenomenology, ethnography, and hermeneutics, it is characterized by a belief in a socially constructed, subjectively-based reality, one that is influenced by culture and history. Nonetheless, it still retains the ideals of researcher objectivity, and researcher as passive collector and expert interpreter of data.

C. Paradigm of Praxis: Though sharing a number of perspectives with the interpretive paradigm, and making considerable use of its related qualitative methodologies, there are some researchers who feel that neither it nor the positivist paradigms are sufficient epistemological structures under which to place action research (Lather 1986, Morley 1991). Rather, a paradigm of Praxis is seen as where the main affinities lie. Praxis, a term used by Aristotle, is the art of acting upon the conditions one faces in order to change them. It deals with the disciplines and activities predominant in the ethical and political lives of people. Aristotle contrasted this with Theoria—those sciences and activities that are concerned with knowing for its own sake. Both are equally needed he thought. That knowledge is derived from practice, and practice informed by knowledge, in an ongoing process, is a cornerstone of action research. Action researchers also reject the notion of researcher neutrality, understanding that the most active researcher is often the one who has most at stake in resolving a problematic situation.

Evolution of Action Research

Origins in Late 1940s: Kurt Lewin is generally considered the 'father' of action research. A German social and experimental psychologist, and one of the founders of the Gestalt School, he was concerned with social problems, and focused on participative group processes for addressing conflict, crises, and change, generally within organizations. Initially, he was associated with the Centre for Group Dynamics at MIT in Boston, but soon went on to establish his own National Training Laboratories.

Lewin first coined the term 'action research' in his 1946 paper "Action Research and Minority Problems", characterizing action research as "a comparative research on the conditions and effects of various forms of social action and research leading to social action", using a process of "a spiral of steps, each of which is composed of a circle of planning, action, and fact-finding about the result of the action".

Eric Trist, another major contributor to the field from that immediate post-War era, was a social psychiatrist whose group at the Tavistock Institute of Human Relations in London engaged in applied social research, initially for the civil repatriation of German prisoners of war. He and his colleagues tended to focus more on large-scale, multi-organizational problems.

Both Lewin and Trist applied their research to systemic change in and between organizations. They emphasized direct professional-client collaboration and affirmed the role of group relations as the basis for problem-solving. Both were avid proponents of the principle that decisions are best implemented by those who help make them.

Current Types of Action Research

By the mid-1970s, the field had evolved, revealing four main 'streams' that had emerged: traditional, contextual (action learning), radical, and educational action research.

Traditional Action Research: Traditional action research stemmed from Lewin's work within organizations and encompasses the concepts and practices of field theory, group dynamics, T-groups, and the clinical model. The growing importance of labour-management relations led to the application of action research in the areas of Organization Development, Quality of Working Life (QWL), Socio-technical systems (e.g., Information Systems), and Organizational Democracy. This traditional approach tends toward the conservative, generally maintaining the status quo with regards to organizational power structures.

Contextual Action Research (Action Learning): Contextual action research, also sometimes referred to as action learning, is an approach derived from Trist's work on relations between organizations. It is contextual, insofar as it entails reconstituting the structural relations among actors in a social environment; domain-based, in that it tries to involve all affected parties and stakeholders; holographic, as each participant understands the working of the whole; and it stresses that participants act as project designers and co-researchers. The concept of organizational ecology, and the use of search conferences comes out of contextual action research, which is more of a liberal philosophy, with social transformation occurring by consensus and normative incrementalism.

Radical Action Research: The Radical stream, which has its roots in Marxian 'dialectical materialism' and the praxis orientations of Antonio Gramsci, has a strong focus on emancipation and the overcoming of power imbalances. Participatory action research, often found in liberationist movements and international development circles, and feminist action research both strive for social transformation via an advocacy process to strengthen peripheral groups in the society.

Educational Action Research: A fourth stream, that of educational action research, has its foundations in the writings of John Dewey, the great American educational philosopher of the 1920s and 1930s, who believed that professional educators should become involved in community problem-solving. Its practitioners, not surprisingly, operate mainly out of educational institutions, and focus on development of curriculum, professional development, and applying learning in a social context. It is often the case that university-based action researchers work with primary and secondary school teachers and students on community projects.

Action Research Tools

Action research is more of a holistic approach to problem-solving, rather than a single method for collecting and analyzing data. Thus, it allows for several different research tools to be used as the project is conducted. These various methods, which are generally common to the qualitative research paradigm, include: keeping a research journal, document collection and analysis, participant observation recordings, questionnaire surveys, structured and unstructured interviews, and case studies.

The Search Conference: Of all of the tools utilized by action researchers, the one that has been developed exclusively to suit the needs of the action research approach is that of the search conference, initially developed by Eric Trist and Fred

Emery at the Tavistock Institute in 1959, and first implemented for the merger of Bristol-Siddley Aircraft Engines in 1960.

The search conference format has seen widespread development since that time, with variations on Trist and Emery's theme becoming known under other names due to their promotion by individual academics and consultants. These include Dannemiller-Tyson's Interactive Strategic Planning, Marvin Weisbord's Future Search Conference, Dick Axelrod's Conference Model Redesign, Harrison Owen's Open Space, and ICA's Strategic Planning (Rouda 1995).

Search conferences also have been conducted for many different circumstances and participants, including: decision-makers from several countries visioning the "Future of Participative Democracy in the Americas"; practitioners and policymakers in the field of health promotion in Ontario taking charge in an era of cutbacks; and Xerox employees sorting out enterprise re-organization.

Eric Trist sums up the process quite nicely:

"Searching...is carried out in groups which are composed of the relevant stakeholders. The group meets under social island conditions for 2-3 days, sometimes as long as five. The opening sessions are concerned with elucidating the factors operating in the wider contextual environment—those producing the meta-problems and likely to affect the future. The content is contributed entirely by the members. The staff is facilitators only. Items are listed in the first instance without criticism in the plenary session and displayed on flip charts which surround the room. The material is discussed in greater depth in small groups and the composite picture checked out in plenary. The group next examines its own organizational setting or settings against this wider background and then proceeds to construct a picture of a desirable future. It is surprising how much agreement there often is. Only when all this has been done, is consideration given to action steps...".

Role of the Action Researcher: Upon invitation into a

domain, the outside researcher's role is to implement the action research method in such a manner as to produce a mutually agreeable outcome for all participants, with the process being maintained by them afterwards. To accomplish this, it may necessitate the adoption of many different roles at various stages of the process, including those of:

planner	leader
catalyzer	facilitator
teacher	designer
listener	observer
synthesizer	reporter

The main role, however, is to nurture local leaders to the point where they can take responsibility for the process. When this point is reached they understand the methods and are able to carry on when the initiating researcher leaves.

In many action research situations, the hired researcher's role is primarily to take the time to facilitate dialogue and foster reflective analysis among the participants, provide them with periodic reports, and write a final report when the researcher's involvement has ended.

Ethical Considerations

Because action research is carried out in real-world circumstances, and involves close and open communication among the people involved, the researchers must pay close attention to ethical considerations in the conduct of their work. Richard Winter (1996) lists a number of principles:

1. "Make sure that the relevant persons, committees and authorities have been consulted, and that the principles guiding the work are accepted in advance by all.
2. All participants must be allowed to influence the work, and the wishes of those who do not wish to participate must be respected.
3. The development of the work must remain visible and open to suggestions from others.
4. Permission must be obtained before making observations

or examining documents produced for other purposes.

5. Descriptions of others' work and points of view must be negotiated with those concerned before being published.
6. The researcher must accept responsibility for maintaining confidentiality."

To this, might be added several more points:

7. Decisions made about the direction of the research and the probable outcomes are collective.
8. Researchers are explicit about the nature of the research process from the beginning, including all personal biases and interests.
9. There is equal access to information generated by the process for all participants.
10. The outside researcher and the initial design team must create a process that maximizes the opportunities for involvement of all participants.

Action Research and Information Technology

In the past ten years or so, there has been a marked increase in the number of organizations that are making use of information technology and computer mediated communications. This has led to a number of convergences between information systems and action research. In some cases, it has been a matter of managers of corporate networks employing action research techniques to facilitate large-scale changes to their information systems. In others, it has been a question of community-based action research projects making use of computer communications to broaden participation.

Much of the action research carried out over the past 40 years has been conducted in local settings with the participants meeting face-to-face with "real-time" dialogue. The emergence of the Internet has led to an explosion of *asynchronous* and *a spatial* group communication in the form of e-mail and computer conferences, and recently, v-mail and video conferencing. While there have been numerous attempts to use this new technology in assisting group learning, both within organizations and among groups in the community [this author has been involved with a dozen or more projects of this kind in the non-profit sector in Canada alone], there is a dearth of published studies on the use of action research methods in such projects. Lau and Hayward (1997), in a recent review of the literature, found that most research on group support systems to date has been in short-term, experimental situations using quantitative methods. There are a few examples, though, of longitudinal studies in naturalistic settings using qualitative methods; of those that did use action research, none studied the use and effects of communication systems in groups and organizations.

Conclusion

This chapter has presented an overview of action research as a methodological approach to solving social problems. The principles and procedures of this type of research, and epistemological underpinnings, were described, along with the evolution of the practice. Details of a search conference and other tools were given, as was an indication of the roles and ethics involved in the research. The case studies gave concrete examples of projects, particularly in the relatively new area of social deployment of information technologies. Further, action research is needed to explore the potential for developing computer-mediated communications in a way that will enhance human interactions.

7

Thesis Writing

Introduction

Thesis writing is considered a complex work by every researcher. This is because, the scholar remains under the impression that while writing the thesis, he has to do something different from what he is normally doing. This impression is because the theses that he would have referred while reviewing literature would have been written and presented in such a way that an ordinary individual will not be able to understand what is stated in the thesis. In reality, thesis writing involves presenting ideas in a logical sequence in a simple language. There is no need to use very flowery language or Elizabethan style. It is suggested that the scholar should place himself in the position of the other readers and use appropriate language. But, while presenting the contents of the thesis there is a structure to be followed. Most of the universities prescribe the structure of the thesis, which is to be closely followed.

One of the questions normally raised by the researchers is when to write and submit the research report. The answer for this question is that depending upon the subject matter of research; the time has to be determined. In a research relating to current economic issues, the thesis should be submitted in time, as otherwise, the contents will be out of date. In the case of theoretical research, time is not a constraint. In the field of medical or science the time taken for submitting the research report is very lengthy because the finding of the study have to be experimented at several stages and only after confirmation of the findings, the report could be presented.

A thesis should contain the following points:

The problem focus of the thesis should be clearly stated;

The research procedure followed, the area of the study, the sources of data, the sampling design, the hypothesis and the tools of analysis must be explained clearly;

The findings and results of the study should be stated; and

The policy options and implications of the results must also be specified.

Thesis writing requires concerted effort and concentration. A large volume of information has to be presented in a sequence in concise manner. The scholar should take care to avoid any duplication of facts anywhere, unless otherwise necessary. Contradictory statements should be avoided. That is, what is stated at one stage is countered in another stage. This would happen usually when the results are interpreted. Hence, the scholar should always have the habit of summarizing the findings of each analysis and then study the summary to identify any contradiction. A very important point is that the scholar should use past tense while referring to the research procedure.

Guidelines for Thesis Writing

While writing a thesis there are a few practices which should be followed without fail. This will ensure uniformity and consistency in the constituents of the thesis. These practices are explained below:

1. Always two or three draft of a thesis should be prepared before the final version is prepared. The draft could be either written manuscripts or typed scripts or computer print outs. Whatever be the form of the drafts, it is essential that it is produced on an A4 size paper, typed in double line spacing, typed on one side of the paper, a margin of one inch at the top and bottom and one and half inch margin on the left and right.
2. The drafts should have sufficient space for noting down the changes and corrections in the subject matter. Corrections and changes should always be indicated in pencil marking, using standard editing practices.

3. When the final draft is prepared it should be printed on an A4 bond paper preferably executive bond paper.
4. Depending upon the objectives and methodology of the thesis, the layout of the thesis should be decided in advance. If emphasis has to be given on any aspect of the thesis, it is better to place it as a separate chapter. While there are no restrictions with regard to the number of chapters in a thesis, it is better to limit it to suit the nature of the work.
5. As regards the size of the thesis, i.e. the number of pages in a thesis, the stipulation of the university concerned must be adhered. There are universities which suggest that the body of the thesis should not exceed 200 pages, while in some other case, the entire thesis should not exceed 250 pages. Depending upon the stipulation of the university, the size of the thesis could be decided.
6. The thesis should be neatly cloth bound and provided in plastic jacket. The outer cover should contain all the details on the title page of the thesis. Here also, universities specify the format for the title page. In some universities, only the name of the candidate has to be given in the title page and the name of the supervisor or guide is not mentioned. So it is advisable to follow such approved formats.
7. In some universities, a rough binding of the thesis in final form is suggested while submitting the thesis. After the evaluation is completed, the suggestions and views of the evaluators could be incorporated in the thesis and then the final corrected version could be bound properly.
8. As regards the foot notes and bibliographical entries, some universities suggest the format and this should be closely followed.
9. It is a good practice to use a number of main headings and sub-headings in the thesis. While using them, appropriate distinction should be given. For example, if the main heading is in bold capital letters, the sub-headings may be

bold, italic and underscored.

10. Special care should be taken while using tables, graphs and diagrammers. Tables should all be numbered and placed before the discussion. On no account, the tables should be split. In case of bigger tables, it is better either to print them on double sheet and place them folded properly in the thesis or break up the contents of the tables into different components and present each one of them through different tables.
11. As regards graphs or diagrams, they should be neatly drawn either with black ink or computer printed. Colour graphs would add to clarity and presentation. But the graphs or diagrammed should fit in an A4 size paper. Sufficient margin should be given around the presentation. Each figure should be numbered and titled. In case of multiple entries, legend should be used. It is a good practice to use different style of lines [like bold, ordinary, dotted, dashed, star, ascetics, etc.] while drawing graphs. Different types of diagrams are available like bar diagrams, pie diagrams, area diagrams, etc. Suitable diagrams should be selected to represent the information. Regarding the placement of graphs or diagrams, it is a good practice to position them after the discussion in the sequence in which the results are discussed.
12. Regarding the assignment of pages, it should be noted that all graphs and diagrams should bear a page number. Appendix should also be numbered in continuation of the body of the thesis. Only the preliminary pages are to be numbered in lower case roman letters.

Footnotes

Footnotes are placed at the bottom of each page to give additional information on the source from where the material used in the text is borrowed. The purpose of the footnote is to indicate the source of information used. Sometimes the material concerned may be an elaboration of the reference used in the text, but not required to be produced in the body of the text. Acknowledgements of the sources may also be given in the form of footnotes. Usually, the footnote number should correspond with the number assigned for the matter in the text of the thesis. The number should be placed slightly above the footnote text. The letter size of footnote text should be lesser than that of the letter size used in the body of the thesis. Footnote is always typed in single line spacing and double line space is given in between footnotes.

Other very useful aspects about footnote is: (1) The first footnote reference should be complete in every respect, containing name of the author, title of the article, the title of the journal or the book, volume number, issue number, date and page numbers. (2) Suppose the same source is referred immediately following the first reference, then the term ibid [means in the same place] is used. Suppose the reference material is in the same place which is already specified, then it is represented by ibid. However, if the source is the same but the page number referred is different, in such cases, it is enough that the page number alone is referred, [example, ibid. p. 7]. (3) Suppose the references to the same work occur within the same chapter, then it is indicated as op. cit. [means, the work cited] or loc. cit. [means, in the place cited]. In this case, the foot note will be shown as: author's name followed by op.cit., p. 401.

There are occasions when more than one person would have authored an article or a book. Suppose the number of authors is two, then the name of both of them is given. If there are more than two authors, then the name of the first alone is given followed by et al. [means and others].

Structure of a Ph.D. Thesis

A Ph.D. thesis has a specific structure. The thesis should adhere to this structure, though the university concerned may suggest a small variation of this structure. However, the general format for the structure includes the following main sections:

1. Preliminary section;
2. Body of the thesis; and
3. Reference or appendix.

Preliminary Section: The preliminary section usually consists of the following pages: 1. Title page, 2. Certificate from the guide, 3. Declaration by the scholar, 4. Acknowledgements, 5. Table of contents, 6. List of tables, 7. List of figures, 8. List of appendices.

Title page: The university concerned suggests normally the format for the title page. In this page, the title of the thesis is printed in bold letters. It is advisable that the title does not exceed two lines. The title should be properly centered. The title should clearly reflect the focus of the study. For example: performance evaluation of drugs and pharmaceutical industry in India; evaluation of export performance of leather industry in India; temporal and spatial variation in the marketing of jingly; evaluation of public distribution in urban centre, etc. In all these titles, the scope of the thesis is clearly indicated.

Certificate from the guide/supervisor: Normally this is issued and signed by the guide/supervisor stating that the thesis is the contribution made by the scholar and that the guide has provided only general guidance in shaping the work.

Declaration by the candidate: This is a certificate submitted by the scholar in whom he states, that the thesis is the result of his own efforts, and is not a copy of any thesis or publication already submitted or published to any agency. Through such an undertaking, the scholar commits himself to whatever is stated in the thesis. In case at a later point of time, any part of the thesis is found to be a reproduction of what has been already published or done by somebody, then the scholar will lose his credibility in the field of research. Universities normally view such plagiarism as very serious. So while signing this certificate, the scholar should be fully aware of the consequences.

Acknowledgements: In this page, the scholar expresses his gratefulness to all those who have helped him in the course of his research work. Sometimes, the scholar may also specify what type of help was extended to him by various people. The contents of this page are the prerogative of the scholar.

Table of contents: In this page, the scholar clearly spells out the contents of the thesis. He specifies the title for each chapter and the page number. It should be noted that in this page, the page number of the guide's certificate, scholar's declaration and acknowledgements should also be included. Normally, the pages in the preliminary section are stated in small roman number and the page number of the body of the thesis is indicated in Arabic number. The contents of the appendix section are also indicated along with their page number.

List of tables: in this page the scholar provides the tables that are used in the body of the thesis. Usually the table number is given continuously in roman numerals right from the first chapter till the last chapter of the thesis, though there is no standard pattern recommended. This is because, some scholars use Arabic numbering of the tables and they assign the table number along with the chapter number. For example: 3.16, means 16th table in the third chapter. Some scholars give Arabic number for the tables in serial order from the 1st to the last chapter. Whatever be the numbering style used, in the list of tables, the scholar would indicate the table number, title of the table and the page number in which the table is located.

List of figures: This is a page in which the scholar would present the list of figures/diagrams used in the thesis. As regards the numbering of the figures, different patterns are followed. For example, if the tables are numbered in roman numerals, than the figures are represented in Arabic numerals. Sometimes, the chapter number is indicated in roman number followed by the figure/diagram number. For example: III.4 means fourth figure in chapter III. Like tables, the figures or diagrams are also numbered continuously, and no chapter number is indicated along with the figure number.

List of appendices: In this part of the contents, the scholar would specify items included under the appendices. He would indicate the items in serial order, its title and the page number where it is found. For example: 1. Bibliography; 2. Questionnaire/schedule used for the study; 3. Government policy relating to the topic of the thesis; 4. Explanatory notes for the mathematical/ econometric models used in the study, etc.

So the preliminary section of the thesis would contain information about the above items. In theism page, arrangement of items may differ from university to university. For instance, in the case of research scholars who are sponsored or getting stipend from University Grants Commission (UGC), a page is included indicating the institution or organization which has provided the sponsorship or financial support. Such a page may also state that the copy right of the subject matter of the thesis is held by the sponsoring institution/funding organization. This page is mandatory for such scholars. In some cases, scholars also devote a page for dedicating their work to somebody.

Body of the Thesis: Body of the thesis includes: 1. Introduction, 2. Review of literature, 3. Methodology, 4. Results and discussion and 5. Summary and conclusions.

The above given contents of the body of the thesis is only indicative. Different scholars follow different patterns. Before dealing with other patterns of the body of the thesis, the above basic contents could be discussed.

A. Introduction: In the opening section of a thesis, the scholar would explain the background necessary for the study. He would deal with the relevant aspects, which provide the backdrop to the subject matter of the thesis. For example, suppose the thesis is on evaluation of export performance of leather industry in India, then the scholar would provide brief details about the leather industry in India in terms of its structure, contribution in terms of employment generation, income generation, value addition, export earnings, technology, etc. After this, the scholar would spell out the justifications of the study, i.e. why the study is undertaken and why is it necessary. The problem focus of the study is spelt out next.

This is followed by the objectives of the study. The scholar may indicate the overall objective or broad objective of the study followed by specific objectives. In this context, it should be noted that wording of the objectives should be very carefully done. Scholars should avoid using subjective terms while laying down the objectives. Sometimes, the scholar uses expressions like 'to study the pattern of exports' 'attempt to examine the pattern of exports' etc. Use of terms like study, attempt, etc. should certainly be avoided. As far as possible, the objectives should be measurable so that the tools of analysis could be determined around the objectives and the data required for the analysis could be collected easily. It is suggested that terms like: 'to examine', 'to analyze', 'to evaluate' and 'to identify' could be used. Another important aspect is that the number of objectives should be limited to four or five.

Following the objectives of the study, the scholar may mention the hypothesis taken up for the study. He might also use two or three hypotheses. All of them could be mentioned with the purpose of framing them.

It is necessary that the limitations of the study are also spelt out in the introduction. While framing the limitations, the scholar could focus on limitations relating to the accuracy of the data if it is collected through survey of secondary sources, the limitations about the models or functions used, limitations with regard to the application of the conclusions to different areas, etc.

This will be normally followed by the chapter outline. That is, the scholar would state the number of chapters in the study, their titles and very brief contents of each of them.

B. Review of Literature: In this chapter, the scholar will present the review of all the previous studies, articles published, books published, etc. The scholar would normally classify this chapter in to three of four parts viz. (i) review of journal articles, (ii) review of books, (iii) review of thesis, and (iv) review of the reports. The purpose of presenting the details of the previous studies is to prepare the relevant background. Through this, the scholar would be able to state the findings of the previous study on the topic being researched by him.

While reviewing the previous study, the scholar should focus on the objectives of such studies viz. concepts used, methodology adopted, and the conclusions arrived at. Theses conclusions may corroborate or contradict the ones arrived at by the scholar. The scholar should present the reviews starting from the earlier ones and ending with the current ones. This will give a clear picture about how the conclusions or the concepts have evolved over a period of time. The scholar should also take care to avoid any duplication and irrelevant literature. The scholar should not reproduce the article or the text, unless otherwise necessary for the context. Normally such reproductions are presented through end notes or footnotes. Always every article reviewed should be backed by the source. While indicating the source, the scholar should follow the sequence: the name of the author, title of the article, name of the journal, volume number, issue number and page number, while reviewing an article from a periodical. The sequence will be different in the case of a book, viz. name of the author, title of the book, name of publisher, place of publication, year of publication, edition and page number. He should follow the rules with regard to name of the author, page number, etc. These are discussed in the topic on bibliography in this book.

Often the researchers used to dispute about the number of

reviews to be made. While no specific number can be spelt out, it is always recommended that the researcher should review as many articles and books as possible. At the same time for the sake of achieving the number, the researcher should not be hasty to include all irrelevant reviews. In this task, the guide/supervisor's role is very important.

C. Methodology: This is easily the most crucial part of any thesis. Any evaluator of a thesis would attach maximum importance to this section. Unless the methodology adopted for the study is satisfactory and rigorous, the evaluator is likely to develop a poor impression of the thesis. Hence, the contents of the methodology chapter should be carefully planned. In this regards, the following points are to be taken into account.

Justification of the study should be stated;
Problem focus must be spelt out; and
Objectives of the study should be clearly stated.

These three aspects are usually explained in the introduction chapter itself. However, .repeating them here would make the remaining aspects of the methodology clearer.

Period of study: This refers to the duration of the study. That is, whether the study is analyzing the facts for a period of 10 years or is it focusing on the current status alone. For example, in a study on export performance of drugs and pharmaceutical industry, it is necessary to analyze the pattern of exports of drugs and pharmaceuticals at least for a period of 10 to 15 years, to comment anything on the pattern of exports. While selecting the period of study, the scholar should support it with a justification.

Area of the study: Suppose a research is on spatial and temporal variation in marketing of gingerly oil. Then as the title suggests, the study is analyzing the marketing of gingerly in different places. Therefore, what is the area included for the study, must be specified. This should also be supported by the reasons why this specific area was taken up for research.

Sources of data: Through this, the scholar indicates where from he has collected the data for the study. If it is the primary data then, how it was collected, was it a census or sample study, what was the method of collecting data [interview or observation or questionnaire/schedule], etc. should be mentioned. If it is the secondary data, the scholar should specify what were the sources—like RBI Bulletin, monthly abstracts of statistics, agricultural situation in India, India Investment Centre Publication, etc. These details would add authenticity to the study.

Sample design: Whatever be the type of data collection, sample design becomes a very significant part of the methodology chapter. Sample design refers to the method of sampling adopted for data collection. Sometimes the scholar collects the data from sample respondents. Here, he should explain how the sample characteristic was established, how the sample size was determined and how the data was collected. Sample size depends on several factors, which have been discussed in detail in the topic on sampling. In methodology, the scholar should explain the details about population and the method by which the sample was selected. This will ultimately decide the reliability and usefulness of the study. On most of the occasions, scholars commit mistakes in determining the sample and adopting the sampling process.

Tools of analysis: This is a very important part of the methodology. In this part, the scholar explains the tools that he has adopted for analyzing the data. The scholar should select the tools of analysis by considering the objectives set for the study. He should examine the type of analysis required for accomplishing each objective set. Based on this, he must explain the features of the tools and how they are applied. Suppose the scholar wants to select functional form for some variables, he should first study the relationship between these variables. This is easily done through scatter. If the scatter indicates linear relationship, then the selection is for linear function, if not, then the non-linear form. Based on this, he should select the linear straight line function or quadratic function. Similarly, if he selects multivariate analysis, then he should first determine what are the relevant variables by working out correlation among them. Those with high degree of positive or negative correlation have to be dropped and the remaining have to be included in the multivariate analysis. No scholar should attempt such analyses if he is not familiar with them. Suppose such an analysis is adopted for the study, then what is the general form of the function, what each letter in the function represents, why each of the variables was selected, the type of test statistics like [F test, t test, R2 etc.] and the limitations of the function, should all be stated clearly. It is advisable to explain these tools in the order in which the objectives are studied through the analysis.

Limitations of the study: In this section, the scholar should be honest to state the limitations of the data used, analysis applied, validity of conclusions etc.

D. Results and Discussion: In this chapter, the scholar will present the result of the analysis he had adopted in his study. Each result will be discussed and interpreted. Side by side, the scholar will also indicate the policy options based on the analysis. While he is interpreting the results of the analysis, he should follow the procedures explained in the topic on interpretation. It is a good practice to summarize the findings and interpretation at the end of discussion of each tool of analysis. He must also arrange the discussion of results in the same sequence in which the objectives are laid down for the study. To add clarity to the discussion, the scholar should make liberal use of graphs and diagrams. He must ensure that sufficient care is taken while handling and presenting graphs and diagrams. These tools of representation should be used to substantiate the conclusions and discussion of the results. There are scholars who use graphs and diagrams as tools of analysis. It is a good practice to use tables to present data. But it is always suggested that tables should precede discussion to facilitate an easy understanding. Tables should never be split. All the rules of tabulation should be followed. The usual practice is that tables will precede discussion and graphs and diagrams will follow the discussion. Discussion part of the thesis should be the lengthiest in a thesis. Some scholars discuss each tool in a separate chapter. While there is nothing wrong in it, while adopting such a practice, the scholar should maintain continuity and carefully avoid any contradiction in the interpretation.

E. Summary and Conclusions: This is the last chapter in the body of any thesis. In this chapter, first a brief of objectives and methodology should be presented in the same order in which they were discussed in the discussion chapter. This will facilitate any reader to understand and place the conclusions in the right perspective. This is then followed by the policy options or suggestions, which will form the basis for policies. The scholar should be positive while giving suggestions and indicate how these suggestions will overcome the problems identified in the course of analysis. It is also very frequently found that the scholar gives suggestions, which are not emerging from the study, as a part of the suggestions. This is certainly a questionable practice.

Documentation

A. Bibliography: Bibliography is an alphabetical arrangement of journals, periodicals, books, reports, theses, etc. It provides additional information about the source of the material used in a research study or a book. It furnishes the author's name, title of the article, journal name, issue number, volume number, page or pages in which the particular article is found in the case of journals or periodicals. As regards books, the bibliography indicated, the name of the author, title of the book, publishers name, place of publication, edition, year of publication, the page or pages in which the material used in the study are found. Similarly, in the case of research reports or published or unpublished theses, all the relevant details about the source are given.

Bibliographical notes are always given in a separate page. Serial number of the item is given. Then the bibliographical note is given in single line spacing. In between items, double line spacing is given.

To make bibliography useful, it is always better to classify it in three or four sections, viz. periodicals/journals, books, published reports, unpublished theses, etc. The presentation of entries in bibliography should be in accordance with the standard practice. This is explained in the following paragraphs.

B. Periodicals/Journals: In the case of articles cited from periodicals and journals, the bibliographical note should be recorded as below:

Balasundaram, S.K., "The Growth of Co-operative Rural Banks for the Rural Community", Tamil Nadu Journal of Co-operation, 78 [8], February, 1989, pp. 463-465.

In the above bibliographical note, first the author of the article is given with the initials, then the title of the article is specified within quotation, then the name of the journal/periodical is stated. This is followed by the volume number [i.e. 78], issue number [i.e. 8], month and year of publication [February, 1989], and finally the page numbers are given. If only one page number is to be given, it is stated as p. 463 and if a few pages are to be continuously referred, then it is shown as pp. 463-465.

Books: In the case of books, the bibliographical note is different in presentation. This would be clear from the following example:

William Emory, c., Business Research Methods, Richard D. Irwin Inc., Homewood, Illinois, 1976, pp. 23-29.

It may be noted in the above example that first, the author of the book is given, followed by the title of the book, which is underscored. Afterwards, the publishers name is given, followed by the place of publication. Then the year of publication is given, followed by the page numbers.

Reports: Reports may be of different types. It could be a seminar report or report of some commission set by the government or it could be a report of some institution like RBI, IMF, etc. The bibliographical note for report is shown below:

Antipathy, B.R., Management of Funds in Co-operative Banks, State Level Seminar on Applied Co-operative Management, Sri Ramakrishna Mission Vidyalaya Arts College, Coimbatore, 1984.

The name of the person who has prepared the report is given first, followed by the title of the report. Then the context of the report [like seminar report, report of commission of inquiry, etc.], then the place where the seminar or conference of commission of inquiry was held is indicated, and finally, the place and the year will follow.

Thesis: Whenever any thesis is used as a reference source in the study, then the bibliographical note should be given as illustrated below:

Devnarayanan, T.S., Export Performance Evaluation of Leather Industry in India, Thesis Submitted to the University of Madras, October, 1997, pp. 150-155.

Name of the author of the thesis is given first followed by the title of the thesis. The university to which the thesis was submitted is indicated next. The month and year of submission of the thesis and page numbers referred in the source follows in sequence.

Use of Appendices: In this third part of a thesis, a scholar will provide the details of all supporting material used in his study. Usually, the appendix may contain four or five sections viz. bibliography, index, additional information, questionnaire and schedule used in the study, supporting data, explanation of models used, etc. By providing this, the scholar would be able to establish authenticity for his work and also facilitate future research.

Bibliography will contain the details of journals and books used and referred in the course of the study. The details of the sources, like, name of the journal, its volume number, issue number and date are also mentioned. In the case of books, name of the author, title of the book, publisher's name, year of publication, place of publication and edition are all provided. These entries would be alphabetically arranged and may be classified into books, periodicals, report, published and unpublished theses, etc. The procedure for developing the bibliography is explained in the topic on bibliography and index in this book.

Index is also provided in some of the thesis. This will facilitate easy location of any important aspect of the thesis. Care should be taken to prepare the index by focusing on important terms and concepts used in the course of the thesis. Page number should be mentioned along with the index entry. Further details on index preparation and uses are explained in the topic on bibliography and index in this book.

Scholars also add a copy of questionnaire or schedule used in the data collection process. This will help the future researchers for preparing their questionnaires or schedules.

Supporting data in the form of tables, policy notes, abstracts, etc. are also appended to provide necessary clarifications for queries on the contents of the thesis. But while providing these, care should be taken to use only related material. For example, a change in policy, which should be known to assess the conclusions arrived at in the thesis could be added. Numerical information or computations supporting the discussion of results could also be provided. Sometimes, scholars also place some photographs as extra evidence for their findings in this section.

Whenever mathematical or econometric modelling is used in the thesis, some explanatory notes or derivation of some functions, etc. could be explained by adding relevant articles in the appendix section. This will enable the future researchers to learn these models and apply them in their work.

Indexing: Index refers to an alphabetical list of name of author or subject matter provided at the end of research reports. The main purpose of such index is to enable the reader to locate the author of subject matter easily. Index plays a very vital role in supporting and aiding the readers. Sometimes definition of a particular technical term may be required. Instead of trying to determine the topic in which it is used, it is easier to find out the locations in the text where the term is used. While in a dictionary or an encyclopaedia, the terms are all arranged in alphabetical order, in a research note or a text book, the technical terms are used at different places. Sometimes, a technical term is used more in a particular context. In such a context, the term is fully explained and defined and by going through this, anyone should be able to understand the usefulness and application of the term. There are some authors who offer author's index and subject index separately. Such a practice is very useful to the readers of the book.

For example, the term marginal propensity to consume is a term used mainly while explaining the consumption function in macro economics. But this term is also used while explaining the concept of a multiplier. So in a book on macro economics, the term marginal propensity to consume will find its place in several locations. But if one wants to get a clear understanding of the concept, one should only refer to the topic on consumption function, where it is fully explained. However, the index would indicate the pages where this term is used and based on this the reader may refer to the particular page or pages and understand the concept. The index may appear as: marginal propensity to consume, 85-91, 120, 134, 256, 285. In this manner the reader will find full details about the concept in pages 85-91. In all the other pages, some reference is made to this concept.

Another example of a general index is the yellow pages, in which the business contact details are provided trade-wise, like audio-systems, radio, compact disk players and recording, etc. The directory will contain the details of the business establishments dealing with such products. Telephone directory is yet another example of index. But these indexes are of general nature.

To prepare an index, the following steps are to be taken:

Prepare a list of author's name/technical terms used, page-wise.

Remove any duplication of author's name/technical term.

Indicate the page numbers in which the author's name/term has occurred.

Arrange the author's name and technical terms in alphabetical order.

Maintain separate index of authors and technical terms, if required.

If a report of the book is very voluminous, then the index is prepared chapter-wise. This gives a better clarity, but duplication of author's name/technical terms cannot be avoided. Such an index is usually found in textbooks or reference material on law, where case laws are arranged chapter-wise.

Regarding the question whether every research report or a book should contain index—it is certainly optional. But provision of index, subject-wise/author-wise would certainly be found useful. Index is different from bibliography. Index will contain only the page number in which a term or the author's name has occurred. It cannot give any source for the technical term or the author. All the details about the author, journal/book, volume number, issue number, publication details, page numbers, etc. index guides one to the specific term or author referred in the book. It is a source of internal search. But bibliography enables one to locate the source of origin in the journal/book and read the origin. Index is optional in a research report but bibliography is a compulsory section to be included in every research report.

Review Questions

1. Account for the major steps followed in planning a research project.

2. Discuss the main considerations that should be taken into account in the mechanics of thesis writing.
3. What are the precautions to be followed in the presentation of aims and objectives in a research report?
4. What are the precautions to be followed in writing a good research report?
5. Explain the rules for arrangements of text, diagrams, references, etc. in a research report.
6. What do you understand by report writing? What are the steps followed in it?
7. What are the main components of report writing in social science research?
8. Describe the importance of review of literature in thesis writing.
9. Discuss the main considerations that should be taken into account in the mechanics of thesis writing.
10. Describe the importance of review of literature.
11. Discuss the need for bibliography and explain the salient points connected with the preparation of bibliography in a research report.
12. What is the purpose of footnotes in a research report? Explain the rules regarding the use of footnotes in a research report.
13. What is the difference between footnotes and end notes. Explain the relative strengths and weaknesses of both.
14. Define index. What are the purposes for which index is provided in any book?
15. Discuss the rules regarding the use of tables and diagrams in a research report.

8

Report Writing

Research Report Writing

Research report is a written document through which, the researcher intimates to the world the findings of his study, the design of his study, his conclusions, the suggestions and recommendations based on his findings, the details of data collected, the method he has adopted for selecting the sample, the tools he has used for analysis, the hypothesis he has set, his objectives, the limitations of his study, etc. Research findings are always meant to be announced and shared. In this processing of communicating to the world, the researcher must make his communication very effective.

There are instances when, even the most useful findings and generalizations were not taken note of, because they were presented in a disorganized manner. Further, researchers normally have a wrong feeling that writing a research report is not a part of the research work. In reality, research report is the last stage in the process of research. But the type of skill required for writing the research report is different from the skill required, at the initial stage of research. Therefore, a research scholar must develop the art of writing and communicating his ideas clearly. This skill is acquired only by practice and experience. In this context, a researcher can also seek the help and guidance of experts. The supervisor of research also could extend his help. In fact, a supervisor should train the researcher in the art of writing and communicating during the course of research, so that the scholar could bring out a well organized and structured research report.

Types of Research Report

There are three different types of research report: (a)

technical report, (b) popular report, and (c) oral presentation. In this, the first two are written while the third one is orally presented.

Technical report: In this type of report, the scholar should focus on the assumptions of his study, methods he had adopted and the findings of his study.

Usually a generalized format is adopted for presenting such reports. It includes, an executive summary of the results, an overview of the study including the problem studied, objectives, hypothesis set, the data used and the tools of analysis adopted, etc. It would also specify the methodology adopted, the sources and extent of data collection, the results of the analysis and findings, the conclusions drawn, etc. It would also give a detailed bibliography, technical explanations through appendices and index to facilitate the user.

Popular report: As the name itself suggests, this is a type of report which is meant for the understanding and use of common public. It should be devoid of any technical jargons and details. It should be in simple but effective language and must be attractive in its presentation. Liberal use of diagrams, pictographs, graphs and others forms of representation is recommended. The content of such a report includes, findings and the implications, objectives and methods of the study, policy options or suggestions and recommendations, results of the study, etc.

Oral presentation: This type of reporting takes place in a public viva voce examination conducted for Ph.D researchers. In this type of reporting, the researcher would present the details of his work orally. He may use different methods of presentation like, overhead projector, slide projector, simple presentation on board, manual drawings, printed matter, etc. The basic objective in this type of reporting is to make an impact on the people who are informed about the findings and suggestions. Unless the researcher is good in his command over language, he would only fail to make any impact.

The flow of language, style adopted, delivery speed,

gestures and gesticulations, body language, etc., will all determine the effectiveness of oral presentation. In such presentations, the researcher should avoid unnecessary elaboration affecting sentiments, recreating controversies, attack on any ideals or beliefs and most important, the details which are not supported by facts or evidences. Alternatively, he must plan his presentation well in advance, by structuring it.

He should maintain a logical sequence in his presentation. By allowing questions in the course of presentation, he would be able to enable the listeners to understand the nuances of some of the intricate and complex ideas. Eye contact with the audience is one important essential requirement of presentation. By being evasive in answering questions, the researcher would only invite more questions. The researcher should be honest enough to accept if he does not know the answer for any question raised or he had not studied that aspect in his research work. To acquire the art of presentation, a researcher should participate in seminars and conferences. Thereby, he would be able to observe how others do it and based on that he could plan his presentation.

Guidelines for Writing a Research Report

There are different stages involved in writing a research report. This is explained below.

1. *Introduction of the subject in a logical manner*: In this stage, the researcher would develop his subject matter in a logical manner. He would study the sequence of his subject matter and accordingly prepare the draft either chronologically or logically. Having decided the plan of his subject matter, the researcher should prepare an outline of his report, by indicating the chapters to be developed, the chapter content in terms of headings, sub-headings, questions to be answered, the type of presentation to be used, etc. Once the outline is ready, it is given a shape through the preparation of rough draft. At this stage, the researcher need not impose any restrictions with regard to

the style, language, presentation, length of report, etc., but he should be careful to include every aspect of his study. This outline only gives unrefined details of the study.

2. *Preparation of second draft:* In this stage, the rough draft is edited, pruned, polished and brought to actual size, by eliminating all that is unwanted or unwarranted in the rough draft. This stage is very important as nothing useful should be left out and details irrelevant should be deleted. Further, the style of presentation, language used, representations used, conclusions presented, etc. are all checked for accuracy and impact. Once the body of the report is finalized, the bibliography should be planned. The bibliography would give useful information for other researchers.
3. *Preparation of the final draft*: In this stage, the scholar should study each statement made. He should avoid contradictory statements and conclusions. He must also avoid statements like 'it is reported', 'it seems', 'it may be believed', etc. Such statements would reduce the authenticity of the study and invite criticisms. He should delete questionable and debatable conclusions. Usually, the urge is to copy the conclusions of the previous studies and report them as part of the report. This is a bad practice. The conclusions should emerge from the research study. They must be original and not borrowed. Sometimes, the conclusions reached in the previous study may be confirmed or substantiated. In that case, it adds to the strength of the conclusions. A scholar should remember that so long the report is not submitted, he has every scope for polishing it and correcting it. Once it is submitted, the scholar should be prepared to accept any critical comments on it.

Layout of a Research Report

Precautions to be taken while writing a research report:

1. The length of the report should be decided in accordance

with the purpose. Usually, it is advisable to be brief and precise rather than lengthy and winding.

2. The report should be interesting to read and must not be loaded with too much of technical jargons.
3. Wherever clarity is to be added, the scholar can make use of tables and figures. But unintelligent use of them will only create a bad impression.
4. The report should be free from any type of mistakes, viz. grammatical, typographical, spelling, usage, etc.
5. Any reference material used in the report should be suitably acknowledged and the details should be given through either footnotes or end notes.
6. The report should be logically structured.
7. It should be a contribution to the field of study rather than repetition of what had been already reported.
8. Originality of the scholar should be clearly evident throughout the report.
9. The page numbering, table and figure numbering, foot note or end note numbering, its position, should all be in conformity with the standard practices or as laid down by the university.
10. Appendices, bibliography and index should be an integral part of the research report.
11. The physical appearance of the report should be attractive, neat and clean.
12. The technical tools applied in the process of analysis should all be explained in detail through the methodology adopted for the study.

Review Questions

1. Discuss the significance of report writing.
2. Explain the layout of a report.
3. What are the different types of report?
4. Examine the precautions to be taken while making oral presentation.
5. Explain the precautions to be taken while writing a

research report.
6. Discuss the need for preparing a rough draft.
7. What precautions are to be taken while preparing a report?
8. Discuss the mechanics of writing a research report.

Part II

Research Methodology: Useful Techniques

9

Statistics for Research

Central Tendency of Data

In many frequency distributions, the tabulated values show small frequencies at the beginning and the end and very high frequency at the middle of the distribution. This indicates that the typical values of the variable lie near the central part of the distribution and other values cluster around these central values. This behavior of the data about the concentration of the values in the central part of the distribution is called central tendency of the data. We shall measure this central tendency with the help of mathematical quantities. A central value which 'enables' us to comprehend in a single effort the significance of the whole' is known as statistical average or simply average. In fact, an average of a statistical series is the value of the variable which is representative of the entire distribution and, therefore, gives a measure of central tendency.

Measures of Central Tendency

There are three common measures of central tendency:

Mean,

Median, and

Mode.

The most common and useful measure of central tendency is, however, the mean. In the following paragraphs, the method of calculation of various measures of central tendency will be discussed. In all such discussion, we need a very useful notation known as summation.

Choice of a Suitable Average

The different statistical averages have different characteristics. There is no all-purpose average. The choice of a particular average is usually determined by the purpose of investigation. Within the framework of descriptive statistics, the main requirement is to know what each average means and then select the one that fulfils the purpose at hand. The nature of distribution also determines the type of average to be used.

Generally, the following points should be kept in mind while making a choice of average for use.

1. **Object:** The average should be chosen according to the object of enquiry. If all the values in a series are to be given equal importance, then arithmetic mean will be a suitable choice. To determine the most stylish or most frequently occurring item, mode should be found out. If the object is to determine an average that would indicate its position or ranking in relation to all the values, naturally, median should be the choice. If small items are to be given greater importance than the big items, geometric mean is the best mean.
2. **Representative:** The average chosen should be such that it represents the basic chrematistics of the distribution.
3. **Nature of form of data:** If the frequently distribution is symmetrical or nearly symmetrical $\overline{X}$, M or Mo may be used almost interchangeably. If there are open-ended class intervals, mean cannot be calculated definitely. In a closed frequently distribution of unequal class intervals, it is impossible to determine mode accurately. If there are a few values, it may not be possible to determine mode. Mean will not give a representative picture, if there are few extremely large or small values at either end of the array, and yet the great majority of the values concentrate around a narrow band. In a variable of non-continuous type, median or mode may be given a value that actually exists in the data.

Davies' Test: Arithmetic mean is considered as an appropriate average for use for data which has a symmetrical distribution or even if it has a moderate degree of asymmetry. Professor George Davis has devised a test which is:

$$\frac{(\text{Log } Q_1 \times \text{Log } Q_3) - (2 \times \text{Log } M)}{\text{Log } Q_3 - \text{Log } Q_1}$$

If this coefficient works out to be more than -0.20, the distribution is symmetrical enough to use arithmetic mean.

4. **Characteristics of an Average:** While choosing a suitable average for a purpose, the merits and demerits of various averages should always be considered and that average which fits into the purpose most should be preferred over others. The following points should be given due consideration in the process of selection of an average.

   In certain commonly encountered applications, the mean is subject to less sampling variability than the median or mode.

   Given only the original observations, the median is sometimes easiest to calculate. Sometimes, when there is no strong advantage for the mean, this advantage is enough to indicate the use of the median.

   Once a frequency distribution has been formed, the mode and the median are mode quickly calculated than the mean. Moreover, when some classes are open-ended, the mean cannot be calculated from the frequency distribution.

   The median is not a good measure when there are very few possible values for the observations as with number of children or size of family.

   The mode and the median are relatively little affected by 'extreme' observations.

   Calculations of geometric mean and harmonic mean are difficult as it involves the knowledge of logarithms and reciprocals.

Hence, "the justification of employing them (averages) must be determined by an appeal to all facts and in the light of the peculiar characteristics of the different types".

Uses of Different Averages

Different averages, due to their inherent characteristics are appropriate in different circumstances. Thus, their use may be guided by the purpose at hand or circumstances in which one is. Here, a brief discussion is being made of uses and of different statistical averages.

1. **Arithmetic Average:** The arithmetic average is used in the study of a social, economic or commercial problem like production, income, price, imports, exports, etc. The central tendency is if these phenomena can best be studied by taking out a 'production' or 'average price', we always mean arithmetic average of all these things. Whenever there is no indication about the type of the average to be used, arithmetic average is computed.
2. **Weighted Arithmetic Average:** When it is desirable to give relative importance to the different items of a series, weighted arithmetic average is computed. If it is desired to compute per capita consumption of a family, due weights should be assigned to children, males and females. This average is also useful in constructing numbers. The weighted average should be used in the following cases:
   If it is desired to have an average of whole group, which is divided into a number of sub-classes, widely divergent from each other.
   When items falling in various sub-classes change in such a way that the proportion which the items bear among themselves also undergoes a change.
   When combined average has to be computed.
   When it is desired to calculate to find an average of ratios, percentages or rates.
3. **Median:** Median is especially applicable to cases which are not capable of precise quantitative studies such as intelligence, honesty, etc. It is less applicable in economic or business statistics, because there is lack of stability in such data.
4. **Mode:** The utility of mode is being appreciated more and more day by day. In the sciences of biology and meteorology, it has been found to be of great value. In commerce and industry it is gaining a greater importance.

Whenever a shopkeeper wants to stock of goods he sells, he always looks to the model size of those goods. Model size of shoes, is of great importance to the businessman dealing in readymade garments or shoes. Many problems of production are related with mode. Many business establishments these days are engaging their attention in keeping statistics of their sale to ascertain the particulars of the model articles sold.

5. **Geometric Mean:** Geometric mean can advantageously be used in the construction of index numbers. It makes the index numbers reversible and gives equal weight to equal ratio of changes. This average is also useful in measuring the growth of population, because increases in geometric progression. When there is wide dispersion, geometric mean is a useful average.
6. **Harmonic Mean:** This average is useful in the class where time, rate and prices are involved. When it is desired to give the largest weight to the smallest item, this average is used.

Summation notation ( )

The symbol E (read: sigma) means summation.

If $x_1, x_2, x_3, \ldots\ldots, x_n$ be the n values of a variable X, then their sum

$x_1 + x_2 + \ldots\ldots x_n$ is shortly written as

$\sum_{i=1}^{n} X_i$ or simply □x (sometimes, □x_1)

Similarly, the sum $w_1x_1 + w_2x_2 + \ldots\ldots\ldots + w_nx_n$ is denoted by

$\sum_{i=1}^{n}$ w_1x_1 or simply □wx (sometimes, □w_1x_1)

Some Important Results

1. $$\sum_{i=1}^{n} (x_i \pm y_i) = \sum_{i=1}^{n} x_i \pm \sum_{i=1}^{n} y_i$$

n

2. $\sum_{i=1}^{n} A = A + A + \ldots + A = nA$ (A is a constant)

$\underbrace{\qquad\qquad\qquad}_{n \text{ terms}}$

3. $\sum_{i=1}^{n} AX_i = Ax_1 + Ax_2 + \ldots\ldots + Ax_n$

$= A(x_1 + x_2 + \ldots\ldots + x_n) = A\sum_{i=1}^{n} x_i$

Mean

There are three types of mean, namely:

1. Arithmetic Mean (A.M.),
2. Geometric Mean (G.M.), and
3. Harmonic Mean (H.M.).

Of the three means, arithmetic mean is most commonly used. In fact, if no specific mention is made, by mean we shall always refer to Arithmetic Mean (A.M.) and calculate accordingly.

Simple arithmetic mean [$\bar{x}$]

Definition: The arithmetic mean ($\bar{x}$) of a given series of values, say, $x_1, x_2, \ldots\ldots x_n$ is defined as the sum of these values divided by their total number; thus

$$\bar{x} = \frac{x_1 + x_2 + x_3 + \ldots\ldots\ldots\ldots + x_n}{n} = \frac{\Sigma x}{n}.$$

Ex. 1: Find the Arithmetic Mean of 3,6,24 and 48.

Sol. The required A. M.

$$\bar{x} = \frac{3 + 6 + 24 + 48}{4} = \frac{81}{4} = 20.25.$$

Weighted arithmetic mean [$\bar{x}$]

Definition: if $x_1, x_2, \ldots\ldots, x_n$ be n values of a variable x and if $f_1, f_2, \ldots\ldots f_n$ he their respective weights (or frequencies), then the weighted arithmetic mean $\bar{x}$ is defined by

$$\overline{x} = \frac{f_1x_1 + f_2x_2 + \ldots\ldots\ldots\ldots + f_nx_n}{f_1 + f_2 + \ldots + f_n} = \frac{\Sigma fx}{\Sigma f} = \frac{\Sigma fx}{N},$$

Where, $N = \Sigma f$ = total frequency.

Skewness

A frequency distribution is said to be symmetrical when the values of the variable equidistant from their mean have equal frequencies.

If a frequency distribution is not symmetrical, it is said to be asymmetrical or skewed. Any deviation from symmetry is called scenes.

In the words of rig leman and Frisbee:

"Skewness is the lack of symmetry. When a frequency distribution is plotted on a chart, skewness present in the items tends to be dispersed more on one side of the mean than on the order."

Skewness may be positive or negative. A distribution is said to be positively skewed if the frequency curve has a longer tail towards the higher values of x, i.e., if the frequency curve gradually slopes down towards the high values of x. For a positively skewed distribution:

Mean > median > mode

(M) (ME) (MO)

A distribution is said to be negatively skewed if the frequency curve has a longer tail towards the lower values of x. For a negatively skewed distribution:

Mean < median < mode

(M) (ME) (MO)

For a symmetrical distribution,

Mean = Median=Mode.

Measures of Skewness

The degree of skewness is measured by its coefficient. The common measures of Skewness are:

Pearson's first measure:

$$\text{Skewness} = \frac{\text{Mean-mode}}{\text{Standard Deviation}}$$

Pearson's second measure:

$$\text{Skewness} = \frac{3(\text{Mean-Mode})}{\text{Standard Deviation}}$$

Bowley's measure:

$$\text{Skewness} = \frac{(Q_3 - Q_2) - (Q_2 - Q_1)}{(Q_3 - Q_2) + (Q_2 - Q_1)} = \frac{Q_3 + Q_1 - 2Q_2}{Q_3 - Q_1}$$

Where Q_1, Q_2, Q_3 are the first, second, and third quartiles respectively.

Moment measure:

$$\text{Skewness} = \frac{m_3}{\sigma^3} = \frac{m_3}{m_2^{3/2}}.$$

Where m_2 and m_3 are the second and third central moments and σ is the S.D.

All the four measures of Skewness defined above are independent of the units of measurement.

Calculate the person's measure of Skewness on the basis of Mean, Mode and Standard Deviation.

X: 14.5 15.5 16.5 17.5 18.5 19.5 20.5 21.5

F 35 40 48 100 125 87 43 22

Key: Pearson's first measure of Skewness if

$$\text{Skewness} = \frac{\text{Mean} - \text{Mode}}{\text{Standard Deviation}}$$

Here, mid-values of the class-intervals are given.

Assuming a continuous series, we construct Table 9.1.

Table 9.1: Calculations for Mean and S.D

Class Intervals	X	F	D = x – 18.5	fd	fd^2
14-15	14.5	35	-4	-140	560
15-16	15.5	40	-3	-120	360
16-17	16.5	48	-2	-96	192
17-18	17.5	100	-1	-100	100
18-19	18.5	125	0	0	0
19-20	19.5	87	1	87	87
20-21	20.5	43	2	86	172
21-22	21.5	22	3	66	198
Total	-	500 = N	-	-217 = □fd	1669 =□fd^2

$$\text{Mean} = A + \frac{\sum fd}{N} = 18.5 - \frac{217}{500} = 18.5 - 0.43 = 18.07$$

$$\text{S.D.} = \frac{1669}{500} - \frac{-217}{500} = \sqrt{3.338 - 0.188}$$

$$= \sqrt{3.150} = 1.775$$

$$\text{Mode} = L + \frac{f_m - f_1}{2f_m - f_1 - f_2} \text{ x } i = 18 + \frac{125 - 100}{2 \times 125 - 100 - 87}$$

$$= 18 + \frac{25}{63} = 18 + 0.4 = 18.4;$$

$$\therefore \text{Skewness} = \frac{18.07 - 18.4}{1.775} = -0.187$$

Types of Frequency Distributions

In general, frequency distributions that form a balanced pattern are called symmetrical distributions, and those that form an unbalanced pattern are called skewed or asymmetrical distributions. In a symmetrical distribution, frequencies go on increasing up to a point and then begin to decrease in the same fashion. A special kind of symmetrical distribution is the normal distribution; the pattern formed is not only symmetrical but also has the shape of a bell. Following are some of the possible patterns of the symmetrical distribution.

In a symmetrical distribution, mean median and mode coincide and they lie at the centre of distribution. As the distribution departs from symmetry, these three values are pulled apart. A distribution in which more than half of the area under the curve is to the right side of the mode, is a positively skewed distribution. In a positively skewed distribution, its right tail is longer than its left tail. Under such a distribution, mean is greater than the median, and the median is greater than the mode ($\overline{X} > M > Mo$), and the difference between upper quartile and median is greater than the difference between median and lower quartile ($Q_3 - M > M - Q_1$). In a negatively skewed distribution, more than half of area under the distribution curve is to the left side of the mode. In such a distribution, the elongated tail us to the left and mean is less than the median and median is less than the mode ($\overline{X} < M < Mo$), and the difference between upper quartile and median is less than the difference between median and lower quartile ($Q^3 -- M < M - Q_1$). Table 9.2 depicts these facts.

Test of Skewness

In order to find out whether a distribution is symmetrical or skewed, the following facts should be noticed.

Relationship between Averages: If in a distribution mean, median and mode are not identical, then it is a skewed distribution. The greater is the difference between mean, median and mode, more will be the skewness in the distribution.

Total of Deviations: If the sum of positive deviations from median or mode is equal to the sum of negative deviation, then is no skewness in the distribution. The extent of difference between the sums of positive and negative deviations from median or mode will determine the extent of skewness in the data.

Table 9.2: Position of Average on Various Distributions

Size	(a)	(b)	(c)
	Frequently	Frequently	Frequently
5	1	1	1
10	3	9	2
15	5	5	3
20	7	4	4
25	5	3	5
30	3	2	9
35	1	1	1
Skewness	(Symmetry) No. of Skewness	Positive Skewness	Negative Skewness
Average	$\bar{X}$=M=Mo=20	$\bar{X} > M > Mo$ $16.8 > 15 > 10$	$\bar{X} < M < Mo$ $23.8 < 25 < 30$
Quartiles	$(Q_3$-M) = (M-Q1)	$(Q_3$-M)>(M-Q1)	$(Q_3$-M)<(M-Q1)
Curve	Normal	Skewed to the Right	Skewed to the left

The Distance of Partition Values from Median: In a symmetrical distribution, Q1 and Q2, D1 and D9, and P10 and P90 are equidistant from median. In an asymmetrical distribution it is not so.

The Frequencies on Either Side of the Mode: In an asymmetrical distribution, frequencies on either side of the mode are not equal.

The Curve: When the data is plotted on a graph paper, the curve will not be bell shaped, or when cut along a vertical line through the centre, two halves will not be identical.

Conversely stated, in the absence of skewness in the distribution:

Values of mean, median and mode will coincide.

Sum of the positive deviations from the median or mode will be equal to the sum of negative deviations.

The two quartiles, decile one and nine, and percentile ten and ninety will be equidistant from the median.

Frequencies on the either side of the mode will be equal.

Data when plotted on a graph paper will take a bell-shaped form.

Measures of Skewness

To find out the direction and the extent of asymmetry in a series, statistical measures of skewness are calculated. These measures can be absolute or relative. Absolute measures of skewness tell us the extent of asymmetry and whether it is positive or negative. The absolute skewness can be known by taking the difference between the mean and the mode. Symbolically,

Absolute $SK = \bar{X} - Mo$

If the value of mean is greater than the mode ($\bar{X} >$ Mo), skewness will be positive. In case the value of mean is less than the mode ($\bar{X} <$ Mo), skewness will be negative. The greater is the amount of skewness, the more the mean and mode would differ because of the influence of extreme items. The reason why the difference between mean and mode is taken for the measure of skewness is that in a symmetrical distribution, both the values along with median coincide, but in an asymmetrical distribution, mean moves away from the mode. The more is skewness in the distribution, greater will be the difference between the mean and the mode.

Thus, the difference between the mean and the mode, whether positive or negative, indicates that the distribution is asymmetrical. However, such an absolute measure of skewness is unsatisfactory, because, the difference between the mean and mode may be more in one series and less in another, yet the frequency curves of the two distributions may be similarly skewed.

For comparison, the absolute measures of skewness are changed to relative measures, which is called the coefficient of skewness.

These are four measures of relative skewness. They are:

1. The Karl Pearson's coefficient of skewness.
2. The Bowley's coefficient of skewness.
3. The Kelly's coefficient of skewness.
4. Measure of skewness based on moments.

Karl Pearson's Coefficient of Skewness: Karl Pearson has given a formula, for relative measures of skewness. It is known as Karl Pearson's Coefficient of Skewness or Pearsonian coefficient of Skewness. The formula is based on the difference between the mean and mode, divided by the standard deviation. The coefficient is represented by J.

$$J = \frac{\text{Mean - Mode}}{\text{Standard Deviation}} \text{ or } \frac{\bar{X} - Mo}{\sigma}$$

If in a particular frequency distribution, it is difficult to determine precisely the mode, the coefficient of skewness can be determined by the following changed formula:

$$J = \frac{3\text{ (Mean - Mode)}}{\text{Standard Deviation}} \text{ or } \frac{3(\bar{X} - Mo)}{\sigma}$$

This is based on the relationship between different averages in a moderately asymmetrical distribution. In such a distribution:

$$Mo = X + 3(M - X)$$

Or $Mo = \bar{X} - 3(X - M)$

As $Mo = \bar{X} - 3(X - M)$

$\therefore (\bar{X} - Mo) = 3(\bar{X} - M)$ that is why $(\bar{X} - Mo)$ is replaced by $3(\bar{X} - M)$

The Pearsonian coefficient of skewness has an interesting characteristic that it will be positive when the mean is larger than the mode or the median, and it will be negative when the arithmetic mean is smaller than the mode or the median. In a symmetrical distribution, the value of Pearsonian coefficient of skewness will be zero. There is no theoretical limit to this measure, however, in practice the value given by this formula is rarely very high and usually lies between +1. The direction of the skewness is given by the algebraic sign of the measure, i.e. if it is plus, then the skewness is positive and if it is minus, the skewness is negative. The degree of skewness is obtained by the numerical figure such as 9, 0.4, etc. Thus, this formula gives both the direction as well as the degree of skewness.

There is another relative measure of skewness based on the position of averages. In this, the difference between two averages is divided by the mean deviation. The formula is:

$$\frac{\bar{x}-Mo}{\delta\bar{x}} \text{ or } \frac{\bar{x}-Mo}{\delta Mo}; \frac{\bar{x}-M}{\delta\bar{x}} \text{ or } \frac{\bar{x}-Mo}{\delta M}; \frac{M-Mo}{\delta M} \text{ or } \frac{M-Mo}{\delta Mo}$$

These formulas are not very much used in practice, because of the demerits of mean deviation.

Dispersion

Measures of Dispersion: An average may give a good idea of the type of data, but it alone cannot reveal all the characteristics of data. It cannot tell us in what manner all the values of the variable are scattered/dispersed about the average.

Meaning of Dispersion: The variation or scattering or deviation of the different values of a variable from their average is known as dispersion. Dispersion indicates the extent to which the values vary among themselves. Professor W.I. King defines the term, 'dispersion' as, it is used to indicate the facts that within a given group, the items differ from another in size or in other words, there is lack of uniformity in their sizes. The extent of variability in a given set of data is measured by comparing the individual values of the variable with the average of all the values and then calculating the average of all the individual differences.

Objectives of Measuring Variations:

To serve as a basis for control of the variability itself.

To gauge the reliability of an average.

To serve as a basis for control of the variability itself.

Types of Measures of Dispersion: There are two types of measures of dispersion. The first, which may be referred to as 'distance measures', describe the spread of data in terms of distance between the values of selected observations. The second are those which are in terms of an average deviation from some measure of central tendency.

Absolute and Relative Measures of Dispersion: Measures of absolute dispersion are in the same units as the data whose scatter they measure. For example, the dispersion of salaries about an average is measured in rupees and the variation of time required for workers to do a job is measured in minutes or hours. Measures of absolute dispersion cannot be used to compare to scatter in one distribution with that in another distribution when the averages of the distributions differ in size or the units of measure differ in kind. Measures of relative dispersion show some measure of scatter as a percentage or coefficient of the absolute measure of dispersion. They are generally used to compare the scatter in one distribution with the scatter in other. Relative measure of dispersion is called the coefficient of dispersion

Methods of Measuring Dispersion: There are two meanings of dispersion, as explained above. On the basis of these two meanings, there are two mathematical methods of finding dispersion, i.e. methods of limits and methods of moment. Dispersion can also be studied graphically. Thus, the following are the methods of measuring dispersion:

1. Numerical Methods

A. Methods of Limits

The Range,

The Inter-Quartile Range, and

The Percentile Range.

B. Methods of Moments

The first moment of dispersion or mean deviation,

Second moment of dispersion from which standard deviation is computed, and

Third moment of dispersion.

B. Quartile Deviation

Graphic Method, and

Lorenz Curve.

Range

The simplest measure of dispersion is the range of the data. The range is determined by the two extreme values of the observations and it is simply the differences between the largest and the smallest value in a distribution. Symbolically,

Range (R) = Longest value (L) - Smallest value (S)

or $R = L - S$

The coefficient of range, which is the relative measure of range, is computed by applying the following formula:

$$\text{Coefficient of Range (C.R.)} = \frac{\text{Largest value} - \text{Smallest value}}{\text{Largest value} + \text{Smallest value}}$$

or $$\text{C.R.} = \frac{L - S}{L + S}$$

Quartile Deviation or Semi-interquartile Range

Quartile deviation (Q) is an absolute measure of dispersion and it defined by the formula.

$$Q = \frac{Q_3 - Q_1}{2}$$

Where, Q_1 and Q_2 are the first (or lower) and the third (or upper) quartiles respectively. Here, Q_3-Q_1 is the interquartile range and hence, quartile deviation is called the semi-interquartile range.

As it is based only on Q_1 and Q_3, it does not take into account the variability of all the values and hence it is not very much used for practical purposes.

1. Find the quartile deviation of the following frequency distribution:

Daily Wages: 10-15 15-20 20-25 25-30 30-35
No. of Workers: 6 12 18 10 4
Key:

Table 9.3

Class-boundary Points	Cumulative Frequency ("less than")
10	0
15	6
→ Q1	← 12.5 = N/4
20	18
25	36
Q3	37.5 = 3N/4
→ 30	← 46
35	50 = N

N/4 = 50/4 =12.5 and 3N/4 = 37.5

By simple interpolation,

$$\frac{Q1 - 15}{20 - 15} = \frac{12.5 - 6}{18 - 6}$$

or, $\dfrac{Q_1 - 15}{5} = \dfrac{6.5}{12}$ or $Q1 - 15 = \dfrac{6.5}{12} \times 5 = \dfrac{32.5}{12} = 2.71$

$Q_1 = 15 + 2.71$ or $\mathbf{Q_1 = 17.71}$

Similarly, $\frac{Q_3 - 25}{30 - 25} = \frac{37.5 - 36}{46 - 36}$

or, $\frac{Q_3 - 25}{5} = \frac{1.5}{10}$ or, $Q_3 - 25 = \frac{1.5}{2} = .75$

or $Q_3 = 25.75$

Hence the quartile deviation,

$$\frac{Q_3 - Q_1}{2} = \frac{25.75 - 17.7}{2} = \frac{8.04}{2} = \mathbf{4.02}$$

Mean Deviation (or Average Deviation or Mean Absolute Deviation): Mean deviation of a series of values of a variable is the arithmetic mean of all the absolute deviations (i.e. difference without regard to sign) from any one of its averages (mean, median or mode, but usually mean or median). It is an absolute measure of dispersion.

Mean deviation of a set of n values X_1, X_2...........X_n about their A.M. is defined by,

Where X = Value of mid-value accordingly as the data is ungrouped or grouped and X = Mean

$$\text{Mean Deviation} = \frac{\sum_{i=1}^{n} xi \left| x_i - \bar{x} \right|}{n}$$

$$= \frac{\sum_{i=1}^{n} \left| d_i \right|}{n} = \frac{\Sigma \left| d \right|}{n}$$

Where $\bar{x}$ = A. M. and $|d_i| = |x_i - \bar{x}|$ = absolute deviation of x_i from $\bar{x}$.

$$\text{Mean deviation about median} = \frac{\sum_{i=1}^{n} x_i |x_i - M|}{n}$$

$$= \frac{\sum_{i=1}^{n} x_i |d_i|}{n}$$ where M = Median

For a frequency distribution,

$$= \frac{\Sigma f|x - \bar{x}|}{n} = \frac{\Sigma f|d|}{n}$$

$$\text{Mean Deviation} = \frac{\Sigma f|x - M|}{\Sigma f} = \frac{\Sigma f|d|}{N}$$

Where M = Median and d = X – M = Value (or mid value) - Median.

Similarly, we can define mean deviation about mode.

Note: The expression |d| is read as mod. d and gives only numerical or absolute value of d without regard to sig. Thus,

$$|-3| = 3,\ |+4| = 4,\ |0.56| = 0.56.$$

The reason for taking only the absolute and not the algebraic values of the deviation is that the algebraic sum of the deviations of the value from their mean is zero.

Advantages and Disadvantages

Mean deviation is based on all the values of the variable and sometimes gives fairly good result as a measure of dispersion. However, the practice of neglecting signs and taking absolute deviations for the calculation of mean deviation seems rather unjustified and this makes an algebraic treatment difficult.

2. Find the Mean Deviation about the Arithmetic Mean of the numbers 31, 35, 29, 63, 55, 72, 37.

Key:

$$\text{Arithmetic Mean } (\overline{X}) = \frac{31+35+29+63+55+72+37}{7}$$

$$= \frac{322}{7} = 46$$

Table 9.4: Calculation of Absolute Deviations

Value X	Deviation from mean D= $X-\overline{X} = X-46$	Absolute deviation |d|
31	-15	15
35	-11	11
29	-17	17
63	17	17
55	9	9
72	26	26
37	-9	9
Total	-	104 =$\sum\|d\|$

The required mean deviation about the mean

$$= \frac{\Sigma|d|}{n} = \frac{104}{7} = \mathbf{14.86}$$

Standard Deviation (S.D.)

It is the most important absolute measure of dispersion. Standard Deviation (S.D.) of a set of values of a variable is defined as the positive square root of the arithmetic mean of the squares of all the deviations of the values from their arithmetic mean. It short, it may be defined as the *Square root of the mean of the squares of* deviation from mean.

S.D. is usually denoted by the Greek small letter O (pronounced Sigma).

If X1, X2,..........Xn be a series of values of a variable and $\overline{X}$ their A.M., then S.D. (O) is defined by

$$\sigma = \frac{(x_1 - \overline{x})^2 + (x_2 - \overline{x})^2 + \dots\dots\dots\dots.. + (x_n - \overline{x})^2}{n}$$

$$= \frac{\Sigma(x - \overline{x})^2}{n}$$

The square of standard deviation is known as the variance i.e.,

Variance (σ^2) = $(S.D.)^2$

S.D. is often defined as the positive square-root of variance.

3. Find the standard deviation of the following numbers :
   1, 2, 3, 4, 5, 6, 7, 8, 9

Key:

$$A.M.\ (\overline{X}) = \frac{1 + 2 + 3 + 4 + 5 + 6 + 7 + 8 + 9}{n}$$

$$= \frac{45}{9} = 5$$

The deviations of the numbers from the A.M. 5 are respectively -4, -3, -2, -1, 0, 1, 2, 3, and 4.

The squares of the deviations from A.M. are 16, 9, 4, 1, 0, 1, 4, 9, and 16.

$$S.D. = \frac{\Sigma (X - \overline{X})^2}{n}$$

$$= \frac{16+9+4+1+0+1+4+9+16}{9}$$

$$= \frac{60}{9} = \frac{2}{3}\ 5 = 2.58$$

Advantages and Disadvantages

Standard deviation is the most important and widely used among the measures of dispersion and it possesses almost all the requisites of a good measure of dispersion. It is rigidly defined and based on all the values of the variable.

It is suitable for algebraic treatment. S.D. is less affected by sampling fluctuations than any other absolute measure of dispersion.

S.D. is difficult to understand. The process of squaring the deviations from their A.M. and then taking the square-root of the A.M. of these squared deviations is a complicated affair.

The calculation of S.D. can be made easier by changing the origin and the scale conveniently.

Relative Measures of Dispersion

Absolute measures expressed as a percentage of a measure of a control tendency gives relative measures of dispersion. Relative measures are independent of the units of measurement and hence, they are used for the comparison of dispersion of two or more distributions given in different units.

Co-Efficient of Variation

Co-efficient of variation is the most important relative measure of dispersion and is defined by the following formula:

$$\text{Co-efficient of variation} = \frac{\text{Standard deviation}}{\text{Mean}} \times 100$$

Co-efficient of variation is thus, the ratio of the standard deviation to the mean, expressed as a percentage. In the words of Karl Pearson, co-efficient of variation is the percentage variation in the mean.

Co-efficient of Quartile deviation

Co-efficient of quartile deviation is a relative measure of dispersion and is defined by

$$\text{Co-efficient of Quartile deviation} = \frac{\text{Quartile deviation}}{\text{Median}} \times 100$$

Co-efficient of Mean deviation

It is a relative measure of dispersion. Co-efficient of Mean deviation is defined by

$$\text{Co-efficient of Mean deviation} = \frac{\text{Mean deviation}}{\text{Mean (or) Median}} \times 100$$

4. Find the mean deviation about the median in respect of the following numbers 46, 79, 26, 85, 39, 65, 99, 29, 56, 72

Find also the co-efficient of Mean Deviation.

Key: By arranging the given numbers in ascending order of magnitude, we obtain 26, 29, 39, 46, 56, 65, 72, 79, 85, and 99.

$$\text{Mean} = \left(\frac{n+1}{2}\right)^{th} \text{Value}$$

$$\text{Value} = \left(\frac{10+1}{2}\right)^{th} \text{Value}$$

$= 5.5^{th}$ Value

$$= \frac{5^{th}\text{ Value} + 6^{th}\text{ Value}}{2}$$

$$= \left(\frac{56+65}{2}\right) = \frac{121}{2} = 60.5$$

Absolute deviation of the values from the median 60.5 respectively are:

34.5, 31.5, 21.5, 14.5, 4.5, 4.5, 11.5, 18.5, 24.5, 38.5

M.D. about the median

$= 34.5 + 31.5 + 21.5 + 14.5 + 4.5 + 4.5 + 11.5 + 18.5 + 24.5 + 38.5$

$$= \frac{204}{2} = 20.4$$

$$\text{Co-efficient of M.D.} = \frac{\text{M.D.}}{\text{Median}} \times 100$$

$$= \frac{20.4}{60.5} \times 100$$

$$= \frac{204}{605} \times 100$$

$= 33.72$ percent

Kurtosis

Kurtosis in Greek means 'bulginess'. The degree of kurtosis of a distribution is measured relative to the pealedness of a normal curve. The measure of kurtosis indicates whether the curve of a frequency distribution is flat or peaked.

Kurtosis is the peakedness of the frequency curve. In two or more distributions having same average, dispersion and skewness, one may have high concentration of values near the mode, and in this case, its frequency curve will show a sharper peak than the others. This characteristic of frequency distribution is known a Kurtosis.

According to Clark and Schkade, "Kurtosis is the property of a distribution which expresses its relative peakedness".

Kurtosis is measured by the coefficient B2 which is defined by the formula

$\beta_2 = \frac{m_4}{m_2^2} = \frac{m_4}{\sigma^4}$ or by $\gamma_2 - \beta_2 - 3$, where m_4 are the 2nd and the 4th control Moments and σ = S.D.

A distribution is said to be Platy-Kurtic, Meso-Kurtic and Lepto-Kurtic according as $\beta_2 < 3$, $\beta_2 = 3$ and $\beta_2 > 3$.

$$\text{i.e. } \frac{m_4}{\sigma^4} < 3, \quad \frac{m_4}{\sigma^4} = 3 \text{ and } \frac{m_4}{\sigma^4} > 3.$$

Karl Pearson in 1905 introduced the terms mesokurtic, leptokurtic and platykurtic. A peaked curve is called 'leptokurtic' and a flat topped curve is termed 'platykurtic'. These are evaluated by comparison with intermediate peaked curve with intermediate peaked curve 'meso kurtic' which is a normal curve. These three curves differ widely in regard to convexity. The aforesaid curves are depicted below.

Calculate the Measures of the following Distribution

Age in Years	No. of Employees	Age in Years	No. of Employees
20-25	6	45-50	15
25-30	8	50-55	11
30-35	11	55-60	9
35-40	14	60-65	5
40-45	21		--------
			100

Key:

Class	Mid-value m	f	A=42.5/i=5 d'	Fd'	Fd'^{2}	Fd'^{3}	Fd'^{4}
20-25	22.5	6	-4	-24	96	-384	1536
25-30	27.5	8	-3	-24	72	-216	648
30-35	32.5	11	-2	-21	44	-88	176
35-40	37.5	14	-1	-14	14	-14	14
40-45	42.5	21	0	0	0	0	0
45-50	47.5	15	1	15	15	15	15
50-55	52.5	11	2	22	44	88	176
55-60	57.5	9	3	27	81	243	729
60-65	62.5	5	4	20	80	320	1280
Total		100		0	446	-36	4574

$$v_1 = \frac{\Sigma fd'}{N} = \frac{0}{100} = 0,$$

$$v3 = \frac{\Sigma fd'^3}{N} = \frac{-36}{100} = -.36,$$

$$v_2 = \frac{\Sigma fd'^2}{N} = \frac{446}{100} = 4.36$$

$$v_2 = \frac{\Sigma fd'^4}{N} = \frac{4574}{100} = 45.74$$

$\mu_2 = v_2 - v_1^2 = 4.46 - 0^2 = 4.46$

$\mu_4 = v_4 - 4v_1v_3 + 6v_1^2v_2 - 3v_4^2$

$= 45.74 - (4 \times 0 \times -.36) \times (6 \times 0^2 \times 4.46) - (3 \times 0^4) =$ 45.74

$$\alpha_4 \text{ or } \alpha_2 = \frac{\mu}{\mu_2^2} = \frac{45.74}{4.46^2} = \frac{45.74}{19.8916} = 2.3$$

The value of β_2 is less than 3, hence, the curve is platykurtic.

Self Assessment Questions

1. Explain the special features of measures of central tendency.
2. How will you choose an 'average'?
3. What is dispersion? State its objectives. Explain the various types of measures of dispersion.
4. Explain the various methods of measuring dispersion.
5. Differentiate standard deviation from mean deviation.
6. Define 'skewness'. How will you measure it?
7. Explain the application of averages in research.

10

Measures of Relationship

Objectives of the lesson are:

To study simple, partial and multiple correlation and their appliacation in research,

To study simple and multiple regression and their application in research, and

To explain association of attributes and its application in research.

Measures of Relationship

The following statistical tools measure the relationship between the variables analyzed in social science research:

Correlation

Simple correlation,

Partial correlation, and

Multiple correlation.

Regression

Simple regression, and

Multiple regression.

Association of Attributes: Correlation measures the relationship (positive or negative, perfect) between the two variables. Regression analysis considers relationship between variables and estimates the value of another variable, having the value of one variable. Association of attributes attempts to ascertain the extent of association between two variables.

Correlation

Aggarwal Y.P., in his book 'Statistical Methods' has defined coefficient correlation as, "a single number that tells us to what extent two variable things are related and to what extent variations in one variable goes with variation in the other".

Richard I. Levin in his book, 'Statistics of Management' has defined correlation analysis as "the statistical tools that we can use to describe the degree to which one variable is linearly related to another". He has further stated that "frequently correlation analysis is used in conjunction with regression analysis to measure how well the regression line explains the variation of the dependent variable, Y. Correlation can also be used by itself, however, only to measure the degree of association between the two variables".

Srivastava U.K., Shenoy G.V., and Sharma S.C., in their book 'Quantitative Techniques for Managerial Decision' have stated that, "correlation analysis is a statistical technique that is used to describe the degree to which one variable is related to another. Frequently, correlation analysis is also used along with the regression analysis to measure how well the regression line explains the variations of the dependent variable. The correlation coefficient is the statistical tool that is used to measure the mutual relationship between the two variables."

Coefficient of correlation is denoted by r.

The sign of 'r' shows the direction of the relationship between the two variables X and Y. Positive correlation reveals that there is a positive correlation between the two variables. Negative correlation reveals negative relationship. Levin states that if an inverse relationship exists i.e., if Y decreases as X increases–then r will fall between 0 and -1. Likewise, if there is a direct relationship (if Y increases as X increases), then r will be a value within the range of 0 to 1.

Aggarwal Y.P, has highlighted in his book 'Statistical Methods', the properties of correlation and factors influencing the size of the correlation coefficient. The details are given below.

Properties of the Correlation Coefficient: The range of correlation coefficient is from -1 through 0 and +1. The values of r = -1 and r = +1 reveals a case of perfect relationship, though the direction of relationship is negative in the first case, and positive in the second case.

The correlation coefficient can be interpreted in terms of r^2. It is known as the coefficient of determination. It may be considered as the variance interpretation of r^2.

Example:

r = 0.5

$r^2 = 0.5 \times 0.5 - 0.25$

in terms of percentage: 0.25 x 100 = 25 percent

It refers that 25 percent of the variance in Y scores has been accounted for by the variance in X scores.

The correlation coefficient does not change if every score in either or both distribution is increased or multiplied by a constant.

Causality cannot be inferred solely as the basis of a correlation between two variables. It can be inferred only after conducting controlled experiments.

The direction of the relation is indicated by the sign (+ or -) of the correlation.

The degree of relationship is indicated by the numerical value of the correlation. A value near 1 indicates a nearly perfect relation, and a value near 0 indicates no relationship.

In a positive relationship, both variables tend to change in the same direction: as x increases, y also tends to increase.

The Pearson correlation measures linear (straight line) relationship.

A correlation between x and y should not be interpreted as a cause-effect relationship. Two variables can be related without one having a direct effect on the other (Source: Frederick J. Gravetter and Carry B. Wallnau, *Essentials of Statistics for the Behavioural Sciences*).

Factors Influencing the Size of Correlation Coefficient

1. The size of r is very much dependent upon the variability of measured value in the correlated sample. The greater

the variability, the higher will be the correlation, everything else being equal.

2. The size of r is altered when researchers select extreme groups of subjects order to compare these groups with respect to certain behaviours. Selecting extreme groups on one variable increases the size of r over what would be obtained with more random sampling.
3. Combining two groups which differ in their mean values on one of the variables is not likely to faithfully represent the true situation as far as the correlation is concerned.
4. Addition of an extreme case (and conversely dropping of an extreme case can lead to changes in the amount of correlation. Dropping of such a case leads to reduction in the correlation while the converse is also true (Source: Aggarwal Y.P., *Statistical Methods*, 1998, p. 131).

Types of Correlation

Types of correlation are given below:

Positive or Negative,

Simple, Partial and Multiple, and

Linear and Non-linear.

Positive Correlation: Both the variables (X and Y) will vary in the same direction. If variable X increases, variable Y also will increase; if variable X decreases, variable Y also will decrease.

Negative Correlation: The given variables will vary in opposite direction if one variable increases, other variable will decrease.

Simple, Partial and Multiple Correlation: In simple correlation, relationship between two variables are studied. In partial and multiple correlation, three or more variables are studied. Three or more variables are simultaneously studied in multiple correlation. In partial correlation more than two variables are studied, but the effect on one variable is kept constant and relationship between other two variables is studied.

Linear and Non-Linear Correlation: It depends upon the constancy of the ratio of change between the variables. In linear correlation, the percentage change in one variable will be equal to the percentage change in another variable. It is not so in non-linear correlation.

Methods of Studying Correlation

The various methods of studying correlation are given below:

a) Scatter Diagram Method,
b) Graphic Method,
c) Karl Pearson's Coefficient of Correlation, and
d) Method of Least Squares.

Karl Pearson's Coefficient of Correlation

Karl Pearson's coefficient of correlation is a popular method used to study correlation between two variables. Karl Pearson's coefficient of correlation formula (for actual mean) is:

$$r = \frac{\Sigma xy}{\sqrt{\Sigma x^2 \times \Sigma y^2}}$$

$$x = X - \overline{X}; Y = Y - \overline{Y}$$

Procedure

Compute mean of the X series data.
Compute mean of the Y series data.
Compute deviations of X series from the mean of X. It is denoted as x.
Square the deviations. It is denoted as $\sum x^2$.
Compute deviations of Y series from the mean of Y. It is denoted as y.
Square the deviations. It is denoted as $\sum y^2$.
Multiply deviation (X series, Y series) and compute total. It denoted as Exy.

The above values can be applied in the formula and correlation can be computed.

Karl Pearson's coefficient of correlation-formula (assumed mean) is:

$$r = \frac{N\Sigma dxdy - \Sigma dx \times \Sigma dy}{\sqrt{N\ \Sigma dx^2 - (\Sigma dx)^2}\ \sqrt{N\ \Sigma dy^2 - (\Sigma dy)^2}}$$

dx = sum of deviations of X series from the assumed mean.

dy = sum of deviations of Y series from the assumed mean.

$\sum dxdy$ = total of deviations (X and Y series).

$\sum dx^2$ = deviations of X series from assumed mean are squared.

$\sum dy^2$ = deviations of Y series from assumed mean are squared.

N = Number of items.

The above values can be applied in the above formula and correlation can be computed.

Correlation for the grouped data can be computed with the help of the following formula:

$$r = \frac{N\ f\ dx\ dy - \Sigma fdx \times \Sigma fdy}{\sqrt{N\ \Sigma fdx^2 - (\Sigma fx)^2}\ \sqrt{N\ \Sigma fdy^2 - (\Sigma f\text{dy})^2}}$$

In the above formula, deviations are multiplied by the frequencies. Other steps are the same.

Calculation of Correlation

Raw Score Method:

X	20	16	12	8	4
Y	22	14	4	12	8

X	Y	X^2	Y^2	XY
20	22	400	484	440

16 12 8 4	14 4 12 8	256 144 64 16	196 16 144 64	224 48 96 32
ΣX 60	ΣY 60	ΣX^2 880	ΣY^2 904	ΣXY 840

$$r = \frac{N\Sigma XY - (\Sigma X)(\Sigma Y)}{\sqrt{[N\ \Sigma X^2 - (\Sigma X)^2]}\ \sqrt{[N\ \Sigma Y^2 - (\Sigma Y)^2]}}$$

$$r = \frac{5(840) - (60)(60)}{\sqrt{5\ (880) - (60)^2}\ \sqrt{5\ (904) - (30)^2}}$$

$$r = 0.7$$

Deviation Score Method (Using Actual Mean)

Calculate Karl Pearson Coefficient of Correlation from the following data:

Year	1985	1986	1987	1988	1989	1990	1991	1992
Index of Production	100	102	104	107	105	112	103	99
Number of Unemployed	15	12	13	11	12	12	19	26

Solution: Calculation of Karl Pearson's Correlation Coefficients

Year	Index of Production	$(X-\overline{X})$ X	X^2	No. of Unemployed Y	$(Y-\overline{Y})$ Y	Y^2	Xy
1985	100	-4	16	15	0	0	0
1986	102	-2	4	12	-3	9	+6
1987	104	0	0	13	-2	4	0
1988	107	+3	9	11	-4	16	-12
1989	105	+1	1	12	-3	9	-3

1990	112	+8	64	12	-3	9	-24
1991	103	-1	1	19	+4	16	-4
1992	99	-5	25	26	+11	121	-55
	∑X	∑x	$\sum x^2$	∑Y	∑y	$\sum y^2$	∑xy
	832	0	120	120	0	184	-92

$$X = \frac{\Sigma X}{N} = \frac{832}{8} = 104$$

$$Y = \frac{\Sigma Y}{N} = \frac{120}{8} = 15$$

$$r = \frac{\Sigma xy}{\sqrt{\Sigma x^2 \ \Sigma y^2}}$$

$\sum xy = -92 \quad \sum x^2 = 120 \quad \sum y^2 = 184$

$$r = \frac{-92}{\sqrt{120 \times 184}} = -0.619$$

Correlation between index of production and unemployed is negative.

Calculation of correlation coefficient from the following data:

X	50	60	58	47	49	33	65	43	46	68
Y	48	65	50	48	55	58	63	48	50	70

Calculation of Karl Pearson coefficient of correlation:

X	X – 50 dx	Dx^2	Y	Y-55 Dy	Dy^2	Dx dy
50	0	0	48	-7	49	0
60	+10	100	65	+10	100	+100

58	+8	64	50	-5	25	-40
47	-3	9	48	-7	49	+21
49	-1	1	55	0	0	0
33	-17	289	58	3	9	-51
65	+15	225	63	8	64	+120
43	-7	49	48	-7	49	+49
46	-4	16	50	-5	25	+20
68	+18	324	70	15	225	+270
519	+19	1077	535	5	595	489

$$r = \frac{\Sigma dx\ dy - \dfrac{\Sigma dx\ \Sigma dy}{N}}{\sqrt{\Sigma dx^2 - \dfrac{(\Sigma dx)^2}{N}}\ \sqrt{\Sigma dy^2 - \dfrac{(\Sigma dy)^2}{N}}}$$

$$r = \frac{489 - \dfrac{19 \times 5}{10}}{\sqrt{1077 - \dfrac{(19)^2}{10}} - \sqrt{595 - \dfrac{(5)^2}{10}}}$$

$$r = 0.611$$

Rank Correlation: It is a method of ascertaining co-variability or the lack of it between the two variables. Rank correlation method was developed by the British psychologist Charles Edward Spearman in 1904. Gupta S.P., has stated that "the rank correlation method is used when quantitative measures for certain factors cannot be fixed, but individual in the group can be arranged in order, thereby obtaining for each individual, a number indicating his/her rank in the group".

The formula for Rank Correlation,

$$R = 1 - \frac{6\Sigma D^2}{N(N^2-1)} \qquad or$$

$$1 - \frac{6\Sigma D^2}{N^3 - N}$$

Rank-Difference Coefficient of Correlation (Case of No Tiles)

Student	Score on Test I	Score on Test II	Rank on Test I	Rank on Test II	Difference Between Ranks	Difference Squared
	X	Y	R1	R^2	D	D^2
A	16	8	2	5	-3	9
B	14	14	3	3	0	0
C	18	12	1	4	-3	9
D	10	16	4	2	2	4
E	2	20	5	1	4	16
N = 5						$\Sigma D^2 = 38$

Rank Correlation:

$$R = 1 - \frac{6\Sigma D^2}{N(N^2-1)}$$

$$= 1 - \frac{6 \times 38}{5(5^2-1)}$$

$$= 1 - \frac{228}{120}$$

$$= 1 - 1.9$$

$$= -0.9$$

Relationship between X and Y is very high and inverse. Relationship between score on test I and II is very high and inverse.

Procedure for Assigning Ranks: First rank is given to the student who secured the highest score. [In Test I, student F is given the first rank. His score is the highest].

Second rank is given to the next highest scorer. [In Test I, student E is given the second rank].

Student A and G have similar scores of 20 each and they stand for 6th and 7th. The average of the two ranks [6 and 7, i.e. (6+7)/2=6.5] is given to each of them.

The same procedure is followed to assign ranks to the scores secured by students in Test II.

Calculation of Rank Correlation when Tied Ranks Exist (Rank-Difference Coefficient of Correlation)

Student	Score on Test I	Score on Test II	Rank on Test I	Rank on Test II	Difference Between Ranks	Difference Squared
	X	Y	R_1	R_2	D	D^2
A	20	32	6.5	5.5	1.0	1.00
B	30	32	3	5.5	-2.5	6.25
C	22	48	5	1.5	3.5	12.25
D	28	36	4	4	0	0
E	32	44	2	3	-1.0	1.00
F	40	48	1	1.5	-0.5	0.25
G	20	28	6.5	7.5	-1.0	1.00
H	16	20	9	10	-1.0	1.00
I	14	24	10	9	1.0	1.00
J	18	28	8	7.5	0.5	0.25
N = 10						$\Sigma D^2 = 24$

Rank Correlation:

$$R = 1 - \frac{6 \Sigma D^2}{N(N^2-1)}$$

$$= 1 - \frac{6 \times 24}{10(10^2-1)}$$

$$= 1 - \frac{144}{990}$$

$$= 1 - 0.145$$

$$= 0.855$$

Application of Correlation: Karl Pearson coefficient of correlation can be used to assess the extent of relationship between motivation of export incentive schemes and utilization of such schemes by exporters.

Motivation and Utilization of Export Incentive Schemes–Correlation Analysis

S. No.	Exporters	Correlation
1.	Agriculture Exporters	+0.642
2	Seafood Exporters	+0.423.
3.	Textile Exporters	+0.125
4.	Gems and Jewellery Exporters	+0.898

Opinion scores of the various categories of exporters towards motivation and utilization of export incentive schemes can be recorded and correlated by using Karl Pearson coefficient of correlation and appropriate interpretation may be given on the value of correlation.

Testing of Correlation: 't' test is used to test correlation coefficient. Height and weight of a random sample are six adults.

Height (cm.)	170	175	176	178	183	185
Weight (kg.)	57	64	70	76	71	82

It is reasonable to assume that these variables are normally distributed, so the Karl Pearson correlation coefficient is the appropriate measure of the degree of association between the height and the weight.

$r = 0.875$

Hypothesis test for Pearson's population correlation coefficient;

H_o: p = 0, this implies no correlation between the variables in the population.

H_1: p > 0, this implies that there is positive correlation in the population (increasing height is associated with increasing weight).

5 percent significance level

$$r \frac{\sqrt{n-2}}{1-r^2}$$

test statistic 't' test =

$$0.875 \frac{\sqrt{6-2}}{1-.875^2} = 3.61$$

Table value of 5 percent significance level

4 degree of freedom (6-2) = 2.132
n - 2

Since, the calculated value is more than the table value. Null hypothesis is rejected. There is a significant positive correlation between the height and the weight.

Partial Correlation: Partial correlation is used in a situation where three and four variables are involved. Three variables such as age, height and weight are given. Here, partial correlation is applied. Correlation between height and weight can be computed by keeping age constant. Age may be the important factor influencing the strength of relationship between height and weight. Partial correlation is used to keep constant, the effect of age. The effect of one variable is partially out from the correlation between other two variables. This statistical technique is known as partial correlation.

Correlation between variables x and y is denoted as r_{xy}.

Partial correlation is denoted by the symbol $r_{12.3}$. Here, correlation is between variable 1 and 2, keeping the 3rd variable constant.

The formula for partial correlation,

$$r_{12.3} = \frac{r^{12} - r^{13}\, r^{23}}{\sqrt{1 - r_{13}^2} \times \sqrt{1 - r_{23}^2}}$$

$r_{12.3}$ = partial correlation between variables 1 and 2.
r_{12} = correlation between variables 1 and 2.
r_{13} = correlation between variables 1 and 3.
r_{23} = correlation between variables 2 and 3.

$$r_{13.2} = \frac{r_{13} - r_{12}\, r_{23}}{\sqrt{1 - r_{12}^2} \times \sqrt{1 - r_{23}^2}}$$

$$r_{23.1} = \frac{r_{23} - r_{12}\, r_{13}}{\sqrt{1 - r_{12}^2} \times \sqrt{1 - r_{13}^2}}$$

From the following data, calculate the correlation coefficient between variables 1 and 2 by keeping the effect of variable 3 constant.

$r_{12} = 0.7; \quad r_{13} = 0.6; \quad r_{23} = 0.4$

$$r_{12.3} = \frac{r_{12} - r_{13}\, r_{23}}{\sqrt{1 - (r_{13})^2} \times \sqrt{1 - (r_{23})^2}}$$

$$= \frac{0.7 - 0.6 \times 0.4}{\sqrt{1 - (0.6)^2} \times \sqrt{1 - (0.4)^2}}$$

$$= \frac{0.7 - 0.24}{\sqrt{1 - 0.36} \times \sqrt{1 - 0.16}}$$

$$= \frac{0.7 - 0.24}{\sqrt{0.64} \times \sqrt{0.84}} = \frac{0.46}{0.8 \mathrm{x} 0.92}$$

$$= \frac{0.46}{0.736} = 0.625$$

Calculate r_{23} and $r_{13.2}$ from the following:

$r_{12} = 0.60; \quad r_{13} = 0.51; \quad r_{23} = 0.40$

$$r_{23.1} = \frac{r_{23} - r_{12}\, r_{13}}{\sqrt{1 - (r_{12})^2} \times \sqrt{1 - (r_{13})^2}}$$

$$= \frac{0.40 - 0.60 \times 0.51}{\sqrt{1-(0.60)^2} \times \sqrt{1-(0.51)^2}}$$

$$= \frac{0.40 - 0.306}{\sqrt{1-0.36} \times \sqrt{1-0.260}}$$

$$= \frac{0.094}{\sqrt{0.64} \times \sqrt{0.740}}$$

$r_{23.1} = 0.137$

$$r_{13.2} = \frac{r_{13} - r_{12}\, r_{23}}{\sqrt{1-(r_{12})^2} \times \sqrt{1-(r_{23})^2}}$$

$$= \frac{0.51 - 0.60 \times 0.40}{\sqrt{1-(0.60)^2} \times \sqrt{1-(0.40)^2}}$$

$$= \frac{0.51 - 0.24}{\sqrt{1-0.36} \times \sqrt{1-0.16}}$$

$$= \frac{0.27}{\sqrt{0.64} \times \sqrt{0.84}} = \frac{0.27}{0.736}$$

$= 0.367$

Given following zero order correlation coefficients:

$r_{12} = 0.8$; $r_{13} = 0.6$; $r_{23} = 0.5$

Calculate the partial correction between first and third variables, keeping the second variable constant.

$$r_{13.2} = \frac{r_{13} - r_{12}\, r_{23}}{\sqrt{1-(r_{12})^2} \times \sqrt{1-(r_{23})^2}}$$

$$= \frac{0.6 - 0.8 \times 0.5}{\sqrt{1-(0.8)^2} \times \sqrt{1-(0.5)^2}}$$

$$= \frac{0.6 - 0.40}{\sqrt{1-0.64} \times \sqrt{1-0.25}}$$

$$= \frac{0.2}{\sqrt{0.36} \times \sqrt{0.75}}$$

$r_{13.2} = 0.385$

Coefficient of correlation between variable 1 and 3 was 0.6. It has been reduced to 0.385 after partialling out the effect of variable 2. The difference between the values of r_{13} and $r_{13.2}$,

0.6–0.385 = 0.215 was due to effect of variable 2 or in exact words due to the variability or heterogeneity in variable 2.

Coefficient of correlation between variable 2 and 3 was 0.40. It has been reduced to 0.137 after partialling out the effect of variable 1. The difference between the values of r23 and r23.1, 0.40 -0.137 was due to the effect of variable 1 or in exact words due to the variability or heterogeneity in variable 1.

Coefficient of correlation between variable 1 and 3 was 0.51. It has been reduced to 0.368 after partialling out the effect of variable 2. The difference between the values of r13 and r13.2, 0.51–0.368 was due to the effect of variable 2 or in exact words, due to the variability or heterogeneity in variable 2.

Multiple Correlation: Three or more variables are involved in multiple correlation. The dependent variable is denoted by X_1 and other variables are denoted by X_2, X_3 etc. Gupta S.P., has expressed that "the coefficient of multiple linear correlation is represented by R1 and it is common to add subscripts designating the variable involved. Thus, R1.234 would represent the coefficient of multiple linear correlation between X1 on the one hand, X2, X3 and X4 on the other. The subscript of the dependent variable is always to the left of the point".

The coefficient of multiple correlation for r_{12}, r_{13} an r_{23} can be expressed as follows:

$$R_{1.23} = \sqrt{\frac{r_{12}^2 + r_{13}^2 - 2r_{12}r_{13}r_{23}}{1 - r_{23}^2}}$$

$$R_{2.13} = \sqrt{\frac{r_{12}^2 + r_{23}^2 - 2r_{12}r_{13}r_{23}}{1 - r_{13}^2}}$$

$$R_{3.12} = \sqrt{\frac{r_{12}^2 + r_{23}^2 - 2r_{12}r_{13}r_{23}}{1 - r_{12}^2}}$$

Coefficient of multiple correlation for $R_{1.23}$ is the same as $R_{1.32}$.

A coefficient of multiple correlation lies between 0 and 1. If the coefficient of multiple correlation is 1, it shows that the correlation is perfect. If it is 0, it shows that there is no linear relationship between the variables. The coefficients of multiple correlation are always positive in sign and range from 1.0 to 0.

Coefficient of multiple determination can be obtained by squaring $R_{1.23}$.

Alternative formula for computing $R_{1.23}$ is,

$$R_{1.23} = \sqrt{r_{12}^2 + r_{13.2}^2 \left(1 - r_{12}^2\right)}$$

or

$$R_{1.23} = r_{12}^2 + r_{13.2}^2 \left(1 - r_{12}^2\right)$$

Similarly, alternative formula for $R_{1.24}$, $R_{1.34}$ can be computed.

The following formula can be used to determine a multiple correlation coefficient with three independent variables.

$$R_{1.234} = \sqrt{1 - \left(1 - r_{14}^2\right) \left(1 - r_{13.4}^2\right) \left(1 - r_{12.34}^2\right)}$$

Multiple correlation analysis measures the relationship between the given variables. In this analysis, the degree of association is between one variable considered as the dependent variable and a group of other variables considered the independent variables.

The following zero-order correlation coefficients are given $r_{12} = 0.98$; $r_{13} = 0.44$; $r_{23} = 0.54$.

Calculate multiple correlation coefficient treating first variable as dependent and second and third variables as independent (Source: Gupta S.P., *Statistical Methods*).

Solution: First variable is dependent. Second and third variables are independent. Multiple correlation coefficients are:

$$R_{1.23} = \sqrt{\frac{r_{12}^2 + r_{13}^2 - 2r_{12}r_{13}r_{23}}{1 - r_{23}^2}}$$

$$= \frac{(0.98)^2 + (0.44)^2 - 2(0.98)\,(0.44)\,(0.54)}{1 - (0.54)^2}$$

$= 0.986$

Standard errors of estimate for multiple correlation is given below:

$$S_{1.23} = S_1 \frac{1 - r_{12}^2 - r_{13}^2 - r_{23}^2 + 2r_{23}\; r_{13}\; r_{23}}{1 - r_{23}^2}$$

Regression Analysis

Gupta S.P., in his book, 'Statistical Methods' has defined regression as "the measure of the average relationship between two or more variables in term of the original units of the data".

Morris Hamburg has defined regression analysis as, "the method in which estimates are made of the values of a variable from a knowledge of values of one or more other variables and to the measurement of the involved in this estimation process".

Correlation analysis attempts to study the relationship between the variables x and y. Regression analysis attempts to predict the average x for given y. In regression, it is attempted to quantify the dependence of one variation on the other. *Example:* There are two variables x and y. y depends on x. Dependence is expressed in the form of the following equation:

$$y = a + bx$$

Regression analysis uses to estimate the values of the dependent variables from the values of the independent variables.

Regression analysis is used to get a measure of the error involved using the regression line as a basis for estimation.

Regression coefficient is used to calculate correlation coefficient. The square of correlation coefficient is a measure of the degree of association of correlation that prevails between the given two variables.

Correlation coefficient measures the degree of co-variablility between the given variables x and y. The regression analysis is used to study the 'nature of relationship' between the given variables i.e., the value of one variable is predicted based on another.

Correlation analysis does not study cause and effect relationship of the given variables. It is not stated that one variable is the cause and other the effect. In regression analysis, one variable is taken as dependent and another as independent. Here, there is a possibility to study the cause and effect relationship.

Standard Error of Estimate: The standard error of estimates helps to measure the accuracy of the estimate figures in regression analysis. If the value of the standard error of estimate is small, it shows that the estimate provided by the regression equation is better and closer. If standard error of estimate is zero, it shows that there is no variation about the line and the correlation will be perfect. Gupta, S.P. has explained that "the standard error of estimate is used to ascertain how good and representative the regression line is as a description of the average relationship between the two series".

The standard error of regression of X values from Xc is,

$$Sx.y = \frac{\sqrt{\Sigma(X - X_c)^2}}{N} \qquad \textit{also}$$

$$Sx.y = 6x\sqrt{1 - r^2} \qquad \textit{also}$$

$$Sx.y = \frac{\sqrt{\Sigma X\ 2 - a\Sigma X - b\Sigma XY}}{N}$$

$$Sy.x = \frac{\sqrt{\Sigma (Y - Y_c)^2}}{N}$$

Problem: The following results were worked out from scores in statistics and mathematics in an examination.

	Score in Statistics	Score in Mathematics
Mean	40	48
Standard Deviation	10	15

Karl Pearson's correlation coefficient between x and y = +0.42.

Find both the regression lines. Use these regression lines to estimate value of y for x = 50 and also estimate the value of x for y = 30.

Solution: The following data are given:

$\bar{x}$ =40, $\bar{y}$ =48, σx =10, σy = 15, r = 0.42

The regression lines are:

$$(x - \bar{x}) = r\frac{\sigma x}{\sigma y}(y - \bar{y})$$

$$(x - 40) = 0.42\frac{10}{15}(y\text{-}48)$$

$$x = 40 + 0.279y - 13.392$$

$$x = 0.279y + 13.392$$

$$(y - \bar{y}) = r\frac{\sigma x}{\sigma y}(y - \bar{x})$$

$$(y - 48) = 0.42 \frac{10}{15} (x-40)$$

$y = 48 + 0.63x - 25.20$

$y = 0.63x + 22.80$

Regression Equation x on y

$x = 0.297y + 26.608$

When y = 30

$x = 0.297 \times 30 + 26.608$

$x = 8.91 + 26.608$

$x = 35.518$

Regression Equation y on x

When x = 50

$y = 0.63x + 22.80$

$y = 0.63 \times 50 + 22.80$

$y = 31.5 + 22.80$

$y = 54.3$

Problem: From the following data, obtain two regression equations:

X	12	4	20	8	16
Y	18	22	10	16	14

Solution: (Actual mean is used)

$$\bar{x} = \frac{12+4+20+8+16}{5} = \frac{60}{5} = 12$$

$$\bar{y} = \frac{18+22+10+16+14}{5} = \frac{80}{5} = 16$$

x	y	$x-\bar{x}$ x - 12	$y-\bar{y}$ y - 16	$(x-\bar{x})^2$	$(y-\bar{y})^2$	$(x-\bar{x})(y-\bar{y})$

12	8	0	2	0	4	0
4	22	-8	6	64	36	-48
20	10	8	-6	64	36	-48
8	16	-4	0	16	0	0
16	14	4	-2	16	4	-8
				160	80	-104

$$b = \frac{\Sigma(x-\bar{x})(y-\bar{y})}{\Sigma(x-\bar{x})^2}$$

$$= \frac{-104}{160} = -0.65$$

$$b' = \frac{\Sigma(x-\bar{x})(y-\bar{y})}{\Sigma(y-\bar{y})^2}$$

$$= \frac{-104}{80} = -1.3$$

Regression equation x on y:

$(x-\bar{x}) = b'(y-\bar{y})$

$(x-12) = -1.3\,(y-16)$

$x = 12-1.3y+1.3x16$

$= 12-1.3y + 20.8$

$x = 32.8-1.3y$

Regression equation y on x:

$(y-\bar{y}) = b(x-\bar{x})$

$(y-16) = -0.65\,(x-12)$

$y = 16-0.65x+0.65x12$

$= 16-0.65x + 7.8$

$y = 23.8-0.65x$

$x = 32.8 - 1.3y$

$y = 23.8 - 0.65x$

Problem: The following table gives the height x (in inches) and weight y (in lbs.) of 10 students aged 18 years selected by random sampling from a population.

x	(Height)	61	68	64	65	70	63	62	64	67
y	(Weight)	112	123	115	110	125	100	113	116	123

Calculate the weight of a student whose height is 71".

Solution: (assumed mean is used).

It is required to calculate weight of a student, when height is given. The required regression line is weight on height. The regression line is y on x.

Assumed mean x = 70 y = 125

X	Y	Dx $x - \bar{x}$ x - 70	Dy $y - \bar{y}$ y - 125	Dx^2	Dy^2	Dx dy
61	112	-9	-13	81	169	117
68	123	-2	-2	4	4	4
68	130	-2	5	4	25	10
64	115	-6	-10	36	100	60
65	110	-5	-15	25	225	75
70	125	0	0	0	0	0
63	100	-7	-25	49	625	175
62	113	-8	-12	64	144	96
64	116	-6	-9	36	81	54
67	123	-3	-2	9	4	6
		-48	-93	308	1377	597

$$B = \frac{n\Box dxdy - (\Box dx)(\Box dy)}{n\Box dx2 - (\Box dx)^2}$$

$$= \frac{10 \times 597 - (-48)(-93)}{10 \times 308 - (-48)^2}$$

$$= \frac{5970 - 4464}{3080 - 2304}$$

$$= \frac{1506}{776}$$

$$= 1.94$$

$$\bar{x} = 70 + \frac{\Sigma dx}{n}$$

$$= 70 + \frac{-48}{10}$$

$$= 70 - 4.8 = 65.2$$

$$\bar{y} = 125 + \frac{\Sigma d\bar{y}}{n}$$

$$= 125 + \frac{-93}{10}$$

$$= 125 - 9.3$$

$$= 115.7$$

$y - \bar{y} = b\,(x - \bar{x})$

$y - 115.7 = 1.94\,(x - 65.2)$

$y = 1.94x + 115.7 - 126.488$

$y = 1.94x - 10.788$

When $x = 71$

$y = 1.94 \times 71 - 10.788$

$= 126.952$

Therefore, the weight of a student whose height is 71" is 126.952.

Relationship between Correlation Coefficient and Regression Coefficient

The product of the regression coefficient is equal to the square of the correlation coefficient.

Correlation coefficient is the geometric mean of the regression coefficient.

In the earlier problem,

$b = -0.65$

$b' = -1.30$

$r^2 = bb'$

$= -0.65 \times -1.30$

$r^2 = 0.845$

From the given b and b' value, correlation coefficient is calculated.

Application of Regression Analysis

Regression analysis can be used to investigate the interrelationship between investment returns and inflation rates. The following regression model can be used to test the relationship.

Relationship between stock return and inflation rate is tested by using the following regression model:

$S_{Rt} = a_{Sr} + b_{Sr} P_t + C_{Sr}$

where S_{Rt} = stock retrun at time 't'

a_{Sr} = constant

b_{Sr} = inflationary coefficient

P_t = inflation rate at time 't'

C_{Sr} = error term

Relationship between gold and silver return and inflation rate is tested by using the following regression model:

$G = a_g + b_g P_t + e_g$

$S = a_s + b_s P_t + e_s$

Where G = percentage change in gold price

S = percentage change in silver price

a_g and a_s = constant

b_g and b_s = inflation

e_g and e_s = error terms

Enquiry Returns from Industries and Inflation Rate

Industry	a_{St}	b_{St}	t value
All industries	-0.2501	-0.1335	-0.2387
Agriculture and allied activities	-1.1222	-0.2112	-0.0380
Processing and manufacturing	-1.0382	-0.4295	-0.0374
Others	-0.0171	-0.4066	-0.7188

Note: t values, accepted at 10 percent level of significance.

The value of bst is negative for all groups. It was -0.1335 for overall industries, -0.2112 for agriculture and allied industries, -0.4295 for processing and manufacturing industries, and -0.4066 for other industries. It can be concluded that equity shares are not providing any hedge against inflation (study period of this study covers a period of five financial years starting from 1994-95).

Bullion Investment and Inflation

Investment	a	b	t value
Gold	-0.1506	0.0348	0.1518
Silver	0.3017	-0.0517	-0.1084

The inflationary coefficient values for silver and gold are-0.0517 and 0.0348. It can be concluded that the relationship between investment in silver and inflation is negative and it is not providing any hedge against inflation during the study period. Investment in gold is providing a partial hedge against inflation.

(Source: "An analysis of interrelationship between investment returns and inflation rate", project work submitted by Mr. S. Amilan, lecturer, Department of International Business and Commerce, Alagappa University, Karaikudi, to Indira Gandhi National Open University for his MBA programme).

Multiple Regression Analysis

Multiple regression analysis is an extension of two variable regression analysis. In this analysis, two or more independent variables are used to estimate the values of a dependent variable, instead of one independent variable. Gupta S. P., in his book, *Statistical Methods* has stated the objectives of multiple regression analysis.

The objectives are:

To derive an equation which provides estimates of the dependent variable from values of the two or more independent variables,

To obtain the measure of the error involved in using the regression equation as a basis of estimation, and

To obtain a measure of the proportion of variance in the dependent variable accounted for or 'explained by' the independent variables.

Multiple regression equation explains the average relationship between the given variables and the relationship is used to estimate the dependent variable. Regression equation refers the equation for estimating a dependent variable.

Example: estimating dependent variable x_1 from the independent variables x_2, x_3...... it is known as regression equation of x_1 on x_2, x_3, ...

Regression equation, when three variables are involved, is given below:

(regression equation of x1 on x2 and x3)

$X_{1.23} = a_{1.23} + b_{12.3} X_2 + b_{13.2} X_3$

Where $X_{1.23}$ = estimated value of the dependent variable

X_2 and X_3 = independent variables.

Gupta S.P., has explained the above regression equation in the following way:

$A_{1.23}$ = (constant) the intercept made by the regression plan. It gives the value of the dependent variable, when all the independent variables assume a value equal to zero.

$B_{12.3}$ and $b_{13.2}$ = partial regression coefficients or net regression coefficients.

$B_{12.3}$ = measures the amount by which a unit change in X_2 is expected to affect X_1 when X_3 is held constant.

$B_{13.2}$ = measures the amount of change in X1 per unit change in X3 when X2 is held constant.

(Source: Gupta S.P., 'Statistical Methods').

Deviations Taken From Actual Means

Regression equation for three variables:

$$x_1 = b_{12.3} x_2 + b_{13.2} x_3$$

$$x_1 = (X_1 - \overline{X}_1)$$

$$x_2 = (X_2 - \overline{X}_2)$$

$$x_3 = (X_3 - \overline{X}_3)$$

$b_{12.3}$ and $b_{13.2}$ can be obtained by solving the following equations:

$$\Sigma x_1 x_2 = b_{12.3}\Sigma x_2^2 + b_{13.2}\Sigma x_2 x_3$$

$$\Sigma x_1 x_2 = b_{12.3}\Sigma x_2 x_3 + b_{13.2}\Sigma x_3$$

$$b_{12.3} = r_{12.3} \times \frac{\sigma_{1.23}}{\sigma_{3.12}}$$

$$b_{13.2} = r_{13.2} \times \frac{\sigma_{13.2}}{\sigma_{3.12}}$$

Regression equation of X_1 on X_2 and X_3 is,

$$(X_1 = \overline{X}_1) = \left[\frac{r_{12} - r_{13}\, r_{23}}{1 - r_{23}^2}\right]\left(\frac{S_1}{S_2}\right)(X_2 - \overline{X}_2) + \left[\frac{r_{13} - r_{12}\, r_{23}}{1 - r_{23}^2}\right]\left(\frac{S_1}{S_3}\right)(X_3 - \overline{X}_3)$$

Regression equation of X_3 on X_2 and X_1 is,

$$(X_3 = \overline{X}_3) = \left[\frac{r_{23} - r_{13}\, r_{12}}{1 - r_{12}^2}\right]\left(\frac{S_3}{S_2}\right)(X_2 - \overline{X}_2) + \left[\frac{r_{13} - r_{23}\, r_{12}}{1 - r_{12}^2}\right]\left(\frac{S_3}{S_1}\right)(X_1 - \overline{X}_1)$$

Regression equation when four variables are involved: (Regression equation of X_1 on X_2, X_3 and X_4)

$X_1 = a_{1.234} + b_{12.34} X_2 + b_{13.241} X_3 + b_{14.23} X_4$

The regression equation of X_1 on X_2, X_3 is

$X_1 = a_{1.234} + b_{12.3} X_2 + b_{13.24} X_3$

The values of the constant $a_{1.23}$, $b_{12.3}$ and $b_{13.2}$ are computed by solving the following three normal equations:

$$\Sigma X_1 = N a_{1.23} + b_{12.3}\Sigma X_2 + b_{13.2}\Sigma X_3$$

$$\Sigma X_1 X_2 = a_{1.23}\Sigma X_2 + b_{12.3}\Sigma X_2^2 + b_{13.2}\Sigma X_2 X_3$$

$$\Sigma X_1 X_3 = a_{1.23}\Sigma X_3 + b_{12.3}\Sigma X_2 X_3 + b_{13.2}\Sigma X_3^2$$

Reliability of Estimates

Reliability of estimates, tests the estimated value obtained by applying regression equation, whether or not the estimated value is close to actual observed value. Standard error is used to measure the closeness of estimates derived from the regression equation to actual observed values. Gupta S. P., explains that the measure of reliability is an average of the deviations of the actual value of non-dependent variables from the estimate of the regression equation. Determining the accuracy of estimates from the multiple regression is the reliability of estimates. It is also known as standard error of estimate.

Standard error of estimate of X1 and X2 and X3 is given below:

$$S_{1.23} = \frac{\sqrt{\Sigma(X_1 - \overline{X}_{(last)})^2}}{N-3}$$

$S_{1.23}$= standard error of estimate of X_1 on X_2 and X_3

X_{last}= estimated value of X_1 as calculated from the regression equations.

Application of Multiple Regression

Multiple regressions can be applied to test the factors such as export elasticity, import elasticity and structural changes (contribution of manufacturing sector towards GDP) influencing the employment.

Employment is a dependent variable. Similarly, researchers can attempt to use multiple regressions in their research work appropriately.

Association of Attributes

Certain variables are measured quantitatively. For example, value of exports, imports and balance of payments, height of the students, their weight and marks scored by them etc. Data regarding such details are known as statistics of variables.

Certain variables are not measured quantitatively. For example, blindness, deafness etc. Number of blind persons in a total population can be measured, whereas it is difficult to measure the blindness exactly. Here, direct quantitative measurement is not possible. The study of presence and absence of particular characteristics is known as statistics of attributes.

Gupta S. P., in his book, *Statistical Methods* has stated that the tool of correlation is used to measure the degree of relationship between two variables that are capable of direct quantitative measurement. Association of attributes is employed to measure the degree of relationship between the two variables whose values are not measured quantitatively and presence and absence of a particular attribute is determined.

The available data is classified while studying the statistics of attributes. Classification is based on presence and absence of particular attributes or characteristics.

Two classifications (presence and absence) are made for one attribute.

Examples:

Attribute-employment;

Classification-employed, unemployed;

Four classifications are made for two attributes

Attributes-employment and sex-wise distribution;

Classification-number of males employed;

Number of females employed;

Number of males unemployed;

Number of females unemployed.

Methods of Studying Association

Methods of studying association of attributes are given below:

Comparison of observed and expected frequencies method,

Proportion method,

Yule's coefficient of association,

Coefficient of colligation, and
Coefficient of contingency.

Comparison of Observed and Expected Frequencies Method

Gupta S.P., has explained the application of this method. The application is given below:

If the actual observation is equal to the expectation, the attributes are said to be independent.
If the actual observation is more than the expectation, the attributes are said to be positively associated.
If the actual observation is less than the expectation, the attributes are to be negatively associated.

The application is symbolically expressed as, given two attributes A and B if,

Independent (actual observation):

$$(AB) = \frac{(A) \times (B)}{N}$$

Positively associated (actual observation) if

$$(AB) > \frac{(A) \times (B)}{N}$$

Negatively associated (actual observation) if

$$(AB) < \frac{(A) \times (B)}{N}$$

Find if A and B are independent, positively associated or negatively associated from the actual observation given below:

(A) = 940, (B) = 1240, (AB) = 640,N = 2000

$$\textit{Expected frequency} = \frac{(A) \times (B)}{N}$$

$$= \frac{940 \text{ x } 1240}{2000}$$

Actual observation of (AB) 640 is more than the expected frequency. It is concluded that attributes A and B are positively associated.

Comparison of observed and expected frequencies method is used to determine the nature of association between the two attributes, i.e. positive association, negative association or disassociation. This method does not reveal the degree of association. Yule's coefficient of association helps to ascertain the nature of association and degree of association.

Proportion Method

This method also determines nature of association between the given attributes and not the degree of association. Gupta S.P., has highlighted that, "if there is no relationship of any kind between the two attributes A and B, we expected to have the same proportion of A's amongst the B's as amongst the B's. Association between the two attributes A and B is expressed symbolically as:

(a) $\frac{(AB)}{(A)} = \frac{(A\beta)}{(\beta)}$

The association between the attributes is independent.

(b) $\frac{(AB)}{(B)} > \frac{(A\beta)}{(\beta)}$

The association between the attributes is positive. The attribute is positively associated.

(c) $\frac{(AB)}{(B)} < \frac{(A\beta)}{(\beta)}$

The association between the attributes is negative. The attributes are negatively associated.

In a population of 1000 sales persons, number of sales persons not trained is 400. Out of 300 sales persons, those who failed to achieve their sales target, belonged to the untrained group. Find out whether the attribute of untrained and their failure to achieve the sales target is independent, positively associated or negatively associated.

A = untrained sales persons

a = trained sales persons

B = number of failures (sales persons) in achieving the sales target

β = number of sales persons achieved sales target
N = total number of sales persons.

(A) = 400, (B) = 300, (AB) = 120,(α) = 600, (αβ)= 180

Attributes A and B will be independent if,

$$\frac{(AB)}{(A)} = \frac{(\alpha\beta)}{(\alpha)} = \frac{120}{400} = \frac{180}{600} = 0.3$$

Since the two proportions are the same, it may be concluded that attributes, untrained and failure to achieve sales target, are independent.

The proportion of untrained sales persons who failed to achieve some target is the same as the proportion of trained sales persons who failed achieving sales target.

Yule's Coefficient of Association

Yule's coefficient of association is a popular method among the methods of studying association of attributes. It attempts to determine not only the nature of association (positively associated, negatively associated, independent) but also the degree or extent of association between the given attributes.

The Yule's coefficient of association is denoted by symbol Q and the formula to compute Yule's coefficient of association is,

$$Q = \frac{(AB)(\alpha\beta) - (AB)(\alpha\beta)}{(AB)(\alpha\beta) + (AB)(\alpha\beta)}$$

Yule's coefficient of association lies between +- 1

If the value of Q is +1, it shows that there is a perfect positive association between the attributes.

If the value of Q is -1, it shows that the two attributes are independent.

Problem: The following data relates to literacy and unemployment in a group of persons. Compute Yule's coefficient of association between literacy and unemployment and state the interpretation.

Illiterate unemployed = 440
Literate employed = 40

Illiterate employed = 360

Solutions:

A denotes literacy

B denotes unemployment

α denoted illiteracy

β denotes employment

The following table is constructed with the help of the given values:

	A	α	Total
B	160	440	600
B	40	360	400
Total	200	800	1000

$$Q = \frac{(AB)\,(\alpha\beta) - (A\mathit{B})\,(\alpha\beta)}{(AB)\,(\alpha\beta) + (A\mathit{B})\,(\alpha\beta)}$$

$$= \frac{160 \times 360 - 40 \times 440}{160 \times 360 + 40 \times 440}$$

Coefficient of Colligation

Coefficient of colligation is denoted by symbol y. the formula is

$$y = \frac{1 - \dfrac{\sqrt{(AB)\times(\alpha B)}}{(A\alpha)\times(\alpha\beta)}}{1 + \dfrac{\sqrt{(A\beta)\times(\alpha B)}}{(AB)\times(\alpha\beta)}}$$

Yule's coefficient of association can be computed from the above coefficient.

Application of Association of Attributes–Yule's Coefficient of Association

Yule's coefficient of association is used to assess whether there is association between age and attitude of the budget center managers towards budget setting factors.

Age vs. Attitude

SN	Age	Level of attitude		Total
		High	Low	
		(No. of respondents)		
1.	Below 45	7 (58 percent)	5 (42 percent)	12 (100)
2.	Above 4	9 (50 percent)	9 (50 percent)	18 (100)
	Total	16	14	30

Yule's coefficient of association,

$$Q = \frac{(AB)\,(\alpha\beta) - (A\beta)\,(\alpha\beta)}{(AB)\,(\alpha\beta) + (A\beta)\,(\alpha\beta)}$$

A: denotes budget center managers in the age group of below 45 years,

α: denotes budget center managers in the age group of above 45 years,

B: denotes budget center managers having high attitude towards budget setting factors, and

β: denotes budget center managers having low attitude towards budget setting factors.

$AB = 7, \alpha\beta = 9,\ A\beta = 5, \alpha B = 9$

$$Q = \frac{7 \times 9 - 5 \times 9}{7 \times 9 + 5 \times 9} = \frac{18}{108} = 0.166$$

Yule's value is +0.166.

This signifies that there is a positive association between age and attitude of the budget center managers on budget setting factors, but their level of association is not that strong.

Yule's coefficient of association can be used to ascertain the association between quantitative factors (like age, experience etc.) and attitude of the budget center manages as well as qualitative factors (such as satisfaction regarding joint monetary and non-monetary benefits and employee welfare measures) and that attitude of the budget center managers towards budget setting and reviewing the monitoring.

Quantitative and Qualitative Factors vs. Attitude of the Budget Center Managers towards Budget Review and Monitoring

Factors	Association with the attitude of budget center managers	Level of association
Quantitative factors		
i. Age	Positive	+0.102
ii. Experience	Positive	+0.473
Qualitative factors		
i. Job satisfaction	Positive	+0.636
ii. Monetary satisfaction	Positive	+0.500
iii. Employee welfare measures satisfaction	Negative	-0.400
iv. Work environment satisfaction	Positive	+0.743

Self-assessment Questions

1. What do you mean by 'correlation'? Explain the properties of correlation coefficient?
2. Explain the various methods of studying correlation.
3. A random sample of 10 families had the following annual income and annual saving in thousands of pounds.

Income	5.1	20.3	25.2	15.0	10.3	15.6	16.0	7.3	8.6	12.3
Savings	0.2	0.5	0.3	5.7	0.7	1.3	0.4	4.2	2.0	0.6

Is there a significant positive correlation between income and saving?

4. Calculate rank difference correlation from the following scores.

Mathematics	55	58	51	53	48	49	52	59	60	54
Chemistry	41	61	47	39	38	36	43	49	50	42

5. On the basis of observation made on 39 cotton plants, the total correlation of yield of cotton (X_1), number of balls i.e. seed vessels (X_2) and height of plants (X_3) are found to be:

   $r_{12} = 0.8$; $r_{13} = 0.65$' $r_{23} = 0.7$.

   Compute partial correlation between yield of cotton and the number of balls eliminating the effect of height.

6. In studying the association between the number of farms and the number of tractors in two district of Punjab, a researcher obtained the following data:

   $$□X = 169 \quad □Y = 130 \quad □XY = 3006$$
   $$□X^2 = 3856 \; □Y^2 = 2370 \quad n = 10$$

   From the above information, estimate the regression equation and test the significance of b at 0.1 level of significance.

7. In order to analyse the branch expansion schemes in the semi-urban and rural areas, the management of a nationalized bank wants to determine the relationship between bank deposits and population. The data for seven different semi-urban towns and villages have been collected.

Population per bank/ office	3700	4000	4100	3600	4500	3600	4100
Deposits (₹ in lakh)	13.3	14.5	14.2	13.5	13.8	14.2	14.7

   Use regression analysis to determine the desired relationship.

8. Compute correlation from the following data and test the correlation.

Year	1992	1993	1994	1995	1996	1997
Premium income (₹ in thousands)	44	48	52	57	59	60
Investment (₹ in thousand)	14	18	22	28	30	34

9. Find Karl Pearson's coefficient of correlation from the following index numbers and interpret it.

Wages	100	101	103	102	104	99	97	98	96	96
Cost of living	98	99	99	97	95	02	95	94	90	91

10. Two housewives, asked to express their preferences for different kinds of detergents gave the following replies.

Detergent	A	B	C	D	E	F	G	H	I	J
Neena	1	2	4	3	7	8	6	5	9	10
Meena	1	4	2	3	5	7	6	8	9	10

To what extent the preferences of these two ladies go together?

11. Calculate the Karl Pearson's coefficient of correlation between age and paying habits from the data given below. Comment on the value.

Age	20	21	22	23	24	25
No. of students	500	400	300	240	200	160
Regular players	400	300	180	96	60	24

12. The following calculations have been made for closing prices of 12 stocks (X) on the Bombay Stock Exchange on a certain day along with the volume of sales in thousand or shares (Y). From these calculations find the regression equations.

□X = 580 □Y = 370 □XY = 11494

□X^2 = 41568 □Y^2 = 17206

13. The following figures relate to the advertisement expenditure and sales:

Adv. Exp. (in lakh of ₹)	60	62	65	70	73	75	71
Sales (in crore of ₹)	10	11	13	15	16	19	14

Estimate (i) the sales for advertisement expenditure of ₹ 80 lakh and (ii) the advertisement for a sales target of ₹ 25 crore.

14. Table below shows the power and top speeds of different brands of sports cars:

Brand	:	A	B	C	D	E	F
Power X(kw)	:	70	63	72	60	66	70
Speed Y (km/h)	:	155	150	180	135	156	168
Brands	:	G	H	I	J	K	L
Power X (kw)	:	74	65	62	67	65	68
Speed Y (km/h)	:	178	160	132	145	139	152

Find the best linear relationship that fits the given data. Estimate the speed of a car that has a power of 63kw. And find a 95 percent confidence interval for this estimate. Determine how much of the variability in speed may be explained by the regression hypothesis.

15. An industrial engineer collected the following data on experience and performance rating of 8 operators:

Operator	1	2	3	4	5	6	7	8
Experience (yrs.)	16	12	18	4	3	10	5	12
Performance Rating	87	88	89	68	58	80	70	85

Does the data give evidence that experience improves performance?
Estimate the performance rating of an operator having (a) 9 years and (b) 15 years of experience.

16. A survey was conducted in respect of marital status and success in examinations. Out of 2000 persons who appeared for an examination, 80 percent of them were boys, and the rest were girls. Among 300 married boys, 140 were successful, 1100 boys were successful among unmarried boys. In respect of 100 married girls, 40 were successful, 200 unmarried girls were successful. Construct two separate nine-square tables and find out the Yule's coefficient of association to discuss the association between marital status and the passing of examination.

17. From the following data, find the association between darkness of eye-colour in a father and a son:
Father with dark eyes and sons with dark eyes=1040.
Father with dark eyes and sons with not dark eyes= 160.
Father with not dark eyes and son with dark eyes=180.
Father with not dark eyes and sons with not dark eyes= 120.
What would have been the frequency of fathers with dark eyes and sons with dark eyes of the same total number, had there been complete independence?

11

Hypothesis Testing

Hypothesis is an assumption or some supposition to be proved or disproved. A research hypothesis is a predictive statement capable of being tested by scientific methods that relates an independent variable with some dependent variable. Hypothesis is usually considered as the principal instrument for research. Its main function is to suggest new experiments and observations. In fact, many experiments are carried out with the deliberate object of testing hypothesis. Decision-makers often face situations wherein they are interested in testing hypothesis on the basis of available information and then take decisions on the basis of such testing.

Definition of Hypothesis

A research hypothesis is a predictive statement capable of being tested by scientific methods that relates an independent variable to some dependent variable.

Features

It should be clear and precise.

It should be capable of being tested.

It should state the relationship between variables.

It should be limited in scope and must be specific.

It should be stated in simple terms.

The hypothesis is capable of being objectively verified and tested. Thus, we may conclude that a hypothesis states what we are looking for and it is a proposition which can be put to test to determine its validity.

Basic Concepts

Null Hypothesis (H_a) and Alternative Hypothesis (H_o): Suppose, if one wants to test the hypothesis that the population mean is equal to the hypothesized mean 100. Here, null hypothesis can be stated that H_o: μ H_o = 100.

If our sample results do not support this null hypothesis, we should conclude something else is true. What we conclude rejecting the null hypothesis, it is known as alternative hypothesis. If we accept Ho, then we are rejecting H_a and if reject H_o, then we are accepting H_a.

For H_o: μ = M H_o = 100 we may consider 3 possible alternative hypothesis as follows.

Alternative hypothesis to be read as follows

H_a: μ # μ_{Ho} the alternative hypothesis is that the population mean is equal to 100 (it may be more or less than 100).

H_a: $\mu > \mu_{Ho}$ the alternative hypothesis is that the population mean is greater than 100.

H_a: $\mu < \mu_{Ho}$ the alternative hypothesis is that the population mean is less than 100.

The H_o and H_a are chosen before the sample is drawn. In the choice of H_o, the following considerations are usually kept in view.

H_a is usually the one which one wishes to prove and the H_o is the one which one wishes one wishes to disprove. Thus, H_o represents the hypothesis we are trying to reject and H_a represents all other possibilities.

If the rejection of a hypothesis when it is actually true involves greater risk, it is taken as null hypothesis because then the probability of rejecting it when it is true, is very small.

H_a should always be a specific hypothesis i.e. it should not state about or approximately a certainly value.

The Level of Significance: It is a very important concept in hypothesis testing. It is always some percent (usually 5 percent) which should be chosen with great care, thought, and reason. If we take the significance level at 5 percent, then this implies that H_o will be rejected when the sampling result has a less than 0.05 probability of occurring if H_o is true.

Decision Rule of Test of Hypothesis: Given H_o and H_a we make a rule which is known as decision rule according to which we accept H_a (i.e. reject H_o) or reject H_o (i.e. accept H_a).

Type I and Type II Errors: In the context of testing of hypothesis, there are basically two types of errors we can make. We may reject H_a when H_o is true and we may accept H_o when infect H_a is not true. The former is known as Type I and the latter known as Type II error.

Type I error is denoted by α (alpha) as error.

Type II error is denoted by β (Beta) as error.

The probability of Type I error is usually determined in advance and is understood at the level of significance of testing the hypothesis. If it is fixed at 5 percent, it means that there are about 5 chances in 100 that we will reject H_o when H_o is true. We can control Type I error just by fixing it at a lower level.

But with a fixed sample size n, when we try to reduce type I error, the probability of committing Type II error increases. Both the types cannot be reduced simultaneously. There is a trade-off between these two errors.

To deal with this trade-off in business situations, decisions-makers decide the appropriate level of Type I error by examining the costs or penalties attached to both type of errors.

Two Tailed and One Tailed Tests: In the context of hypothesis testing, these two terms are quite important and must be clearly understood.

A two tailed test rejects the null hypothesis if, say, the sample mean is significantly higher or lower than the hypothesized value of the mean of the population. Such a test is appropriate when the H_o is some specified value and H_a is a value not equal to the specified value of H_o.

Symbolically, two tailed test is appropriate when

H_o: $\mu = \mu_{Ho}$ and H_a: $\mu = \mu_{Ho}$ which may mean $\mu > \mu_{Ho}$ or $\mu < \mu_{Ho}$.

There are situations when only one tailed tests is considered appropriate. This test would be used when we are to test, say, whether the population mean is either lower than or higher than some hypothesized value.

Procedure of Hypothesis Testing

To test a hypothesis means to tell whether or not the hypothesis seems to be valid. In hypothesis testing, the main question is whether to accept the null hypothesis or not and to accept the H_o?

Procedure for hypothesis testing refers to all those steps that we undertake for making a choice between two actions i.e. rejection and acceptance of a null hypothesis.

Various steps involved in hypothesis testing are stated below.

Making a Formal Statement: This step consists of making a formal statement pertaining to H_o and H_a. This means that the hypothesis should be clearly stated considering the nature of the research problem.

Example: Person X of civil engineering department wants to test the load bearing capacity of an old bridge which must be more than 10 tons. In that case, he can state this hypothesis as under:

Null hypothesis H_o: $\mu = 10$ tons.

Alternative hypothesis H_a: $\mu > 10$ tons.

Selecting a Significance Level: The hypothesis is tested on a pre-determined level of significance and as such the same should be specified. Generally in practice, either 5 percent level or 1 percent level is adopted for the purpose.

The factors that affect the significance level are:

The magnitude of the difference between sample means.

The size of the samples.

The variability of measurements within samples.

Whether the hypothesis is directional or non-directional.

Deciding the Distribution to Use: Determining the appropriate sampling distribution is the next step. The choice generally remains between normal distribution and the t-distribution. The rules for selecting the correct distribution are similar to those which we have stated earlier in the context of estimation.

Selecting a Random Sample and Computing an Appropriate Value: Another step is to select a random sample and compute an appropriate value from the sample data concerning the test by utilizing the relevant distribution. In other words, draw a sample to furnish the empirical data.

Calculation of Probability: One has to calculate the probability that the sample result would diverge as widely as possible.

Comparing the Probability: This step consists in comparing the probability thus calculated with the specified value for a. If the calculated probability is equal to or smaller than the a value, in case of one-tailed test (a/2), then reject H_o. However, if the calculated probability is greater than accept H_o. In case we reject H_o, we run a risk of committing an error or Type I, but if we accept H_o then we run some risk of committing an error of Type II.

Measuring the Power of a Hypothesis Test

There are possibilities of committing Type I and Type II errors while testing a hypothesis. The probability of Type I error is denoted by α and that of Type II by β. Usually, the significance level of α test is assigned in advance and once we decide it, there is nothing else we can do above α. But what can we say about β? We all know that hypothesis test cannot be foolproof. Sometimes that test does not reject H_o when it happens to be a false one and this way, a type II error is made. However, we would always like that 1-β to be as large as possible.

If 1-β is very much nearer to unity, we can infer that the test is working quite well, meaning thereby that the test is rejecting H_o–when it is not true and if 1-β is very much nearer to 0.0, then we can infer that the test is poorly working, meaning thereby that is not rejecting H_0 when H_0 is not true. Accordingly, 1-β value is the measure of how well the test is working or what is technically described as the power of the test plotting the values of 1-β for each possible value of the population parameter for which the H_0 is not true. The resultant curve is known as the "power curve" associated with the given test.

The function defining this curve is known as the power function. In other words, the power function of a test is that function defined for all values of the parameters which yields the probability that H_0 is rejected and the value of the power function at a specific parameter point is called the power of the test at that point.

Closely related to the power function, is the operating characteristic function which shows the conditional probability of accepting H_0 for all values of population parameters for a given sample size, whether or not the decision happens to be a correct one.

If power function is represented by H and the operating characteristic function as I, then we have the L = I-H. However, one needs only one of these two functions for any decision rule in the context of testing hypotheses.

Test of Hypothesis

Hypothesis testing determines the validity of the occupation with a view to choose between two conflicting hypothesis about the value of a population parameter. Hypothesis testing helps to decide on the basis of a sample data whether a hypothesis population is likely to be true or false. Statisticians have developed several tests of significance for the purpose of testing of hypotheses, which can be classified as:

Parametric test, and

Non-parametric test.

A detailed discussion about various parametric and non-parametric tests are given below.

Parametric Test: Parametric test usually examines certain properties of the population (parent) from which we draw samples. Assumptions like observation comes from a normal population, sample size is large, assumptions about population parameters like mean, variance etc. must hold good before the parametric test can be used.

These tests usually assume certain properties of the parent population from which we draw samples. Assumptions like observations come from a normal population, sample size is large, assumptions about the population parameters like mean, variance etc., must hold good before the parametric test can be used.

Hypothesis testing determines the validity of the assumption with a view to choose between two conflicting hypotheses about the value of the population parameter.

It helps to decide on the basis of a sample data, whether hypotheses about the population is likely to be true or false.

Several tests of hypotheses (also known as tests of significance developed by statisticians) can be classified as:

Parametric tests or standard test of hypothesis.

Non-parametric tests or distribution free test of hypothesis.

A brief description about some important parametric tests is given here.

The important parametric tests are:

1. Z-test;
2. T-test; and
3. F-test.

All these tests are based on the assumption of normality i.e. the source of data is considered to be normally distributed.

Z-test: It is based on the normal probability distribution and is used for judging the significance of several statistical measures, particularly the mean. This is a most frequently used test in research studies.

T-test: It is based on t-distribution and is considered an appropriate test for judging the significance of a sample mean or for judging the significance of difference between the means of two samples; in case of small samples when population variance is not known.

X2-test (Chi-square): It is based on chi-square distribution and as a parametric test, can be used for comparing a sample variance to a theoretical population variance.

F-test: It is based on F-distribution and is used to compare the variance of the two independent samples. This is also used in the context of analysis of variance for judging the significance of more than two sample means at the same time. It is also used for judging the significance of multiple correlation coefficients.

Detailed discussions on the several parametric tests are given below with relevant illustrations.

The 'F' test has been named in honor of the great statistician R. A. Fisher. The object of the 'F-test' is to find out whether the two independent estimate of population variance differ significantly, or whether the two samples may be regarded as drawn from the normal population having the same variance.

F is defined as:

$$F = \frac{S_1^2}{S_2^2} \text{ ; Where } S_1^2 = \frac{(X - X_1)^2}{n_1 - 1}$$

$$S_2^2 = \frac{\Sigma(X_2 - X_2)^2}{n_2 - 1}$$

$S_1^2 > S_2^2$ *or*

$$F = \frac{\text{Larger estimate of variance}}{\text{Smaller estimate of variance}}$$

V_1 = degree of freedom for sample having larger variance.

V_2 = degree of freedom for sample having smaller.

Since F test is based on the ratio of two variances, it is also known as variance ratio test.

Assumptions: 'F' test is based on the following assumptions:

1. Normally, i.e., the values in each group are normally distributed.
2. Homogeneity, i.e., the variance within each group should be equal for all groups (021 = 022 = ……..= 0c2). This assumption is needed in order to combine or pool the variances within the groups into a single source of variation.
3. Independence of error: It states that the error should be independent for each value.

For the sake of clarity of technique of analysis of variance, we discuss the following points:

One-way classification, and

Two-way classification.

One-Way Classification

H_o: $\mu_1 = \mu_2 = \mu_3 \ldots\ldots = \mu_k$

H_o: $\mu_1 \neq \mu_2 \neq \mu_3 \ldots\ldots \neq \mu_k$

All the means are not equal.

The steps in carrying out the analysis are:

Calculate the variance between the samples;

Calculate the mean of each sample i.e., X_1, X_2 etc.; and

Calculate the gravel average X, pronounced X double bar.

"Its value is obtained as follows:

$$= \frac{X_1 + X_2 + X_3 + \ldots\ldots}{N_1 + N_2 + N_3 + \ldots\ldots}$$

Take the difference between the means of the various samples of the ground average.

Divide the total obtained by the degrees of freedom. The degree of freedom will be one less than the number of samples.

Calculate variance within the samples:

Calculate the mean value of each sample i.e., X1, X2, X3 etc.;

Take the deviations of the various items in a sample from the mean values of the respective sample;

Divide this total obtained in step above by the degrees of freedom. The degree of freedom is obtained by deviation from the total number of items the number of samples i.e. V = N-K, where k refers to the number of samples and N refers to the total number of all observations.

Calculate ratio F as:

$$F = \frac{\text{Between-Column variance}}{\text{Within-Column Variance}}$$

Compare the calculated value of F with the table value of F for the degrees of freedom at a certain critical level. If the calculated value of F is greater than the table value, it is concluded that the difference in sample means significant.

Two-way Classification Model: In a two-way classification, the data is classified according to two different criteria or factors. Under two-way classification, the F values are calculated as follows.

Interpretation: The calculated value of 'F' is compared with the table value of V1 and V2 at 5 percent or 1 percent level of significance. If calculated value of F is greater than them the table value then F ratio is considered significant and the null hypothesis is rejected. On the other hand, if the calculated value of F is less than the table value the null hypothesis is accepted.

$$F(V_1, V_2) = \frac{MSC}{MSE}$$

Where $V_1 = (C-1)$ and $V_2 = (C-1)(r-1)$

$$F(V_1, V_2) = \frac{MSR}{MSE}$$

Where $V_1 = (r-1)$ and $V_2 = (C-1)(r-1)$

It should be carefully noted that V_1 may be not be same in both cases-in one cases.

V_1 - (C-1) and another case $V_1 = (r-1)$

Interpretation

The calculated value of 'F' is compared with the table value for V_1 and V_2 at 5 percent or 1 percent level of significance. If calculated value of F is greater than the table value, then F ratio is considered significant and the null hypothesis is rejected. On the other hand, if the calculated value of F is less than the table value, the null hypothesis is accepted.

Illustration

Two random samples drawn from two normal populations are:

Sample 1: 20 16 26 27 23 22 18 24 25 19.

Sample 2: 27 33 42 35 32 34 38 28 41 43 30 37.

Test using variance ratio at 5 percent and 1 percent level of significance whether the two populations have the same variances.

Solution

We take the null hypothesis that the two populations from where the samples have been drawn have the same variances i.e., H_o: $\sigma^2_{p1} = \sigma^2_{p1}$. From the sample data we work out $\sigma^2_{s1} = \sigma^2_{s2}$ as under;

Xli	Sample $(Xli - X_1)$	$(X_{1i} - X_1)^2$	X_{2i}	Sample $(X_{2i} - X_2)$	$(X_{2i} - X_2)$
20	-2	4	27	-8	64
16	-6	36	33	-2	4
26	4	16	42	7	49
27	5	25	35	0	0
23	1	1	32	-3	9
22	0	0	34	-1	1
18	-4	16	38	3	9
24	2	4	28	-7	49
25	3	9	41	6	36
19	-3	9	43	8	64
			30	-5	25
			37	2	4

$\sigma X_{1i} = 220$	$\sigma(X_{1i} - X_1)^2 = 120$	$\sigma X_{2i} = 420$	$\sigma(X_{2i} - X_2)^2 = 314$
$n_1 = 10$		$n_2 = 12$	

$$X = \frac{\Sigma X_{1i}}{n_i} = \frac{220}{10} = 22$$

$$X_2 = \frac{\Sigma X_{2i}}{n_2} = \frac{420}{12} = 35$$

$$\therefore \sigma^2_{s1} = \frac{\Sigma(X_{1i} = X_1)^2}{n_1 - 1} = \frac{120}{10-1} = 13.33$$

and

$$\sigma^2_{s1} = \frac{\Sigma(X_{2i} = X_2)^2}{n_2 - 1} = \frac{314}{12-1} = 28.55$$

Hence, $\frac{\sigma^2_{s2}}{\sigma^2_{s1}} \quad (\because \sigma^2_{s2} > \sigma^2_{s})$

$= \frac{28.55}{13.33} = 2.14$

Degrees of freedom in sample 1 = $(n_1 - 1) = 10 - 1 = 9$

Degrees of freedom in sample 2 = $(n_2 - 1) = 12 - 1 = 11$

As the variance of sample 2 is greater variance, hence,

$$V_1 = 11 : \frac{1}{2} = 9$$

The table value of F at 5 percent level of significance for $v_1 = 11$ $v_2 = 9$ is 3.11 and the table value of F at 1 percent level of significance for $v_1 = 11$ and $v_2 = 9$ is 5.20.

Since the calculated value of F=2. 14 which is less than 3.11 and also less than 5.20, the F ratio is insignificant at 5 percent as well as at 1 percent level of significance and as such we accept the null hypothesis and conclude that sample have been drawn from two populations having the same variances.

'Z'-test

Professor Fisher has given a method of testing the significance of the correlation coefficient in small samples. Z-test is based on the normal probability distribution and is used for judging the significance of several statistical measures, particularly the mean. Z is worked out and compared with its probable value at a specified level of significance for judging the significance of the measure concerned. This is the most frequently used test in research studies.

This test is used even in binomial distribution. Z test is generally used for comparing the mean of a sample to some hypothesized mean for the population in case of large sample or when population variance is known, Z-test is also used for judging the significance of difference between means of two independent samples in case of large samples or population variance is known.

Formula

If the absolute value of this statistics exceeds 1.96, the difference is significant at 5 percent level.

$$\frac{Z - \Sigma}{1 / \sqrt{n - 3}}$$

$$Z = ½ \log_e \frac{1+r}{1-r} \text{ or } 1.1513 \log_{10} \frac{1+r}{1-r}$$

$$\Sigma = ½ \log_e \frac{1+p}{1-p} \text{ or } 1.1513 \log_{10} \frac{1+p}{1-p}$$

P: refers to population correlation coefficient.

$$S.E_2 = 1 / \sqrt{n-3}$$

To test the significance of the difference between two independent correlation coefficients, we have to compare the difference of the two corresponding values of Z with the standard error of that difference remembering that the standard error of the difference of two statistical qualities is the square root of the sum of their variances.

$$Z = \frac{Z_1 - Z_2}{\sqrt{1/(n_1 - 3) + (1/n_2 - 3)}}$$

Where $Z_1 = \frac{1}{2} \log (1 + r_1 / 1 - r1)$ or $1.153 \log_{10} (1+r_1 / 1 - r_1)$

And $Z_2 = \frac{1}{2} \log (1 + r_2 / 1 - r2)$ or $1.153 \log_{10} (1+r_2 / 1 - r_2)$

$$S.E, (Z_1\text{-}Z_2) = \frac{Z_1 - Z_2}{\sqrt{1/(n_1 - 3) + 1/(n_2 - 3)}}$$

Interpretation

If the absolute value of this statistic is greater than 1.96, the difference will be significant at 5 percent level. When the calculated value of Z is less than the table value then the hypothesis is accepted and vice-versa.

Illustration 1

The mean produce of wheat of a sample of 100 fields is 200 lbs each with a standard deviation of 10 lbs Another sample of 150 fields gives the mean of 220 lbs with a standard deviation of 12 lbs. Can the two samples be considered to have been taken from the same population whose standard division is 11 lbs. Use 5 percent level of significance.

Solution

Taking the null hypothesis that the means of two populations do not differ, we can write:

$H_o: \mu 1 = \mu_2$

$H_o: \mu 1 \# \mu_2$

And the given information as $n_1 = 100$; $n_2 = 150$

$\overline{X}_1 = 200$ lbs.; $\overline{X}_2 = 220$ lbs.

$\sigma_{s1} = 10$ lbs.; $\sigma_{s2} = 12$ lbs.;

And $\sigma_p = 11$ lbs.

Assuming the population to be normal, we can work out the test statistic z as under:

$$z = \frac{X_1 - X_2}{\sqrt{\sigma_p^2 (1/n_1 + 1/n_2)}} = \frac{200 - 220}{\sqrt{(11)^2 \ (1/100 + 1/150)}}$$

As H_a is two-sided, we shall apply a two-tiled test for determining the rejection regions at 5 percent level of significance which come to as under, using normal curve area table:

$$R: |z| > 1.96$$

The observed value of z is –14.08 which falls in the rejection region and thus we reject H_o and conclude that the two samples cannot be considered to have been taken at 5 percent level of significance from the same population whose standard deviation is 11 lbs. This means that the difference between means of two samples is statistically and not due to sampling fluctuation.

Illustration 2

A simple random sampling survey in respect survey in respect of monthly earning of semi-skilled workers in two cities gives the following statistical information.

City	Mean monthly earning (₹)	Standard deviation of sample data of monthly earnings (₹)	Size of sample
A	695	40	200
B	710	60	175

Test the hypothesis at 5 percent level.

Solution

Taking the null hypothesis that there is no difference in earnings of workers in the two cities, we can write:

H_o: μ1 = μ2

H_o: μ1 # μ2

and the given information as

Sample 1 (City A) Sample 2 (City B)

X_1 = ₹ 695 X_2 = ₹ 710

σ_{s1} = ₹ 40 σ_{s2} = ₹ 60

$n_1 = 200$ $n_2 = 175$

As the sample size is large, we shall use Z-test for difference in means assuming the population to be normal and shall work out the test statistic Z as under:

$$Z = \frac{X_1 - X_2}{\sqrt{(\sigma_{s_1}^2 / n_1) + (\sigma_{s_2}^2 / n_2)}}$$

(since the population variances are not known, we have used the sample variance, considering the sample variances as the estimates of population variances.)

Hence,

$$Z = \frac{695 - 710}{\sqrt{(40)^2 + 200 + (60)^2 / 175}} = - \frac{15}{\sqrt{8 + 20.7}} = - 2.809$$

As H_a is two-sided, we shall apply a two-tailed test for determining the rejection region at 5 percent level of significance which comes to as under, using the normal curve area table:

$$R: |Z| > 1.96$$

The observed value of z is –2.809 which falls in the rejection region and thus, we reject H_0 at percent level and conclude that earnings of workers in the cities differ significantly.

'T' test

Theoretical work on t-distribution was done by W.S. Gosset. 't' test is based on 't' distribution and is considered an appropriate test for judging the significance of a sample mean or for judging the significance of difference between the means of two samples in case of small sample(s), when population variance is not known.

The t-distribution is used when sample size is 30 or less and the population standard deviation is unknown.

Formula:

$$t = \frac{X - \mu}{S} x \sqrt{n}$$

Where, $S = \frac{\Sigma(X - X)^2}{n-1}$

The t-distribution has been derived mathematically under the assumption of a normally distributed population.

F (t) = C (1 + t^2 / v) - (v + 1) / 2

Where $t = \frac{X - \mu}{S} \sqrt{n}$

C = a constant required to make the area under the curve equal to unit.

V = n – 1, the no. of degrees of freedom.

Properties of t-Distribution

1. The variable t-distribution ranges from minus infinity to plus infinity.
2. The constant C is actually a function of V, so that for a particular value of v, the distribution of f (t) is completely specified. Thus, f (t) is a family of functions, one for each value of V.
3. Like the standard normal distribution, the t-distribution is symmetrical and has a mean zero.
4. t-distribution approaches the variance of the standard normal distribution as the sample size increases.

Application of t-Distribution

To test significance of the mean of a random sample, the following illustration is useful.

$$t = \frac{(X - \mu)\sqrt{n}}{S}$$

$$S = \frac{\Sigma(X - X)^2}{n-1} \text{ or } S = \frac{\Sigma d^2 - n(d)^2}{n-1}$$

$$= \frac{1}{(n-1)} [\Sigma d^2 - (\Sigma d)^2 / n]$$

Interpretation

If |t| > t 0.05, difference between X and μ is significant at 5 percent or vice versa.

If |t| > to 0.01, difference between X and μ in significant at 1 percent or vice versa.

Testing difference between means of two samples (independent samples)

$$t = \frac{X_1 - X_2}{S} x \frac{n_1 n_2}{n_1 + n_2}$$

$$S = \frac{\Sigma(X_1 - X_1)^2 + \Sigma(X_2 - X_2)^2}{n_1 + n_2 - 2}$$

Testing difference between means of two samples (Dependent samples) is illustrated below.

$$t = \frac{d - 0}{S} \times \sqrt{n} \quad \text{or} \quad \frac{d\sqrt{n}}{S}$$

$$S = \frac{\Sigma(d - d)^2}{n - 1} \quad \text{or} \quad \frac{\Sigma d^2 - n(d)^2}{n - 1}$$

Testing the significance of an observed correlation coefficient is presented below.

$$t = \frac{r}{\sqrt{1 - r^2}} \; x \; \sqrt{n} - 2$$

Uses

Similar to normal curve tables, there exists, the t-distribution tables. However, the properties of the normal curve are constant for all normal curves where as the t-distribution varies according to the number of items in the sample. These tables, therefore, contain values for all possible sample size up to 30 and are given with references to the degrees of freedom.

Degree of Freedom

The t-value is one given for various significance level over a range of D of F i.e. (n-1).

Also the columns of figures in main body of the table come under the handicap t_{10}, t_{03}, $t^{.03}$, $t^{.02}$, to $t^{.01}$ and $t.^{001}$.

t_v (0.05) for single tailed test,

$= t_v$ (0.10) for two tailed test.

and,

t_v (0.01) for single tailed test,

$= t_v$ (0.02) for two tailed test.

Illustration 1

Memory capacity of 9 students was tested before and after training. State at 5 percent level of significance whether the training was effective from the following score.

Student	1	2	3	4	5	6	7	8	9
Before/	10	15	9	3	7	12	16	17	4
After	12	17	8	5	6	11	18	20	3

Use paired t-test as well as A-test for your answer.

Solution

Take the score before training as X and the score after training as Y and then taking the null hypothesis that the mean of difference is zero, we can write:

H_o: μ2 which is equivalent to test H_o; $\overline{D} = 0$

H_o: μ1 < μ2 (as we want to conclude that training has been effective).

As we are having matched pairs, we use paired t-test and work out the test statistic t as under:

$$t = \frac{\overline{D} - 0}{\sigma_{diff\,!}\sqrt{n}}$$

To find the value of t, we shall first have to work out the mean and standard deviation of difference as shown below.

Student	Score after Training X_i	Score for Training Y_i	Difference ($D_i = X_i - Y_i$)D	Difference Squared D_i^2
1	10	12	-2	4
2	15	17	-2	4

3	9	8	1	1
4	3	5	-2	4
5	7	6	1	1
6	12	11	1	1
7	16	18	-2	4
8	17	20	-3	9
9	4	3	1	1
N = 9			$\Sigma D_i = -7$	$\Sigma D_i^2 = 29$

Mean of Differences of $D = \frac{\Sigma D_i}{n} = -7/9 = -0.778$
and standard deviation of differences or

$$\sigma_{diff!} = \sqrt{\frac{\Sigma D_i^2 - (D)^2 . n}{n-1}}$$

$$= \sqrt{\frac{29 - (-.778)^2 \times 9}{9-1}}$$

$$= \sqrt{2.944} = 1.715$$

$$\text{Hence, } t = \frac{-0.778 - 0}{1.715/\sqrt{9}} = \frac{-.778}{0.572} = -1.361$$

Degrees of freedom = n - 1 = 9 - 1 = 8.

As H_o is one-sided, we shall apply a one-tailed test (in the left tail because H_o is of less than type) for deterring the rejection region at 5 percent level which comes to as under, using the table of t-distribution for 8 degrees of freedom.

$$R: t < -1.860$$

The observed value of t is –1.361, which is in the acceptance region, and thus, we accept H_o and conclude that the difference in score before and after training is insignificant i.e., it is only due to sampling fluctuation. Hence, we can infer that the training was not effective.

Illustration 2

The sales data of an item in six shops before and after a special promotional campaign are.

Shop	A	B	C	D	E	F
Before the promotional campaign	53	28	31	48	50	42
After the campaign	58	29	30	55	56	45

Can the campaign be judged to be a success? Test at 5 percent level of significance. Use paired t-test as well as A-test.

Solution

Let the sales before campaign be represented as X and the sales after campaign as Y and then taking the null hypothesis that campaign does not bring any improvement in sales, we can write:

H_o: $\mu_1 = \mu_2$ which is equivalent to test H_o: D = 0

H_o: $\mu_1 = \mu_2$ (as we want to conclude that campaign has been a success).

Because of the matched pairs, we use paired t-test and work out the test statistic 't' as under:

$$t = \frac{\overline{D} - 0}{\sigma\ diff\ !\ \sqrt{n}}$$

To find the value of 't', we first work out the mean and standard deviation of difference as under.

Shops	Sales before Campaign X_1	Sales after Campaign Y_1	Difference ($D_i = X_i - Y_i$)	Difference Squared $D2_i$
A	53	58	-5	25
B	28	29	-1	1
C	31	30	1	1
D	48	55	-7	49
E	50	56	-6	36
F	42	45	-3	9
N = 6			$\Sigma D_i =$ - 21	$\Sigma D^2_i =$ -121

Degrees of freedom = (n-1) = 6-1 = 5

$$D = \frac{\Sigma D_i}{n} = -\frac{21}{6} = -3.5$$

$$\sigma\, diff = \frac{\Sigma D_i^2 - (D)^2 . n}{n-1} = \sqrt{\frac{121 - (-3.5)^2 \times 6}{6-1}} = 3.08$$

Hence, $$t = \frac{-3.5 - 0}{3.08/\sqrt{6}} = \frac{-3.5}{1.257} = -1.361$$

As H_o is one-sided, we shall apply a one-tailed test (in the left tail because H_o is of less than type) for determining the rejection region at 5 percent level of significance which comes to as under, using table of t-distribution for 5 degrees of freedom:

R: t< -2.015

The observed value of t is -2.784 which falls in the rejection region and thus, we reject H_o at 5 percent level and conclude that sales promotional campaign has been a success.

Illustration 3

Sample of sales in similar shops in two towns are taken for a new product with the following results.

Town	Mean sales	Variance	Size of sample
A	57	5.3	5
B	61	4.8	7

Is there any evidence of difference in sales in the two towns? Use 5 percent level of significance for testing this difference between the means of two samples.

Solution

Taking the null hypothesis that the means of two populations do not differ we can write:

H_o: $\mu 1 = \mu 2$

H_o: μ1 # μ2
and the given information as follows:

Sample from town A as sample one	$X_1 = 57$	$\sigma^2_{s1} = 5.3$	$n_1 = 5$
Sample from town B as sample two	$X_2 = 61$	$\sigma^2_{s2} = 4.8$	$n_1 = 7$

Since in the given question variances of the population is not known and the size of sample is small, we shall use t-test for difference in means, assuming the population to be normal and can work out the test statistic 't' as under:

$$t = \frac{X_1 - X_2}{\sqrt{\frac{(n_1 - 1)\sigma^2_{s1}(n_2 - 1)\sigma^2 s_2}{n_1 + n_2 - 2}} \times \sqrt{(1/n_1 + 1/n_2)}}$$

With d. f. = (n_1+n_2-2)

Degrees of freedom = $(n_1 + n_2 - 2) = 5+7-2 = 10$.

As H_a is two-sided, we shall apply a two-tailed test for determining the rejection region at 5 percent level, which comes to as under, using table of t-distribution for 10 degrees of freedom:

$$R : |t| > 2.228$$

The observed value of t is -3.053 which falls in the rejection region and thus, we reject H_o and conclude that the difference in sales in the two towns is significant at 5 percent level.

Chi-Square Test

The χ^2 test is one of the simplest and most widely used parametric as well as non-parametric tests in statistical work. The symbol χ^2 is from the Greek letter Chi. The Chi-square test was first used by Karl Pearson.

The Chi-square value is often used to judge the significance of population variance i.e., we can use the test to judge if a random sample has been drawn from a normal population with mean (μ) and with a specified variance (σ_p^2).

Formula

$$\chi^2 = \Sigma \frac{(O - E)^2}{E}$$

Steps

Calculate the expected frequencies. In general, the expected frequency for any cell can be calculated from the following equation.

$$E = \frac{RT \times CT}{N}$$

E = expected frequency,
RT = row total,
CT = column total,
N = total no. of observations.

Take the difference between observed and expected frequencies and obtain the squares of these differences $(O-E)^2$.

Divide the values of $(O-E)^2$ obtained in step (2) by the respective expected frequency and obtain the total $\Sigma [(O - E)^2/E]$.

Interpretation

After ascertaining X^2 value, the X^2 table comprises columns headed with symbols X 0.05 for 5 percent level of significance and X 0.01 for 1 percent level of significance; while rows refer to the degrees of freedom. If the calculated value falls in acceptance region, H_o is accepted or vice-versa.

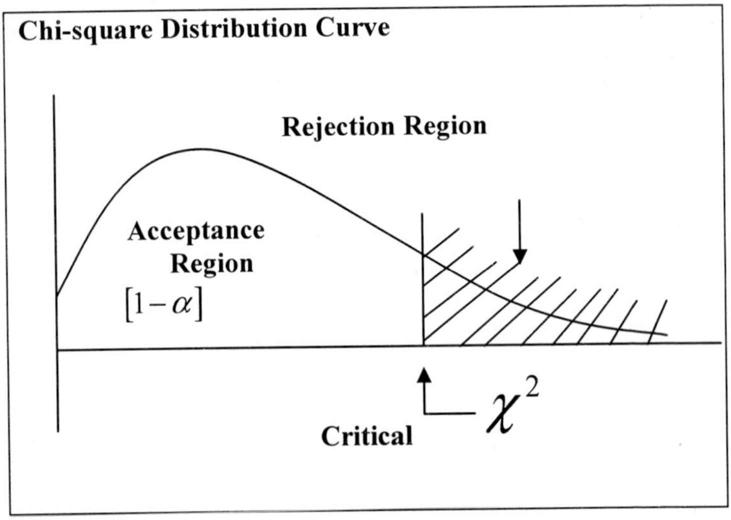

Chi-square Distribution

The square of a standard normal variate is called a chi-square variate with 1 degree of freedom, i.e. if X variable is normally distributed with mean u and standard deviation S.

$$\left(\frac{X - \mu}{\sigma}\right)^2 \quad \text{is a } \chi^2 \text{ variate with d. f.}$$

If $X_1, X_2, \ldots\ldots\ldots\ldots X_n$ are n independent random variables following normal distribution with mean μ and standard deviation σ respectively, then the variate would be:

$$X^2 = \left(\frac{X_1 - \mu}{\sigma}\right)^2 + \left(\frac{X_1 - \mu}{\sigma}\right)^2 + \ldots\ldots\ldots\ldots\ldots\ldots + \left(\frac{X_n - \mu}{\sigma}\right)^2$$

which is the sum of squares of n independent standard normal variates.

The probability functions of chi-square distribution with v degrees of freedoms is as follows.

$$p(\chi^2) = Y_0 (\chi^2)^{½ (V-2)} e^{-½ \chi^2}$$

Where Y_0 is a constant depending on V and V = n – 1, is the d. f.

Properties of Chi-square Distribution

1. Mean of χ^2 distribution = Degrees of freedom = V.
2. Standard deviation of χ^2 distribution = $\sqrt{2v}$.
3. Median of χ^2 distribution divides the area of the curve into two equal parts each part being 0.5.
4. Mode of χ^2 distribution is equal to degrees of freedom less 2, i.e. (V–2).
5. Chi-square values are always positively skewed.
6. Chi-square value increases with the increase in the degrees of freedom. There is a new chi-square distribution with every increase in the number of degree of freedom.
7. The lowest value of chi-square is zero and the highest value is infinite, i.e. $0 < \chi^2 < \alpha$.
8. When two chi-squares χ_1^2 and χ_2^2 are independent, following χ^2 –distribution with n_1 and n_2 degrees freedom, their sum $\chi_1^2 + \chi_2^2$ will follow χ^2 – distribution with n_1+n_2 degrees freedom.
9. When V > 30, $\sqrt{2X^2} - \sqrt{2V-1}$ approximately follows the standard normal distribution.

Conditions

1. The frequencies used in chi-square test must be absolute and not in relative terms.
2. The total number of observations collected for this test must be large.
3. Each of the observations which make up the sample for this test must be independent of each other.

4. As χ^2 -test is based wholly on sample data, no assumption is made concerning the population distribution.
5. χ^2 -test is wholly dependent on degrees of freedom.
6. The expected frequency of any item or cell must not be less than 5, the frequencies of adjacent items or cells should be pooled together in order to make it 5 or more than 5.
7. The data should be expressed in original units for convenience of comparison and the given distribution should not be replaced by relative frequencies or proportions.
8. This test is used only for drawing inferences through test of the hypothesis so that it cannot be used for estimation of parameter value.

Uses

The chi-square test is used broadly for purposes listed below:

Test of goodness of fit for one-way classification or for one variable only.

Test of independence or interaction for more than one row or column in the form of a contingency table concerning several attributes.

Test of population variance (σ^2) through confidence intervals suggested by χ^2 -test.

Test of homogeneity.

Few illustrations relating to testing of hypothesis by applying chi-square method are given below.

Problem 1

A personnel manager is interested in trying to determine whether absenteeism is greater on one day of the week than on others. His records for the past years show the sample.

Days of a week:	Mon	Tue	Wed	Thurs	Fri
No. of absentees:	66	57	54	48	75

Solution

Let the H_0 be: absence is uniformly distributed over the week.

Apply χ^2 test.

On the basis of this hypothesis we should expect 60 days (66 + 57 + 54 + 48 + 75 = 300/5) of absence on each day of a week.

O	E	O – E	$(O-E)^2$	$(O-E)^2/E$
66	60	+6	36	0.60
57	60	-3	9	0.15
54	60	-6	36	0.60
48	60	-12	144	2.40
75	60	15	225	3.75
300				7.50

$$\chi^2 = \Sigma(O - E)^2 / E = 7.50$$

$V = n - 1 \quad = 5-1 = 4$

$$\chi^2_{0.05} = 9.49$$

The calculated value of χ^2 is less than the table value. Hypothesis H_0 is accepted.

Conclusion

Hence, we may conclude that the H_0 i.e. the absenteeism is spread uniformly and distributed over the week.

Given below is a contingency table for production in three shifts and the number of defective good that turn out. Find the value of 'C'. Is it possible that the number defective goods depend on the shifts run by them?

Number of shifts

Shift	I Week	II Week	III Weak	Total
I	15	5	20	40
II	20	10	20	50
III	25	15	20	60
	60	30	60	150

H_0: Defective goods does not depend upon the shift run by the factory.

O	E	$(O-E)^2$	$(O-E)^2/E$
15	16	1	0.063
20	20	0	0
25	24	1	0.042
5	8	9	1.125
10	10	0	0
15	12	9	0.750
20	16	16	1.000
20	20	0	0
20	24	16	0.667
			$\Sigma(O-E)^2/E =$ 3.647

Since, the calculate value of χ^2 is less than the table value, the hypothesis is accepted.

Hence, the number of defectives goods does not depend on shifts run by the factory.

Problem 2

The contingency table below summarizes the results obtained in a study conducted by a research organization, with respect to the performance of four competing brands of toothpaste among the users.

	Brand A	Brand B	Brand C	Brand D	Total
No. cavities	9	13	17	11	50
One of five cavities	63	70	85	82	300

More than five cavities	28	37	48	37	150
Total	100	120	150	130	500

Test the hypothesis that incidence of cavities is independent of the brand of the toothpaste used. (The table value of χ^2 for d.f. are 12.59 and 16.81 at 5 percent and 1 percent levels of significance respectively).

Solution

Our hypothesis is that incidence of cavities is independent of the brand of the toothpaste used.

Applying χ^2 test:

$E_{11} = 50/500 \times 100 = 10$; $E_{21} = 300/500 \times 100 = 60$

$E_{12} = 50/500 \times 120 = 12$; $E_{22} = 300/500 \times 120 = 72$

$E_{13} = 50/500 \times 150 = 15$; $E_{23} = 300/500 \times 150 = 90$

The table expected frequencies shall be:

10	12	15	13	50
60	72	90	78	300
30	36	45	39	150
100	120	150	130	500

O	E	$(O-E)^2$	$(O-E)^2/E$
9	10	1	0.100
63	60	9	0.150
28	30	4	0.133
13	12	1	0.083
70	72	4	0.056
37	36	1	0.028
17	15	4	0.267
85	90	25	0.278
48	45	9	0.200
11	13	4	0.308
82	78	16	0.205
37	39	4	0.103
			□ $(O-E)^2/E =$ 1.911

$\acute{v} = (r-1)(c-1) = (3-1)(4-1) = 6$

For v=6; $\chi^2_{0.05} = 12.59$. The calculated value of χ^2 is less than the table value. Our hypothesis holds true. Hence, incidence of cavities is independent of the brand of the toothpaste used.

Problem 3

The following table gives the number of good and bad parts produced by each of three shifts in a factory.

Shift	Good	Bad	Total
Day	900	130	1030
Evening	700	170	870
Night	400	200	600
	2000	500	2500

Is there any association between the shift and the quality of parts produced?

(Given for v=2; $\chi^2_{0.05} = 5.991$).

Solution

Let us take the hypothesis that there is no association between the shift and the quality of parts produced.

Expected value corresponding to first row and first column, i.e.,

E_{11}= 1030/2500 × 2000 = 824

E_{21}= 870/2500 × 2000 = 696

The table value of expected frequencies shall be as follows:

824	206	1030
696	174	870
480	120	600
2000	500	2500

Applying χ^2 test:

O	E	$(O-E)^2$	$(O-E)^2/E$
900	824	5776	7.099

700 400 130 170 200	696 480 206 174 120	16 6400 5776 16 6400	0.023 13.333 28.039 0.092 53.333
			□ (O – E)2 /E = 101.829

$$\chi^2 = \Sigma\left[(O - E)^2 / E\right] = 101.829$$

v = (r – 1) (c -1) = (3 -1) (2-1) = 2

For v =2; χ^2 = 0.05 = 5.991

The calculated value of χ^2 is much higher than the table value. Hence, the hypothesis is rejected and we conclude that there is association between the shift and the quality of parts produced.

Problem 4

The following data relates to the sales during the time of trade depression of a certain article, normally in wider demand. Does the data suggest that the sales were significantly affected by depression?

District where sales are:

	Not hit by depression	Hit	Total
Satisfactory Not Satisfactory	140 40	60 60	200 100
Total	180	120	300

Solution

Let us take the hypothesis that the sales were not significantly affected by depression. Applying χ^2 –test.

Expectation of (AB) = 200/300×180 = 120.

The table of expected frequencies shall be as follows.

120	80	200
60	40	100
180	120	300

O	E	$(O-E)^2$	$(O-E)^2/E$
140	120	400	3.3333
40	60	400	6.667
60	80	400	5.000
60	40	400	10.000
			□ $(O-E)^2/E = 25$

V = (r – 1) (c – 1) = (2 -1) (2 -1) = 1

For v = 1; $\chi^2_{0.05} = 3.84$.

The calculated value of X^2 is less than the table value. The hypothesis is rejected. Hence, the sales were significantly affected by depression.

Non-Parametric Test

Most of the statistical tests require an important assumption to be met if they are to be correctly applied. This assumption is, that population of data from which a sample is drawn is normally distributed. These statistical tests allow considerable latitude and deviation from normality. But there are situations when the researcher cannot or does not want to make such assumptions. In such situations, we use statistical methods for testing hypothesis which are called "non-parametric" tests because such tests do not depend on any assumption about the parameters of the parent population.

Statisticians have devised alternate procedures which can be used to test hypothesis about data which are not normal or for which meaningful statistics cannot be calculated. Since these tests do not depend on the shape of the distribution, they are called distribution-free tests. These tests do not depend upon the population parameters such as the mean and the variance; they are also called non-parametric tests.

Advantages of Non-parametric test

They do not require any assumption to be made about population following normal or any other distribution.

Simple to understand and easy to apply when the sample sizes are small.

Most non-parametric tests do not require lengthy computations.

It is less time-consuming.

Non-parametric tests are applicable for all types of data.

It makes possible to work with very small samples.

Non-parametric methods make fewer and less stringent assumptions.

Disadvantages of Non-parametric test

They ignore a certain amount of information.

They are not considered as efficient as parametric test.

Types of Non-parametric test

Some of the commonly used non-parametric tests are:

1. Sign test;
2. Rank sum test;
3. One sample run test;
4. Kruskal-Wallis or H test; and
5. Spearman Rank Correlation.

A detailed discussion of these tests along with illustration is given below.

Sign test: The sign test is the simplest of non-parametric test. Its name comes from the fact that it is based on the direction of a part of observation and not on their numerical magnitude.

In any problem in which sign test is used we count.

Number of + signs

Number of – signs

Number of O's

We take H_o: P = 0.05 (Null hypothesis).

If the difference is due to chance effects, the probability of a+ sign for any particular pair is ½ as is the number of times the less frequent sign occurs, then S has the binomial distribution with P = ½. The critical value for a two-sided alternative at x = 0.05 can be conveniently found by the expression.

$$K = \frac{(n-1)}{2} - (0.98).\sqrt{}$$

H_0 is rejected as $S \leq K$ for the sign test.

Two types of sign test are:

The one sample.

The paired sample.

One Sample: In a one sample sign test, we test null hypothesis $\mu = \mu_0$ against an appropriate alternative on the basis of a random sample size n. We replace each sample value greater than μ_0 with a plus sign and each sample value less than μ_0 with a minus sign and discard sample value exactly equal to (pvt-O) random variable having binomial distribution with P = ½.

Paired Sample: This sign test has important application in problems involving paired data such as data relating to the collection of an accounts receivable before and after a new collection policy etc.

Since S > k the null hypothesis is accepted. There is no significant difference before and after the new collection policy in the accounts receivable. For large samples, generally considered n > 25 for the sign test, the normal approximation on the binomial may be used, correcting for continuity. Since P = 0.50, for this we have the mean equal to ½ n and the standard deviation equal to ½ √ n. The actual value of Z can be computed using the formula.

$$Z = \frac{X - nP_0}{\sqrt{nP_0(1-P_0)}}$$

Where, X is the number of plus sign. The value obtained can then be compiled to the critical value of Z which is appropriate for the direction of the test. As mentioned before, in the event of ties, all sign changes of O are dropped before evaluating the results.

Illustration

A market researcher was interested in testing the preference of consumers for a brand of detergent soap. Consumers were asked to rate the brand on cleanliness it provides, by giving them numbers from 1 to 4. The data of the consumers' response and the corresponding sings is given below.

Consumer Number	Score Brand X	Score Band Y	Sing (X–Y)
1.	4	2	+
2.	2	3	-
3.	1	2	-
4.	4	3	+
5.	3	2	+
6.	3	4	-
7.	4	2	+
8.	2	1	+
9.	1	1	0
10.	4	3	+
11.	1	2	-
12.	1	2	-
13.	2	2	0
14.	2	3	-
15.	4	3	+
16.	3	2	+
17.	3	3	0
18.	4	2	+
19.	4	1	+
20.	4	23	+
21.	4	4	0
22.	3	2	+
23.	3	3	0
24.	3	1	+
25.	4	1	+

26.	4	3	+
27.	4	1	+
28.	1	2	-
29.	3	2	+
30.	3	4	-
31.	2	3	-
32.	2	1	+
33.	2	3	-
34.	3	4	-
35	3	2	+

Will you conclude that the effectiveness of the two brands is the same?

Solution

The total numbers of respondents are 35. We find that the numbers of positive signs are 19, numbers of negative signs are 11 and the number of zeroes are 5. We exclude the ties; this gives us a total of 30 usable responses. The hypothesis to be tested H_o: P=0.5.

H_o: P = 0.5 i.e., there is no difference between the two brands.

H_a: P # 0.5 i.e., there is a difference between the two brands.

The sample information gives us the sample proportion

$$P = \frac{19}{30} = 0.633$$

The std. error of proportion is $\sqrt{0.5 \times 0.5/30 = 0.01}$

We want to know whether the true proportion is larger or smaller than the hypothesized proportion, this is a two- tailed test. To standardize the sample proportion p, by subtracting $_pH_o$, the hypothesized proportion, and dividing by σp the standard error proportion and therefore, the test statistic is given by:

$$Z = \frac{p - p}{\sqrt{pq/n}} = \frac{0.633 - 0.5}{\sqrt{(0.5 \times 0.5)/30}} = \frac{0.133}{\sqrt{0.091}} = 1.46$$

At 5 percent level of significance, the acceptance region is $-1.960 \leq Z \leq 1.960$. As the calculated value falls in the acceptance region, the hypothesis H_o is accepted, i.e., the consumers perceive no difference between the two brands of the detergent soaps.

We want to know whether the true proportion is larger or smaller than the hypothesized proportion in this two-tailed test.

Rank Sum Test: Rank sum test is a whole family of tests. Here, we shall discuss only two member of the family, the Mann-whitened U test and the Kruskal-Wallis test. This U test can test H_0: $\mu_1 = \mu_2$ without assuming whether the population samples have rough distribution. It is applicable only when two populations are involved. The K test can be applied when more than two populations are involved.

This test helps us to determine whether two samples have come from identical populations. If it is true that the samples have come from the same populations, it is reasonable to assume that the means of the ranks assigned to the value of the two samples are more or less the same. The alternative hypothesis is that the means of the population are not equal and if this is the case most of the smaller rank will go to those of the other sample.

If the sample sizes are n_1 and n_2, the sum of R_1 and R_2 is simply the sum of first $n_1 + n_2$ positive integers, which is known to be.

$$\frac{(n_1 + n_2)(n_1 + n_2 + n_1)}{2}$$

This formula enables us to find R_2 if we know R_1 and vice-versa.

When the use of the rank sums was first proposed as a non-parametric alternative to the two samples, t-test, the decision was based on R_1 or R_2, but now the decision is usually based on either of the calculated statistics.

$$U_1 = n_1 n_2 + \frac{n_1(n_1 + 1)}{2} - R_1$$

$$U_2 = n_1 n_2 + \frac{n_2(n_2+1)}{2} - R_2$$

Where, n_1 and n_2 are the size of the samples and R_1 and R_2 are the rank sums of the corresponding samples. For small samples, if both n1 and n2 are less, than 10 special tables must be used and if U is smaller than the critical value, H_o can be related to the standard normal curve by the statistic.

$$Z = \frac{U - n_1 n_2 / 2}{\sqrt{n_1 n_2 (n_1 + n_2)/12}}$$

Illustration

A manufacturer wants to test the hypothesis that the mean life time of two machines of different brands is equal. The life time is measured by the number of operating hours between the overhauls. The manufacturer keeps overhaul statistics on all his machines. A random sample of 15 machines gives the following details.

Brand X
1050,1150,850,800,1000,1350,1100,1450,900,1200,1250, 1550,825,650.
Brand Y
1700,970,880,1410,700,775,940,1650,950,1190,600,1600, 975,450,1290.

Using the Mann-Whitney test, will you conclude that the lifetimes of two brands are equal?

Solution

We pool together the data of brand Y and arrange it in ascending order. The array of pooled data from the lowest value of the highest in ascending order is:

450	800	940	1050	1200	1410
600	825	950	1100	1250	1450
650	850	970	1150	1290	1550
700	880	975	1170	1300	1600
775	900	1000	1190	1350	1650

We assign the ranks and also label each figure by its brand. The result is given in the following table.

Ranked Data

Rank	Op. hours	Brand	Rank	Op. hours	Brand.
1.	450	Y	11.	940	Y
2.	600	Y	12.	950	Y
3.	650	X	13.	970	Y
4.	700	Y	14.	975	Y
5.	775	Y	15.	1000	X
6.	800	X	16.	1050	X
7.	825	X	17.	1100	X
8.	850	X	18.	1150	X
9.	880	T	19.	1170	Y
10.	900	X	20.	1190	Y

Contd...

Rank	Op. hours	Brand.
21.	1200	X
22.	1250	X
23.	1290	Y
24.	1300	X
25.	1350	X
26.	1410	Y
27.	1450	X
28.	1550	X
29.	1600	Y
30.	1650	Y

The rank list for each of the brands is given below, as extracted from the table.

Ranks for Brand X: 3, 6, 7, 8, 10, 15, 16, 17, 18, 21, 22, 24, 25, 27, 28.
Ranks for Brand Y: 1, 2, 4, 5, 9, 11, 12, 13, 14, 19, 20, 23, 26, 29, 30.
Total of Rank:
For X = 247
For Y = 218

Thus, we have the following sample information:

$n_1 = 15, n_2 = 15, R_1 = 247, R_2 = 218$

The U statistic is given by:

$$U = n_1 n_2 + \frac{n_1(n_1+1)}{2} - R_1$$

$$= 15 \times 15 + \frac{15 \times 16}{2} - 247$$

$$= 225 + 122 - 247 = 98$$

The mean and standard deviation of the U statistic is calculated as below:

$$\text{Mean} = \frac{n_1 n_2}{2} = \frac{15 \times 15}{2} = 112.5$$

$$\text{Standard deviation} = \sqrt{\frac{n_1 n_2 (n_1 + n_2 + 1)}{12}}$$

$$= \sqrt{\frac{15 \times 15(15+15+1)}{12}}$$

$$= \sqrt{581.25} = 24.1$$

As the values of n_1 and n_2 are greater than 10, the U statistic can be approximated by the normal distribution with mean 112.5 and standard deviation 24.1. We calculate the value of the unit normal variate using these values and for U = 98, we have,

$$Z = \frac{98 - 112.5}{24.1} = \frac{-14.5}{24.1} = -0.60$$

For α = 0.05, and two-tail test, the acceptance region is–1.960 $\leq Z \leq$ 1.960. As the calculated value falls in the acceptance region, H_o is accepted, i.e., two brands of machines have the same mean life times.

One Sample Run Test: A number of methods have been developed for judging the randomness of a sample on the basis of the order in which the observations are taken. It is possible to determine whether the samples that look suspiciously non-random may be attributed to chance. The technique discussed below is based on the theory of runs. A run is a succession of identical letter which is followed or preceded by different letter or no letters at all. To illustrate, consider the following arrangements of letters.

AAA BBBB CCCC DDDDDD KK NNN

The number of runs or r is a statistic with its own special sampling distribution and its own test. To derive the mean of the sampling distribution of r statistic the following formula is used.

$$\mu_1 = \frac{2 n_1 n_2}{n_1 + n_2} + 1$$

μ_1 = mean of the r statistic.

The standard error of r statistic is calculated by the formula distribution with K – 1 d.f. Consequently, we can reject the H_o, that $\mu_2 = \mu_k$ and accept the alt that the μ 's are not all equal at the level of significance α , if $H > \chi a^2$ for K -1 degrees of freedom. The calculated value is less than the table value. The H_0 is separated to conclude that the 3 months are equally effective.

Run Test

The run is used to the samples for randomness of their order. For applying this test, we take the help of the theory of runs. We first combine the two sets of observation and arrange them in ascending order. A run is defined as a sequence of elements of the same type. Thus, if the order is as $X_1,X_2,X_3,Y_1,Y_2,X_3,X_4,Y_3,Y_4$........then the first three elements X_1,X_2,X_3 are from the 1st sample and so it defines one run. If the runs are well mixed, we accept the null hypothesis and if there is a long run of X's or Y's at the extremes, we reject H_0. Also if there are few runs we reject H_0.

For n_1 and n_2 each > 10, where n_1 number of occurrence of type X and n_2 is numbers of occurrence of type Y, the distribution of runs (r) is asymptotically normal.

If Z falls in the rejection, we reject H_0 otherwise accept H_0.

Illustration

The personal director of a company wishes to select applicants for advanced training without regards to the set. Let W denote women and M denote men and the pattern of arrival be:

W,	M,	W,	W,	W,	M,	M,	M,	W,	W,	M,	W,	W,	W,	M,
M,	M,	M,	W,	M,	W,	M,	M,	W,	W,	W,	M,	M,	W,	M,
M,	M,	M,	W,	W,	M,	W,	W,	M,	M,	M,	M,	M,	W,	W,
W,	W,	W,	W,	M,	M,	W,	W,	M,	W,	M,	W,	W,	W,	M,

Will you conclude that the applicants have arrived in a random fashion?

Solution

The null hypothesis is that the applicants have arrived in a random fashion. Here,

$n_1 = 29$, number of men.

$n_2 = 31$, number of women.

$r = 29$, number of runs.

As n_1 and n_2 are greater than 10, we can use the normal approximation for the sampling distribution of numbers of runs. The expected value of r is given by,

$$E(r) = \frac{2n_1n_2}{n_1+n_2} + 1 = \frac{2 \times 29 \times 31}{29+31} + 1 = 30.97$$

And the standard deviation $= \sqrt{Var(r)} = \sqrt{\dfrac{2n_1n_2(2n_1n_2 - n_1 - n_2)}{(n_1+n_2)^2(n_1+n_2-1)}}$

$$= \sqrt{\frac{2 \times 29 \times 31(2 \times 29 \times 31 - 29 - 31)}{(29+31)^2(29+31-1)}}$$

$$= \sqrt{\frac{1798 \times 1738}{3600 \times 59}}$$

$= \sqrt{14.71} = 3.84$

Thus, the Z statistic is given by

$$Z = \frac{r - E(R)}{\sqrt{Var(r)}} = \frac{29 - 30.97}{3.84} = \frac{-1.97}{3.84} = -0.513$$

For $\alpha = 0.05$ the acceptance region is $-1.960 \leq Z \leq 1.960$.

As the calculated value of Z falls in the acceptance region. H_0 is accepted i.e., applicants have arrive in fashion.

Spearman's Rank Correlation

Among the various statistical methods based on ranks, the Spearman's Rank correlation procedure was the earliest to be developed. This method is simple to use and easy to apply. Also is has proved to be almost as powerful as its classical counterpart. The Pearson's product moment correlation method under conditions is favorable to the latter and even more powerful than the parametric method when its assumptions are violated.

The spearmen co-efficient of rank correlation r_s is given by the formula:

$$r_s = 1 + \frac{6 \Sigma D^2}{N^2 - N}$$

The coefficient of rank correlation is a relative measure which varies from -1 to +1. The close r_3 is to these extremes.

$$\sigma_1 = \frac{2 n_1 n_2 (R n_1 n_2 - n_1 - n_2)}{(n_1 - n_2)^2 (n_1 + n_2 - 1)}$$

If may be noted that the sampling contribution of r can be closely approximated by the normal distribution if either n_1 or n_2 is larger than 20.

$$Z = \frac{r - \mu_r}{\alpha_r}.$$

Kruskal-Wallis H Test: An alternative technique was developed called the Krushal-Wallis One way analysis of variance or H-test. This test helps in testing the H_0—that K independent random samples come from identical population against the alternative hypothesis that the means of these samples are not all equal.

As is done in the Mann-Whitney U-test, all data are ranked as if they were in one sum, from lowest to highest, the rank sums of each sample are calculated. The H-statistic is calculated from the formula:

$$H = \frac{12}{N(N+1)} \Sigma \frac{R_1^2}{n_1} + \frac{R_2^2}{n_2} .... \frac{R_k^2}{n_k} - 3(N+1)$$

If the null hypothesis is true and each sample has at least five observations, the sampling distribution of H can be approximated closely with a chi-square. The stronger is the relationship between X and Y and the close r_1 is to v, the weaker is the relationship between X and Y.

The standard error of the rank correlation coefficient is given by:

$$Z = r_2 \sqrt{n - 1}$$

It is possible to calculate the probability that r_1 assumes a large positive or negative value due solely to chance and thereby suggests an association between population when none exists.

Problem

The scores of a sample of 20 student pilots on their Federal Aviation Agency (FAA) written examination have been arranged according to the method used in their training, viz. video cassette (VC), audio cassette (AC) or classrooms training (CT).

Written examinations scores for 20 student pilots trained by three different methods are:

VC 74 88 82 93 55 70

AC 78 80 65 57 89 -

CT 68 83 50 91 84 77 94 81 92

Solution

Rank all the scores in order.

Ties are handled by arranging ranks.

Learn symbols used in Krushkal-Walli's test

n_j => No. of items in sample j

R_j => Sum of ranks of all items in sample j.

K = No. of Samples

N = $n_1 + n_2 + \ldots\ldots\ldots\ldots n_k$ the total no. of observations in all samples.

$$\text{Kruskal-Wallis statistics is } H(\text{or } K) = \frac{12}{N(N+1)}\Sigma\frac{R_j^2}{n_j} - 3(N+1)$$

$$H = \frac{12}{20(20+1)}\Sigma\frac{(61)^2}{6} + \frac{(42)^2}{5} + \frac{(107)^2}{9} - 3(20+1)$$

$$=(.02857)[620.2+352.8+1272.1]-63$$

$$=1.143$$

The written examination scores are ranked from the lowest to the highest as follows:

Rank	Score	Training Methods	Rank	Score	Training Method
1.	50	C	11	81	C
2.	55	VC	12	82	VC
3.	57	AC	13	83	C
4.	65	AC	14	84	C
5.	68	C	15	88	VC
6.	70	VC	16	89	AC
7.	74	VC	17	91	C
8.	77	C	18	92	C
9.	78	AC	19	93	VC
10.	80	AC	20	94	C

Data and rank arranged by training method is as follows:

VC	Rank	AC	Rank	CT	Rank
74	7	78	9	68	5
85	15	80	10	83	13
82	12	65	4	50	1

93	19	57	3	91	17
55	2	89	16	84	14
70	6			77	8
				94	20
				81	11
				92	18
	61		42		107

d.f = K – 1= 3 – 1 = 2

H_0: $_1$ = $_2$ = $_3$; there is no difference between three populations.

H_1: $_1$, $_2$, $_3$ are not equal.

Level of significance is 10 percent i.e., 0.10.

K statistic can be approximated by Chi-square distribution when all the sample size is at least 5.

The calculated value of Kruskal-Wallis test at 0.10 level of significance as per Chi-square distribution is 4.605

Notice that the acceptance region for the null hypothesis extends from 0-4.065. The sample k value 1.143 is within this acceptance region; therefore, the FAA should accept the H_0 and conclude that there was no difference is the results obtained by using the three training methods.

Kolmogorov-Smironov One Sample Test

This test is similar to the chi-square test of goodness of fit, but it is chosen for comparing the distribution on an ordinal scale. This test is also concerned with the degree of agreement between the distribution of observed values and some specific theoretical distribution (expected frequencies).

The test involves specifying the cumulative frequency distribution that would occur under the null hypothesis (theoretical distribution) and comparing it with the observed cumulative frequency distribution. If $F_0(x)$ is the theoretical cumulative distribution under H_0 and $S_n(x)$ is the cumulative distribution of the observed values, the test statistic is given by:

$$D = Maximum\,|F_0(X) - S_n(X)|$$

For $\alpha = 0.05$, the critical value of D for large samples is given by

$$1.36/\sqrt{n}$$

Where n is the sample size. If the calculated value exceeds the critical value, H_o is rejected.

Illustration

A paint manufacturer is interested in developing a new color: very light, light, bright and dark. Each color differs slightly in shade from the other so the four colors can be discerned from the darkest to the lightest. A sample of 200 people was shown these four shades and the following results were obtained: 80 preferred very light shade, 60 preferred light shade, 40 preferred the bright shade and 20 preferred the dark shade.

Do these results indicate a preference towards the shade?

Solution

H_0: There is no preference of shades. Under H_0, as there is no preference of shades, it means that the theoretical distribution will be that 50 people out of 200 will show preference for each shade. The theoretical and observed values are given in table.

The calculated value of $D = Maximum\,|F_0(X) - S_n(X)|$ is 0.20. The critical value is given by:

$$\frac{1.36}{\sqrt{n}} = \frac{1.36}{\sqrt{200}} = 0.096$$

	Shade Chosen			
	Very light	Light	Bright	Dark
f = observed number of people choosing that Shade	80	60	40	20
F_o (x) = theoretical cumulative distribution under H_0	0.25	0.50	0.75	1.00
Sn (x) = cumulative distribution of observed values	0.40	0.70	0.90	1.00

$\lvert F_0(X) - S_n(X) \rvert$	0.15	0.20	0.15	0.00

As the calculated value is greater than critical value, H_o is rejected. Thus, the results show significant preferences among the color shades.

Limitations of Hypothesis Testing

The test only presents useful aids for decision-making but not the decision-making itself.

The test does not indicate the reasons for the differences between means of two samples or populations.

The results of significance test are based on probability and hence does not express with full certainty.

The significance test for making statistical inferences cannot be entirely true.

Conclusion

Thus, we have discussed how tests concerning statistical hypotheses can be designed and used. A statistical hypothesis is a statement about a population parameter or about a population distribution. As these tests are conducted on the basis of evidence thrown up by sample, errors cannot be totally eliminated. The null and alternative hypotheses are set up such that one of them, and only one of them, is always true. There are two types of errors in any testing of hypothesis;, viz., type one error and type two error. All tests of hypotheses are conducted in two phases–in the first phase a test is designed where we decide as to when can the null hypothesis be rejected –and in the second phase, the designed test is used to draw the conclusion.

Self Assessment Questions

1. What is a hypothesis? What are the characteristics of a good research hypothesis?
2. The procedure of testing hypothesis requires a researcher to adopt several steps. Describe them briefly.

3. What do you mean by the power of a hypothesis test? How can it be measured?
4. Ten young recruits were put through a strenuous physical training programme by the army. Their weights (in kg.) were recorded before and after with the following results:

Recruit	1	2	3	4	5	6	7	8	9	10
Weight before	127	195	162	170	143	205	168	175	197	136
Weight after	135	200	160	182	147	200	172	186	194	141

Using a 5 percent level of significance, should we conclude that the programme affects the average weight of young recruits (Answer using t-test as well as A-test)?
5. A personnel manager has received complaints that the stenographers in the company have become slower and do not have the requisite speeds in stenography. The company expects the stenographers to have a minimum speed of 90 words per minute. The personnel manager decides to conduct a stenography test or a random sample of 15 stenographers. However, he is clear in his mind that unless the sample evidence is strongly against it, he would accept that the mean speed is at least 90 w.p.m. After the test, it is found that the mean speed of the 15 stenographers tested is 86.2 w.p.m. What should the personal manager conclude at a significance level of 5 percent, if it is known that the standard deviation of the speed of all stenographers is 10 w.p.m.
6. The situation is the same as in 2 above. However, suppose that instead of selecting 20 shops, the marketing manager selects only 10 shops and he introduces both the products in all the 10 shops. At the end of 15 days, he finds that the total sales in each of these 10 shops has been as follows:

Shop *(sales in kg.)*

	1	2	3	4	5	6	7	8	9	10
Product p1	14	17	12	9	13	15	13	13	10	9

Product p2 12 12 12 11 16 12 16 17 10 11

What should his conclusion be?

7. A production manager is certain that the output rate of experienced employees is better than that of the newly appointed employees. However, he is not sure if the variability in output rates for these two groups is same or not. From previous studies it is known that the mean output rate per hour of new employees at a particular work centre is 20 units with a standard deviation of 4 units. For a group of 15 employees with three year's experience, it was found that the sample mean of output rate per hour was 30 units with a sample standard deviation of 6 units. Is it reasonable to assume that the variability of output rates at these two experience levels is not different? Test at a significance level of .01.
8. A survey of industrial sales persons included questions on the age of the respondent and the degree of job pressure the sales person felt in connection with the job. The data is presented in the table below. Using a significance level of .01, examine if there is any relationship between the age and the degree of job pressure.

Age (years)	Degree of job pressure		
	Low	Medium	High
Less than 25	32	25	17
25-34	22	19	20
35-54	17	20	25
55 and above	15	24	26

For each of the statements below, choose the most appropriate response from among the ones listed.

12

Parametric Tests

Parametric tests are concerned with testing population parameters like mean, standard deviation, correlation regression, proportion, etc. Parametric tests assume normal distribution of the population, else go for large samples.

In this unit, testing of hypothesis with particular reference to parametric tests is attempted. First, testing of significance of difference between hypothesized population, mean, proportion, variance or correlation from the same or a random sample drawn from that population in order to judge the truth or otherwise of the hypothesized value of population is taken up. Next, the significance of difference between the means, proportions, variances or correlation coefficients of two populations is tested from significance of difference between sample mean, proportions, variances or correlation coefficients of two random samples drawn from the two populations. Before proceeding further, certain fundamentals of hypothesis testing is done.

Fundamentals of Hypothesis Testing

Hypothesis testing begins with an assumption, called a 'hypothesis' that we make about a population parameter. Then we collect sample data, produce sample statistics, and use this information to decide how likely it is that our hypothesized population parameter is correct. Say that we assume a certain value for a population mean. To test the validity of our assumption, we gather sample data and determine the difference between the hypothesized value and the actual value of the sample mean. Then we judge whether the difference is significant. The smaller the difference, the greater the likelihood that our hypothesized value for the mean is correct.

The larger difference, the smaller is the likelihood. But the question is, what is the yardstick to decide whether the difference is smaller or larger?

Unfortunately, the difference between the hypothesized population parameter and the actual statistic is more often neither so large that we automatically reject our hypothesis nor so small that we just as quickly accept it. So, in hypothesis testing, clear-cut solutions are difficult.

Concepts of Hypothesis Testing

Now we discuss a number of terms which are most commonly used in tests of significance.

Null Hypothesis: It is a hypothesis which assumes that there is no difference between two values such as sample means or sample proportions and in case there is any difference that is attributed to sampling fluctuations and is unimportant.

In many situations, we set up a hypothesis simply for the purpose of rejecting or to nullify it. For example, to know whether fertilizer manufactured by one firm will produce a higher yield of corn than fertilizer B manufactured by a second firm, the null hypothesis concerning the yield of corn of two fertilizers. This is stated as: "there is no difference between the yield of corn from fertilizer –A manufactured by one firm and the yield of corn from fertilizer–B manufactured by second firm".

Such hypotheses are referred to as null hypothesis and are denoted by H_o. *The null hypothesis is a hypothesis which reflects no change or no difference.*

A hypothesis that differs from a null hypothesis is called an alternative hypothesis. As the name implies, an alternative hypothesis is a statement which will be accepted when the null hypothesis is rejected. An alternative hypothesis is denoted by 'H_i': Regarding the yield of corn of two fertilizers A and B: the yield of corn from fertilizer–A is different from yield of corn from fertilizer–B.

The alternative hypothesis is the statement which reflects the situation anticipated to be correct if the null hypothesis is wrong.

The null hypothesis is that there is no difference between the mean yields of corn (μ_1, μ_2) of two fertilizers 'A' and 'B'. In symbols, it may be written as:

$$H_0 \quad \mu_1 = \mu_2$$

or

$$H_0 \quad \mu_1 - \mu_2 = 0$$

The alternative hypothesis is stated that the mean yields of corn $(\mu_1 - \mu_2)$ of two fertilizers are not equal. In symbols, it may be written as

$$H_i \quad \mu_1 \neq \mu_2$$

either $H_1 \quad \mu_1 > \mu_2$

or $H_i \quad \mu_1 < \mu_2$

Level of Significance

As a matter of practical convenience, experiments and research workers have used probability levels for deciding whether to accept or to reject a null hypothesis. These probability levels are called the levels of significance. It is defined as the probability of rejecting a null hypothesis, which is in fact true. In fact, two most commonly used levels of significance are 0.5 (5 percent) level and 0.01 (1 percent) levels. These levels correspond to the confidence coefficients of 0.95 (95 percent) and 0.99 (99 percent) respectively.

The level of significance is the maximum probability of rejecting a correct null hypothesis.

Suppose, a sample of 100 items is taken from a population with mean 136. The mean the sample works out is 128 and the standard error of mean is 2.5. Here, we formulate the null hypothesis, that there is no difference between sample mean and population mean and whatever difference in there may be attributed to sampling fluctuations. Now, we specify 0.05 probability at which we will reject the null hypothesis. This figure means that if the difference between the sample mean and population mean is such that it would occur only 5 percent or less than 5 percent of the times, the null hypothesis would wrongly be rejected. Here, the experimenter or the research worker runs the risk of making wrong decisions only in 5 out of 100 cases. In other words, the correct null hypothesis would be rejected in 5 out of 100 cases.

If we specify 0.01 (1 percent) level of significance, this figure (0.01) implies that if the difference between the sample mean and the population mean is such that it would occur only 1 percent or less than 1 percent of times, the null hypothesis would be wrongly rejected. Here, the experimenter runs the risk of making a wrong decision only in one out of 100 cases.

Regions of Acceptance and Rejection

The level of significance is mainly employed in decision-making problems because it distinguishes between two regions known as region of acceptance and region of rejection.

The region of acceptance may be defined as a range of values such that if the sample statistic falls in the range, the null hypothesis is accepted. On the contrary, the region of rejection may be defined as a range of values such that if the sample statistic falls in this range, the null hypothesis is rejected.

Standard Error

The standard error is an indispensable tool in the kit of a research worker because it is used in testing the validity of statistical hypothesis. The standard deviation of the sampling distribution of a statistical is called the standard error of a statistic. The standard error is important in dealing with statistics (measures of samples) which are normally distributed.

Here, the use of the word error is justified in this connection by the fact that we usually regard the expected value to be the true value and the divergence from it as error of estimation due to sampling fluctuations. The term standard error has a wider meaning than merely the standard deviation of simple sampling because of the following reasons:

1. The standard error is mainly employed for testing the validity of a given hypothesis. Mostly, two levels of significance (0.05 and 0.01) are used for testing the validity of hypotheses. At 0.05 level of significance, if the difference between expected and observed values is more than 1.96 standard errors, the difference is considered significant. Such a difference could not have arisen due to sampling fluctuations but due to the operation of other causes. On the contrary, if this difference is less than 1.96 standard errors, it is considered not significant, arising due to sampling fluctuations. In this case, the result of an experiment supports the null hypothesis. Similarly, at 0.01 level of significance, if the differences between observed and expected values is more than 2.58 standard errors, the difference is considered significant. Such a difference could have arisen not due to sampling fluctuations but due to other causes. On the other hand, if the difference is less than 2.58 standard errors, it may be attributed to sampling fluctuations and can be ignored. In this case, the result of the experiment supports the null hypothesis at 0.01 (1 percent) level of significance.

The standard error may fairly be taken to measure the unreliability of the sample estimate. The greater the standard error, the greater the difference between observed and expected values and greater the unreliability of the sample estimate. On the other hand, the smaller value of the standard error, the smaller the difference between observed and expected values and greater the reliability of the sample estimate.

2. The reciprocal of the standard error may be regarded as a measure of reliability. The reliability of an observed proportion varies as the square root of the number of observations on which it is based. The larger the sample size, the smaller the standard error and the smaller the sample size, the larger the standard error. In case we want to double the precision, the number of observations in the sample should be increased four times.
3. The most important use of the standard error is in the construction of confidence intervals within which parameter values are expected to fall. For a sufficiently large sample size, the sampling distribution tends to be normal. Therefore, at 5 percent level of significance, the population mean is expected to lie within the interval of:

$\overline{X} \pm 1.9$ Standard error of mean

Similarly, at 1 percent level of significance, the population mean is expected to fall within the interval of:

$\overline{X} \pm 2.58$ Standard error of mean

In the same way, other confidence intervals may be constructed.

Two-tailed and One-tailed Tests

Depending on choice of alternative hypothesis, tests are classified into two-tailed and one-tailed tests. Below, we highlight these tests in detail.

Two-tailed Test: When two tails of sampling distribution of the normal curve are used, the relevant test is called a two-tail test. Here, we are concerned with values that are higher as well as lower than the hypothetical value. For example, we may like to find whether the sample mean is significantly different from the hypothetical mean or not.

In the language of statistics it may be expressed as:

H_0; = a specified value

H_i; = a specified value

That is either > a specified value or < a specified value.

It may also be interpreted as that either very high values or very low values of sample mean (X) tend to support the alternative hypothesis (H_i) and cause the rejection of null hypothesis (H_0). Therefore, we have two rejection regions in a two-tail test.

If it is decided to use 5 percent level of significance for a two-tail test, the null hypothesis would be rejected if the value of the testing statistic is equal to or less than -1.96 and greater than or equal to +1.96.

One-tail Test: When only one tail of the sampling distribution of the normal curve is used, the test is described as one-tail test. Here, we are concerned only with values that are lower or only with values that are higher than the hypothetical value. For example, we may wish to determine whether the population mean is greater than a specified value i.e. a hypothetical value. In statistical language, it may be represented as:

H_0; = a specified value

H_i; > a specified value

It implies that very high values of sample means tend to support the alternative hypothesis (H_i) and cause the rejection of null hypothesis (H_o). Here, we are not concerned with low values of sample means, therefore, we have one rejection number in one tail-test.

Suppose, it is decided to use 5 percent level of significance for one tail-test, the null hypothesis (H_o) would be rejected if the value of testing statistic is greater than + 1.645.

Type-1 Error and Type-II Error

In testing hypothesis, there is a possibility of making a wrong decision because the decision is based on a sample data. If the hypothesis H_0 is true, we accept and if the hypothesis is wrong, we reject it then we will be making a right decision. If the hypothesis, H_o is true and we reject it, we will be committing an error of type-1. On the other hand, if the hypothesis is false and we accept it, we will be committing an error of type-II.

Type-I error is committed when we reject a null hypothesis – H_o by marking differences significant when actually no such difference exists. In fact, null hypothesis is true but the sample data leads to the rejection of null hypothesis. Thus, type-I error may be defined as the probability of rejecting a H_o, which in fact, is true. It is represented by the Greek letter 'α' (called alpha), which is also the level of significance.

Similarly, type-II error is committed when we accept a H_o by making difference not significant when actually the difference does exist. In fact, H_o is false but sample data leads to the acceptance of hypothesis. In other words, sample data do not seem to disagree with the hypothesis. Thus, type-II error may be defined as the probability of accepting a null hypothesis which is false. It is denoted by Greek letter 'β' (called beta).

1. For a given sample size, the probability of an error of second type is determined once the probability of an error of the first kind is decided.
2. If we want to decrease the probability of an error of first kind, the probability of type-II error is correspondingly increased.
3. If you want to reduce type-II error keeping type-I error at a fixed level, the size of sample must be increased. Thus, the four situations that arise in test procedure are described in the following table:
4. Decisions:

   H_0 – True H_0 – False

   H_0 Accepted Correct decision (No Error) Type-I, Error:

   H_0 Rejected Type-II, Error Correct decision (No Error)

   Test Procedures

   First, we have to state the null hypothesis.

Second, we have to state the alternative hypothesis.

Third, we have to state the level of significance. Level of significance refers to chance or probability of committing type I error.

Fourth, we have to calculate standard error of the relevant statistic.

Fifth, we have to calculate the test statistic depending on the problem.

Sixth, if need be "degrees of freedom" is to be chosen.

Seventh, we have to get critical value from appropriate theoretical probability distribution.

Eighth, if the calculated test statistic (as in step 5 above) is less than critical value read from table, null hypothesis is accepted. Otherwise it is rejected.

Large vs. Small Samples vis-à-vis Distributions Used

Statistically, a sample is large when the size exceeds 30. In other words, when $n > 30$ it is large sample, similarly when $n \leq 30$, it is a small sample.

When $n > 30$, i.e., for large samples normal distribution is generally used and for small samples 't' distribution is used in respect of testing of means, correlation coefficient, regression coefficients, etc. For testing of proportions, 'Z' test is used generally. For testing of mean and difference between means, normal distribution is used even in the case of small samples, if population standard deviation is known. In other words, 't' distribution is used only when population standard deviation is not known and the sample is small.

Testing for Mean: Here, testing of equity of population mean to a hypothesis value of the same is done. Three test situations are involved.

Large Sample Test of Mean: A foreign institutional investment house puts that high rated debt return in India is 14 percent. A random sample of 100 "AAA" bonds gives a return of only 12.8 percent. The standard deviation of population return is known to be 4 percent. *Test appropriate null hypothesis against suitable alternative hypothesis.*

Solution

Two-tailed test

Null hypothesis: H_0: = 14

(Where = population mean return)

Alternative hypothesis: H_1: # 14

Alpha = level of significance = 5 percent

N = 100 and X = 12.8 percent

Standard deviation = 4

SEx = Standard error of mean =

$\sigma / \sqrt{N} = 4 / \sqrt{100} = 0.4$

Test statistic $Z = (\overline{X} - \mu) / SE$

$= (12.8 - 14) / 0.4 = -3 = 3$

The normal distribution table value for alpha of 5 percent is 1.96 (for two-tailed tests).

The null hypothesis is to be rejected as the calculated "Z" = 3 is > critical value = 1.96.

[Note: even if population standard deviation is not known here, you can take sample standard deviation as surrogate for population value].

One-tailed Test: The above problem may be solved for alternative hypothesis that < 14 percent

So, H_0: = 14 percent, $\overline{X}$ = 12.8; Alpha = 5 percent

H_1: < 14 percent; N = 100; σ = 4 percent

SE mean = $\sigma / \sqrt{N} = 4/\sqrt{100} = 0.4$

$Z = (\overline{X} - \mu) / SE$ of mean = (12.8 – 14) / 0.4 = 3

The table value for 5 percent significance level for one-tailed test (one-tailed test has alternative hypothesis of the form > or <, at against two-tailed test where alternative hypothesis is of the "not equal to" form) is 1.645.

So, the null hypothesis stands rejected.

Small Sample Test with Known Population Standard Deviation

Since, population standard is known, normal distribution is used.

Let H_0: = 7 (average no. of equity scrip in middle – class portfolios)

H_1: $\neq 7$

$\overline{X} = 6; S = 2; n = 25$

Alpha = 5 percent

SE mean = $S/\sqrt{n}$ = $2/\sqrt{25} = 0.4$

$Z = (\overline{X} - \ )/SE = (6-7)/0.4 = 2.5$

The calculated value is > critical value = 1.96 and then null hypothesis is rejected. The H_i: < 7, also does not help in accepting the null hypothesis as the critical value is 1.645, while calculated value stands at 2.5.

Small Sample, Population Standard Deviation is not Known

When $n \leq 30$, and S is not known,'t' distribution is used. Except this, computational procedure is same.

The dividend payout ratio is assumed to be 40 percent in textile industry. A sample of 10 mills produced 30 percent, 32 percent, 40 percent, 45 percent, 35 percent, 50 percent, 28 percent, 30 percent, 42 percent and 28 percent. *Test the null hypothesis against (i) H_i that the ratio is not equal to 40 percent and (ii) H_i that the ratio has declined.*

Solution

X:	30	32	40	45	35	50	28	30	42	28
$X-\overline{X}$:	-6	-4	4	9	-1	14	-8	+6	-56	-8
$(X-\overline{X})^2$:	36	16	16	81	1	196	64	36	36	64

$\overline{X} = \Sigma X/N = 360/10 = 36$

$S = \sqrt{(X - \overline{X})^2 / n - 1} = \sqrt{556/9} = 7.93$

H_0: μ = 40 percent

(i) H_1: $\mu \neq 40$ percent

(ii) H_1: $\mu < 40$ percent

Alpha = 5 percent; $\overline{X}$ = 36 percent; S = 7.93 percent; N = 10.

SE of Mean = $S\sqrt{N} = 7.93\sqrt{10} = 2.51$

$t = (\overline{X} - \mu)/SE$ = (36-40)/2.51 = 1.594

DF= Degree of freedom = N-1 = 10-1 = 9

For two tail test for 9 DF and 5 percent significance level, "t" value = 2.262

The computed value is less than 2.262. So, H_0 is accepted.

For one-tailed test, the "t" value = 1.833. Here too the H_0 is accepted.

Testing of Difference between Population Means

To test whether two populations have different means, a test procedure is followed. The same is dealt below.

The H_0 is taken as: $\mu_1 = \mu_2$

The H_1 can be any of the three:

(i) $\mu_1 \neq \mu_2$

(ii) $\mu_1 < \mu_2$

(iii) $\mu_1 > \mu_2$

The SE of difference between mean is given by: $\sigma\sqrt{1/n_1 + 1/n_2}$ where "σ" is population standard deviation, n_1 = size of sample one and n_2 = size of sample two.

If "σ "is not available and sample standard deviations are available, the SE is calculated as $\sqrt{S_1^2/n_1 + S_2^2/n_2}$

The test statistic $(\overline{X}_1 - \overline{X}_2)/SE$ if this value is less than table value, H_0 is accepted otherwise rejected.

Testing of Difference between Means-Large Samples

In testing difference between means, if both n_1 and n_2 are greater than 30, we use normal distribution, whether "σ " is known or only "s" values are known.

Case of Combined Population S.D Known

The mean EPS of a sample of 50 southern textile mills is ₹ 8 while that of northern textile mills is ₹ 7. The σ for all textile mills is ₹ 2.6. Can we say the two regions differ in mean?

$H_0: \mu_1 = \mu_2$

$H_1: \mu_1 \neq \mu_2$

Alpha = 5 percent; $\sigma = 2.6$

$\overline{X}_1 = 8$; $\overline{X}_2 = 7$; $n_1 = n_2 = 50$

S.E. of diff. in means = $S\sqrt{1/n_1 + 1/n_2}$

$= 2.6\sqrt{1/50 + 1/50} = 0.52$

Test statistics = $(\overline{X}_1 - \overline{X}_2)/SE$ = (8-7)/0.52 = 1.92.

At 5 percent significance level, the table value is 1.96. The calculated value is less than table value. So, H_0 is accepted. That is, the mean EPS of southern mills is equal to mean EPS of northern mills.

If we had adopted one-tailed test with the $H_i: \mu_1 > \mu_2$, the H_0 will get rejected since, calculated value > the critical value 1.645.

Case of Individual Population S.D Known

A sample of 100 firms is Tamil Nadu produced a dividend payout ratio of 0.42 while a sample of 200 firms in Karnataka produced a dividend payout ratio of 0.45. The standard deviations is 0.1 and 0.2 for the two states respectively. *Test the H_0 that the two means are equal, against H_i that, the former mean is less than the latter.*

Testing of Difference between Means-Small Samples

When any of the samples is a small sample, and population standard deviation is not known, the 't' distribution is used for testing the difference between means.

Prices of scrip for 11 days and that of another for 21 days are as under.

Scrip A price: 38 40 42 40 55 56 40 46 49 50 61.

Scrip B price: 39 45 40 41 45 50 42 48 50 40

55 40 40 40 49 36 52 47 46 50 50.

Whether the mean prices of the two scrips are the same?

The following test procedure is adopted:

$\overline{X}_1$ = The mean of scrip A = 47

$\overline{X}_2$ = The mean of scrip B = 45

S_1 = The standard deviation of scrip A = 7.47

S_2 = The standard deviation of scrip B = 5.22

(All these values are computed).

H_0: $\mu_1 = \mu_2$

H_1: $\mu_1 \neq \mu_2$

$n_1 = 11$; $n_2 = 21$

S.E. of diff. between mean = $\sqrt{S_1^2/n_1 + S_2^2/n_2}$

$\sqrt{(7.47)^2/11 + (5.22)^2/21}$

$\sqrt{55.8/11 + 27.2/21}$

$\sqrt{5.072 + 1.295} = 2.523$

Test statistics = $(\overline{X}_1 - \overline{X}_2)/SE$ = (47-45)/2.523 = 0.79

The table 't' value for degrees of freedom = $n_1 + n_2 - 2$ = 11 + 21 – 2 = 30, for two-tailed test it is = 2.086. The calculated value is less than table value. So, H_0 is accepted.

Testing of Difference between Means-Paired Test

Paired test refers to, testing sample means, where the two sample figures come from the same set of units but observed twice.

The figures of ROI of firms before and after a policy change introduced by the Government are as below:

Before: 14 18 22 10 19 25 26 31

After: 21 21 20 17 22 25 30 35

Here, testing involves, whether or not the policy change has changed the mean ROI. For that, the change in ROI, firm wise is obtained and that is tested for H_0—that there is no change against H_i—that there is change.

So, the test involves just one series of figures, being the "change" in ROI.

The "change" being, "after" minus "before". We get change in ROI, i.e. "d"

d: 7 3 -2 7 3 0 4 4

d_2: 49 6 4 49 6 0 16 16

$\bar{d} = \Sigma d / N = 26/8 = 3.25$

Standard deviation =

$\sqrt{\Sigma d^2 / n-1} = \sqrt{152/8-1} = 4.66$

H_0 = Mean Change = $\bar{d}$ = 0

H_i = Mean Change ≠ 0

N = 8; S = 4.66

SE = 4.66/√8 = 1.65

Test statistics = d/SE = 3.25/1.65 = 1.97

The 't' value, N-1 = 8-1 = 7 and degree of freedom is 2.365. The calculated value is less than table value. So, H_0 is accepted.

Testing for Significance of Standard Deviation

The standard deviation of a population is assumed to be 5. A sample of 50 units produced a sample standard deviation of 4. Is there significant difference we can test and tell.

H_0: σ = 5

H_i: σ ≠ 5

S=4; α =5 percent

The SE of SD is given by = S/√2n = 4/√2×50 = 4/√100 = 0.4

Test Static = (S- σ)/SE = (4-5)/0.4 = 2.5.

The calculated value, viz. 2.5 is more than the table value of "Z", at 5 percent significance level being 1.96. So, H_0 is rejected. That is, the hypothesized value of standard deviation is rejected as it is not true. The value is not equal to 5.

Testing for Difference between Standard Deviations

The significance of difference between two standard deviations can be tested given the sample sizes, sample standard deviations and the table values.

The S.E. of difference between standard deviations = $\sqrt{S_1^2/2n_1 + S_2^2/2n_2}$

Test statistic = $(S_1 - S_2)/SE$

The mean price of a scrip over a 100 trading days period and the standard deviation were: ₹ 540 and ₹ 30. For another scrip, for an 80 days period, the mean and standard deviation were ₹ 552 and ₹ 25. Test for equality of standard deviation against,

Set I

$$H_0 = \sigma_1 = \sigma_2$$
$$H_1 = \sigma_1 \neq \sigma_2$$

S_1=30; S_2= 25
N_1= 100; N_2= 80
Alpha = 5 percent

Set II

$$H_0 = \sigma_1 = \sigma_2$$
$$H_1 = \sigma_1 > \sigma_2$$

S_1=30; S_2= 25
N_1= 100; N_2= 80
Alpha = 5 percent

$$\text{S.E.} = \sqrt{S_1^2/2n_1 + S_2^2/2n_2}$$
$$\sqrt{(30)^2/2\times100 + (25)^2\,2\times80}$$
$$\sqrt{900/200 + 625/160}$$
$$= 2.899$$

Test statistics = (S1-S2)/SE = (30-25)/2.899 = 1.72. The table value for 5 percent significance level = 1.96. The calculated value is less than table value. So, null hypothesis is accepted. In the 2nd set of hypothesis, the null hypothesis is rejected, because calculated test statistic is –1.72, which is greater than 'Z' value for 5 percent significance level under one-tailed test, which is equal to 1.645.

Testing for Variance

Testing for variance, i.e. standard deviation squared, is done using chi-square distribution in the case of one population problems and F-distribution for two population problems. The two problems already done using z-test, are now done using chi-square test and F-test as well.

Testing for significance of variance: χ^2 test

Given:

H_0 : =5

H_1 : −5

S : 4

α : 5 percent

n : 50

X^2 : (n-1) $S^2/\ ^2$ = (50-1) × $4^2/5^2$=31.36

The calculated value must fall between lower and upper χ^2 values obtained from table for given degrees of freedom and level of significance for accepting the H_0 in the case of two-tailed test.

The critical χ^2 for 49 degrees of freedom and 5 percent level is 32.4 on right tail and 71.4 on the left tail. Since the calculated χ^2 is within the two critical values, H_0 is accepted. So, the assumed population variance of 25 (i.e. 5x5) is the correct value.

For one tailed test with H_1: <5, the critical χ^2 =37.7 for 10 percent level and 49 degrees of freedom. The calculated value falls in the rejection region, being less than 37.7, the critical value. So, H_0 is rejected.

Testing for Significance of Difference in Variances: F-test

The problem on significance of difference between population variances is tested through an 'F' test. We have to calculate F-ratio, given as S_1^2/S_2^2, where S_1^2 is the larger variance of the given two sample variances and S_2^2 is the other one. In our case,

$$F=S_1^2/S_2^2=30^2/25^2=900/625=1.44$$

For one-tailed test, critical value is 30-1 = 29 df for numerator and 25-1 = 24 df for denominator at 5 percent level is 1.94. The calculated value falls in the acceptance region. H_0 is accepted. That is $_1 = {}_2$.

For two-tailed test, we have to state lower and upper 'F' critical ratios. If the actual value falls within these, H_0 is accepted.

In our problem, the acceptance region extends from F (29, 24, 0.95) to F (29, 24, 0.05).

We can get F (29, 24, 0.05) directly from F table and is equal to 1.94. We cannot get F (29, 24, 0.95) directly from table but that is equal to

$$1/ F(24,29,0.05) = 1/1.9 = 0.53$$

So, the calculated 'F' value 1.44 falls between the critical F values viz. 0.53 and 1.94. So, H_0 is accepted.

Testing the Significance of Correlation Coefficient– Large Sample

To test the significance of correlation coefficient, the following steps are involved;

Calculate of standard error of correlation coefficient.

The standard error of correlation coefficient denoted by S.E., is calculated by the expression:

$$S.E.r = \frac{1 - r^2}{\sqrt{N}}$$

Calculate of critical ration Z.

The critical ratio z is defined by the relation.

$$Z = \frac{r}{S.E.r}$$

At 5 percent level of significance, the rejection region consists of Z values equal to or less than -1.96 and equal to or greater than +1.96. If the computed value of Z falls in the rejection region, then the formulated null hypothesis is rejected otherwise it is accepted.

95 percent confidence limits of correlation coefficient are given by:

$r \pm 1.96 S.E.r$

Lower limit=r-1.96 S.E.r

Upper limit-=r+1.96 S.E.r

And 99 percent confidence limits are:

r$\pm$2.58 S.E.r

Illustration

A random sample of 900 pairs from a bivariate normal population showed a correlation coefficient of +0.67. Is this value significant for correlation in the population?

Solution

We setup the null hypothesis that the given correlation coefficient is not significant.

The Standard error of correlation coefficient is given by

$$S.E.r = \frac{1-r^2}{\sqrt{N}} \frac{1-0.67^2}{\sqrt{900}} = 0.018$$

The critical ratio Z is given by

$$Z = \frac{r}{S.E.r} = \frac{0.67}{0.018} = 37.22$$

At 5 percent level of significance, the rejection region consists of Z value equal to or less than -1.96 and equal to or greater than +1.96. The computed value of Z=37.22 falls in the rejection region and the formulated null hypothesis is wrong.

Testing the Significance of an Observed Correlation Coefficient-Small Sample

Assuming that the two variables X and Y are distributed normally in a bivariate distribution with means X and Y and standard deviations ax and ay have a correlation coefficient P (rho). These values are independent as well as random. Here, we have to test the hypothesis that the coefficient of correlation is significant. The statistic 't' is hypothesis that the coefficient of correlation is significant. The statistic 't' is defined by:

$$t = \frac{r}{Sr}$$

R = coefficient of correlation.

Sr = standard error of the coefficient of correlation .

The standard error of the coefficient of correlation is given by:

$$Sr = \sqrt{\frac{1 - r^2}{N - 2}}$$

Thus, the critical ratio 't' may be written as:

$$Sr = \frac{r\sqrt{N - 2}}{\sqrt{1 - r^2}}$$

The degree of freedom is computed by:

$$v = N - 2$$

Lastly, we have to compare the computed value of 't' with table value of 't' for given degrees of freedom at a specified level of significance to test the formulated null hypothesis.

Illustration

A random sample of 15 from a normal population gives a correlation coefficient of -0.5. Is the significant of the existence of correlation in the population?

Solution

We set up the null hypothesis that r = -0.5 is not significant of the existence of correlation in the population:

H_o:'r' is not significant

H_i:'r' is significant

Thus the critical ratio 't' may be written as'

$$t = \frac{-0.5\sqrt{15 - 2}}{\sqrt{1 - (-0.5)^2}} = \frac{-0.5\sqrt{13}}{\sqrt{0.75}} = -2.08$$

The number of degrees of freedom

$$t = \frac{r\sqrt{N - 2}}{\sqrt{1 - r^2}}$$

v = N – 2

= 15 – 2 = 13

The table value of 't' for 13 degrees of freedom at 5 percent level of significance is 2.16. But the computed value of t = -2.08 is greater than table value of t = -2.16 and falls in the acceptance region. Hence, the formulated null hypothesis is correct.

Illustration

Find the least value of the coefficient of correlation (R) in the sample of 18 pairs from a bivariate normal population, significant at 5 percent level.

Solution: The statistics 't' is defined by

$$t = \frac{r\sqrt{N-2}}{\sqrt{1-r^2}}$$

The no. of degrees of freedom V = N – 2 = 18 – 2 = 16

The table value of 't' for 16 degrees of freedom at 5 percent level of significance is 2.12.

For Significance at 5 percent level, we have

$16r^2 > 4.5(1.1\text{-}r^2)$

or

$16r_2 + 4.5r_2 > 4.5$

or $20.5r^2 > 4.5$

$r^2 > 4.5/20.5$

$r > \sqrt{4.5/2.5}$

$r > 0.474$

Testing the Significance of the Difference between Two Independent Correlation Coefficients

Suppose two independent samples of sizes N1 and N2 give correlation coefficients 'r1' and 'r2' respectively. Here, we have to test the hypothesis such that the samples are drawn from the same bivariate normal population.

On the assumption that the samples are drawn from the same bivariate normal population, the difference between the values of Z for two tests of significance (small samples) is:

S.E

Z_1-Z_2=

The test statistic 'z' is defined by the relation: $\sqrt{\frac{1}{N_1-3}+\frac{1}{N_2-3}}$

And is normally distributed with mean zero and unit standard deviation where:

Z_1=(1.1513) $\left(\frac{1+r_1}{1-r_1}\right)$ $\log_{10}$

and

Z_2=(1.1513) $\left(\frac{1+r_2}{1-r_2}\right)$ $\log_{10}$

The computed values of Z is compared with table value of Z at a specified level of significance and conclusion drawn.

Testing of Significance of Population Proportion

Suppose that the promotable employees in an organization is 40 percent. A random sample of employees from that population reveals that 50 percent are promotable or only 32 percent promotable. We now doubt whether the assumption of 40 percent of employees as promotable is correct or not. In other words, whether the true population proportion of promotable employees is 40 percent or some other figure.

Similarly, suppose that the percent of defectives be 5 percent in a process. Whether truly the defectives percent is 5 percent, testing of significance of proportion can be done.

Test Procedure

Set the H_0: P = A specific value

Set the H_1: p $\neq$ A specific value(or)

p > A specific value(or).

P < A specific value.

Set the level of significance

Get the sample proportion

Compute the standard error or proportion: the formula is

Where, P is assumed population proportion, Q = 1 – P and n is the size of sample.

Test statistic:

$$S.E. = \sqrt{\frac{P.Q}{n}}$$

Compare the test statistic with the critical 'z' value.

$$Z = \frac{\overline{p} - p}{SE_{\overline{p}}}$$

If the calculated z value is less than critical z value, H_o is accepted. If calculated value is equal to or greater than critical Z, H_o is rejected.

Self-Assessment Questions

1. Explain the procedure of hypothesis testing.
2. What do you mean by testing for significance of mean and difference between means? Explain with an example.
3. What do you mean by testing for significance of proportion and difference between proportions? Explain with an example.
4. What do you mean by testing for significance of variance and difference between variances? Explain with an example.
5. What do you mean by testing for significance of standard deviation and difference between standard deviations? Explain with an example.
6. What do you mean by testing for significance of correlation and difference between correlation coefficients? Explain with an example.
7. The assumed population mean is 75. A sample of size 100 gives a mean of 78 and standard deviation of 2. Test whether the population mean has increased?
8. The assumed population proportion is 0.8. A sample of 25 gives a proportion of 0.72. Test at 5 percent level whether the population proportion has decreased.

9. 2 samples dawn from 2 normal populations have means of 25 and 29. Test whether the 2 populations have identical means.
10. 2 samples drawn from 2 normal populations have proportions of 0.25 and 0.29, the sample sizes being 42 and 38. Test whether 2 populations have identical proportions.
11. 2 samples drawn from 2 normal populations have variances of 25 and 36, the sample sizes being 42 and 38. Test whether 2 populations have identical variances.
12. 2 samples drawn from 2 normal populations of bivariate relationship have correlation coefficient of 0.8 and 0.7, the sample sizes being 42 and 38. Test whether 2 populations have identical correlation coefficients. Use Z transformation model.

13

Anova and Chi-square Test Analysis of Variance

Testing Significance of Difference between more than Two Sample Means

Analysis of variance is a statistical technique used to test whether the effects of several factors are equal or not. It therefore, tests whether given samples can be considered as having been drawn from populations with some mean or all from the same population. Analysis of variance technique was mainly used in agricultural research. Now, the technique finds useful application in the field of both natural and social sciences.

The statistical test used in analysis of variance is 'F-test'. The null hypothesis 'sample means are equal'. If the null hypothesis is accepted, it is concluded that the effects of the different factors which cause variation are the same.

One Way Classifications of Data

In one way classification, observations are classified into groups on the basis of single criterion. In such a classification, there are k samples, one from each of k normal populations with common variance.

For example, consider an experiment to compare the effects of two fertilizers, say A and B, on the yield of a particular variety of paddy. Then, the two populations are the two kinds of paddy fields, one where fertilizer A is applied and the other where fertilizer B is applied. From both these populations, samples of size n1 and n2 are selected. The observations thus collected form one way classification, since only aspect namely the effect of fertilizer is to be examined.

'Anova' Table in One Way Analysis of Variance

'ANOVA' table presents the various results obtained while carrying out the analysis of variance. A specimen of ANOVA table is given below.

Source of variation	Sum of squares	Degree of freedom	Mean square
Between samples Within samples	SSC SSE	K – 1 N – K	MSC MSE
TOTAL	SST	N – 1	

Example:

Below are given the yield (in kg.) per acre for 5 trial plots of 4 varieties of treatment.

Plot No.	Treatment			
	1	2	3	4
1.	42	48	68	80
2.	50	66	52	94
3.	62	68	76	78
4.	34	78	64	82
5.	52	70	70	66

Carry out an analysis of variance and state conclusion.

Plot no.	I (X1)	II (X2)	III (X3)	IV (X4)
1.	42	48	68	80
2.	50	66	52	94
3.	62	68	76	78
4.	34	78	64	82
5.	52	70	70	66
TOTAL	240	330	330	400

T= Sum of all the observations =42+50+...........+66=1300

SST = Sum of the squares of all the observations

$$\frac{T^2}{N} = \frac{(1300)^2}{20} = 84500$$

$$=(42^2+50^2+62^2+.....+66^2)-84500=4236$$

$$=\frac{(\Sigma X_1)^2}{n^2}+\frac{(\Sigma X_2)^2}{n^2}+........\frac{T^2}{N}$$

$$=\frac{(240)^2}{5}+\frac{(330)^2}{5}+\frac{(330)^2}{5}+\frac{(400)^2}{5}-84500=2580$$

SSE=SST-SSC=4236-2580=1656

$$\text{MSC} =\frac{SSC}{K-1}+\frac{2580}{3}=860$$

$$\text{MSE} =\frac{SSC}{N-1}+\frac{1656}{20-4}=103.5$$

The degree of freedom = (K – 1, N – K) = (3, 16). {K is the number of column and N is the total number of observations}.

The Analysis of Variance Table

Source of variation	sum of squares	Degree of freedom	Mean square
Between samples Within samples	SSC = 2580 SST = 1656	K – 1 = 3 N – K = 16	MSC = 860 MSE = 103.5
Total	SST = 4236	N – 1 = 19	

The table value of F at 5 percent level of significance for (3,16) degree of freedom is 3.24. The calculated value of F is more than the table value of F. Therefore, the null hypothesis is rejected.

Two Way Classification

In the two way classification, observations are classified into groups on the basis of two criteria.

Procedure for Carrying out the Two Way Analysis of Variance

Steps:

1. Assume the means of all columns are equal. That is the effects of all factors in one kind of treatment are equal. i.e., ${}_1 = {}_2 \ldots\ldots\ldots {}_c$
2. Assume the means of all rows are equal. That is, the effects of all factors in the second kind of treatment are equal. i.e., ${}_1 = {}_2 \ldots\ldots\ldots {}_r$
3. Compute T = sum of all the values.
4. Find SST=Sum of Squares of all observations $-\frac{T^2}{N}$
5. Find SSC where $= \frac{(\Sigma X_1)^2}{n^1} + \frac{(\Sigma X_2)^2}{n^2} + \ldots\ldots\frac{T^2}{N}$ X1, X2..... are column Totals
6. Find SSR where $= \frac{(\Sigma X_1)^2}{n^1} + \frac{(\Sigma X_2)^2}{n^2} + \ldots\ldots\frac{T^2}{N}$ X1, X2..... are row totals.
7. SSE = SST-SSC-SSR
7. MSC $= \frac{SSC}{MSE}; MSR = \frac{SSR}{r-1}; MSE = \frac{SSE}{(c-1)(r-1)}$ where 'c' is the number of columns and 'r' is the number of rows.
8. $F_c = \frac{MSC}{MSE}$ and $F_R = \frac{MSR}{MSE}$

Degree of freedom for $F_C = [c-1, (c-1)x(r-1)]$

Degree of freedom for $F_R = [r-1, (c-1)x(r-1)]$

F_c is for column wise and F_R is for row wise comparison.

If $F_c <$ table value of F, then ${}_1 = {}_2 = \ldots\ldots\ldots\ldots$

If $F_R <$ table value of F, then ${}_1 = {}_2 = \ldots\ldots\ldots$

Anova Table for Two Way Analysis of Variance

Sources of variation	Sum of squares	d.f.	Mean square	F. ratio
Between columns Between rows Residual	SSC SSR SSE	C – 1 R – 1 (C-1) × (R-1)	MSC MSR MSE	F_C F_R
Total	SST	N – 1		

Example:

Three varieties of crops A, B, C are tested in a randomized block design with four replications–the yields are given below:

Variety	Replications			
	1	2	3	4
A	6	4	8	6
B	7	6	6	9
C	8	5	10	9

Test whether there is difference between replications. Test also whether varieties differ significantly.

Solution:

Variety	Replications				Total
	1	2	3	4	
A	6	4	8	6	24
B	7	6	6	9	28
C	8	5	10	9	32
Total	21	15	24	24	84

N = 12,

T = Sum of all values = 6+7+……+9+9= 84

$$\therefore \frac{T^2}{N} = \frac{84^2}{12} = 588$$

$$SST = \text{Sum of all values} - \frac{T^2}{N}$$

SST $= 6^2 + 7^2 = \ldots\ldots + 9^2 - 588$

For $= 624 - 588$ columns, SSC

$= 36$ $\quad = \frac{(\Sigma X_1)^2}{n^1} + \frac{(\Sigma X_2)^2}{n^2} + \ldots\ldots\ldots \frac{T^2}{N}$

SSC $= \left[\frac{(21)^2}{3} + \frac{(15)^2}{3} + \frac{(24)^2}{3} + \frac{(24)^2}{3}\right] - 588$

MSC $= \frac{1818}{3} - 588$

For $= 18$ rows, SSR

$= \frac{SSC}{c-1} = \frac{18}{3} = 16$ $\quad = \frac{(\Sigma X_1)^2}{n^1} + \frac{(\Sigma X_2)^2}{n^2} + \ldots\ldots - \frac{T^2}{N}$

SSR $= \left[\frac{(24)^2}{4} + \frac{(28)^2}{4} + \frac{(32)^2}{4}\right] - 588$

MSR $= \frac{2384}{4} - 588$

SSE $= 8$ $\quad$ = SST – SSC – SSR = 36 – 18 – 8

= 10 $\quad = \frac{SSR}{r-1} = \frac{8}{2} = 4$

$$\text{MSE} = \frac{SSE}{(r-1)(c-1)} = \frac{10}{6} = 1.667$$

Anova Table

Sources of variation	Sum of squares	Degree of freedom	Mean squares	F
Between columns	18	3	6	$F_c = \frac{6}{1.667} = 3.6$
Between rows	8	2	4	$F_R = \frac{4}{1.667} = 2.4$
Residual	10	6	1.667	

Total	36	11	-	

Between Columns:

Degree of freedom (3.6)

Table value of F = 4.757

Calculated value of F = 3.6 which is less than the table value.

Therefore, we accept the hypothesis that there is no significant difference between replications.

Between Rows

Degree of freedom (2.6)

Table value of F= 5.143

Calculated value of F = 2.4 which is less than the table value.

Therefore, we accept the hypothesis that is no significant difference between the varieties.

χ^2 Test and Goodness of Fit

In many business problems, we are required to ascertain the frequency of events falling in specified categories, e.g. in market research we counter the number of people who prefer a particular brand of detergent power, in quality control we count the number of defectives produced by a machine during a certain period, in socio-economic studies we count the number of children in families at different income levels. There are, thus, many situations of this type where measurements are by counting of numbers or frequency in each category. Chi-square test is applied to such frequencies of occurrence as against the expected ones without reference to population parameters, which was being done earlier in test of significance.

χ^2 Defined

The χ^2 test (pronounced as chi-square test) is one of the simplest and most widely used non-parametric tests in statistical work. The symbol χ^2 is from the greek letter chi. The χ^2 test was first used by Karl Pearson in the year 1990. The quantity χ^2 describes the magnitude of the discrepancy between theory and observation. It is defined as:

$$\chi^2 = \Sigma \frac{(O - E)^2}{E}$$

Where O refers to the observed frequencies and E refers to the expected frequencies.

Steps

To determine the value of χ^2, the steps required are:

Calculate the expected frequencies. In general, the expected frequency for any cell can be calculated from the following equation:

RT = the row total for the row containing the cell.

CT = the column total for the column containing the cell

N = the total number of observations.

Take the difference between the observed and expected frequencies and obtain the squares of these differences, i.e. obtain the values of $(O - E)^2$.

Divide the values of $(O - E)^2$ obtained by the respective expected frequency and obtain the total Σ $[(O - E)^2/ E]$. This gives the value of χ^2 which can range from zero to infinity. If χ^2 is zero, it means that the observed and expected values coincide. The greater the discrepancy between the observed and expected frequencies, the greater shall be the value of χ^2.

The calculated value of χ^2 is compared with the table value of χ^2 for given degrees of freedom at a certain specified level of significance. If at the stated level (generally 5 percent level is selected), the calculated value of χ^2 is more than the table value of χ^2, the difference between the or and observation is considered to be significant, i.e., it could not have arisen due to fluctuations of simple sampling. If, on the other hand, the calculated value of χ^2 is less than the table value, the difference between theory and observation is not considered as significant i.e. it is regarded as due to fluctuation of simple sampling and hence ignored.

The computed value of χ^2 is a random variable which takes on different values from sample to sample. That is χ^2 has a sampling distribution just as to the other test statistics.

It should be noted that the value of χ^2 is always positive and its upper limit is infinity. Also since χ^2 is derived from observations, it is a statistic and not a parameter (there is no parameter corresponding to it). The χ^2 test is therefore, termed non-parametric. It is one of the great advantages of this test that it involves no assumption about the form of the original distribution from which the observations come.

Points to Note

The following points about the χ^2 test are worth noting:

1. The sum of the observed and expected frequencies is always zero. Symbolically,

$$(O - E) = \quad O - \quad E = N - N = 0$$

2. Needles to say that this provides an important check on the calculation in the computation of χ^2.
3. The χ^2 test depends only on the set of observed and expected frequencies and on degrees of freedom. It is a non-parametric test, also known as distribution free test, since no assumptions are made about the parameters of the population.
4. χ^2 distribution is a limiting approximation of the multinomial distribution.
5. Though χ^2 distribution is essentially a continuous distribution. The χ^2 test can be applied to discrete random variables whose frequencies can be counted and tabulated with or without grouping.

Yates' Correction

One of the conditions for the application of χ^2 test is that not all frequency should be less than 5 in any case, though 10 is better. This requirement is to avoid inflated chi-square values due to the division of the squared differences by a small size of the expected frequency. When the theoretical frequencies are less than 10 and especially less than 5, the ordinary table values of χ^2 are less reliable. This is especially true for one degree of freedom; it is true to a lesser extent for two or three degrees of freedom. However, the error is negligible for more than three degrees of freedom.

The Yates' connections for continuity, are introduced because the theoretical chi-square distribution is continuous whereas the tabulated values are based on the distribution of discrete χ^2 statistic. The correction has the effect of reducing the calculated value of χ^2 as continuous compared to the corresponding value without correction.

In a special case of 2 × 2 contingency table, approximation may be improved, and bias arising out of the use of small theoretical frequencies may be reduced, by means of a correction proposed by F. Yates in 1934. The correction involves the reduction of the deviation observed from theoretical frequencies which of course reduces the value of χ^2. The working rule for the application of the correction is to adjust the observed frequency in each cell of the 2 × 2 table in such a way as to reduce the absolute deviation of the observed from the theoretical frequency for that cell by ½. Adjustments for all the cells are to be made without changing the marginal totals. This operation will increase the observed frequency by ½ in each of two cells, and will reduce by ½ in each of two cells (please refer to following).

Another method of adjustment which gives the same result as the above procedure is:

$$^2 \text{ (corrected)}$$

or

$$\Sigma \frac{\left[(O_1 - E_1) - 0.5\right]^2}{E_1} + \frac{[(O_2 - E_2) - 0.5]^2}{E_2} + \frac{[(O_k - E_k) - 0.5]^2}{E_k}$$

In general, $\chi^2 = \frac{[(O - E) - 0.5]_2}{E}$ correction is made only when the number of degrees of freedom or V= 1 and N is small. For large samples where each expected frequency is between 5 and 10, it is perhaps best to compare both the corrected and uncorrected values of χ^2. If both values lead to the same conclusion regarding a hypothesis, such as acceptance or rejection at 0.05 level, difficulties are rarely encountered. If they lead to different conclusions, one can either resort to increasing sample size or if this proves impractical, one can employ exact methods of probability involving the multinomial distribution.

Significance Test

The χ^2 test is used in the following ways:

1. To indicate the null hypothesis and alternate hypothesis.
2. To list the observed frequencies resulting from a given investigation.
3. To calculate the expected frequencies which would have applied if the investigated data had followed a given theoretical distribution which we assume to apply to the situation in hand.
4. To calculate the difference between the observed frequency and the corresponding expected frequency for each class or group in the series, we express the square of the difference as a fraction of the expected frequency concerned.
5. To add together all the fractions obtained from step 4.

Illustration

A marketing research department of a television manufacturing company has chosen seven cities. It is believed that each city has the same sale potential. The actual number of television sets sold by the company in each city, during one month period, is given in the following table. We have to test the hypothesis that the seven cities have equal sales potential, using a level of significance of 0.05.

City	Number of sets sold
A	120
B	185
C	260
D	190
E	210
F	175
G	260
Total	1400

With the hypothesis that each city has the same sales potential, the expected number of television sets sold in each city is 200. To test the hypothesis, we calculate the χ^2 statistic. If the calculated value of χ^2 is equal to zero, there is perfect agreement between observed and expected frequencies. In other words, we are testing that $\chi^2 = 0$.

Calculations for χ^2 Statistic

City	Observed frequency	Expected frequency	(O – E)	$\frac{(O-E)^2}{E}$
A	120	200	-80	32000
B	185	200	-15	1125
C	260	200	+60	18000
D	190	200	-10	0.500
E	210	200	+10	0.500
F	175	200	-25	3.125
G	260	200	+60	18000
Total	1400	1400		$\chi^2 = 73.25$

Since the sum of the seven observed frequencies must equal 1400, the expected frequency for the seventh cell can be determined as soon as the expected frequencies for the first six cells are known. Thus, the number of degrees of freedom is V $= 7 - 1 = 6$.

Using a 0.05 level of significance, the table value of $\chi^2_{0.005}$ is 10.64.

Since the calculated $\chi^2 = 61.25$ is much greater than the table value, the hypothesis that the seven cities have equal sale potential is rejected.

Using OK χ^2 Test

The χ^2 test is one of the most popular statistical inference producers today. It is applicable to a very large number of problems in practice which can be summed up under the following heads:

χ^2 *test as a test of independence*: With the help of χ^2 test, we can find out whether two or more attributes are associated or not. Suppose, we have N observations classified according to some attributes, we may ask whether the attributes are related or independent. Thus, we can find out whether quinine is effective in controlling fever or not, whether there is no association in the attributes under study, in other words, the two attributes are independent, if the calculated value of χ^2 is less than the table value at a certain level of significance (generally 5 percent level),we say that the results of the experiment proved no evidence for doubting the hypothesis or, in other words, the hypothesis that the attributes are not associated holds good. On the other hand, if the calculated value of χ^2 greater than the table value at a certain level of significance, we say that the results of the experiment do not supports the hypothesis or, in other words, the attributes are associated. It should be noted that χ^2 is not a measure of the degree or form of relationship, it only tell us whether two principles of classification are or are not significantly related without reference to any assumptions concerning the form of relationship.

χ^2 *test as a test of goodness of fit*: χ^2 test is very popularly known as the test of goodness of fit for the reason that it enables us to ascertain how approximately the theoretical distributions such as binomial, position normal etc. fit into empirical distributions, i.e. those obtained from sample data. When an ideal frequency curve whether normal or some other type is fitted to the data, we are interested in finding out how well this curve fits with the observed facts. A test of concordance (goodness of fit) of the two can be made just by inspection, but such a test is obviously inadequate. Precision can be secured by applying the χ^2 test.

The following are the steps in testing the goodness of fit:

1. A null and alternative hypothesis is established and a significance level is selected for rejection of the null hypothesis.
2. A random sample of observations is drawn from a relevant statistical population.
3. A set of expected or theoretical frequencies is derived under the assumption that a particular probability distribution is applicable to the statistical population under consideration.
4. The observed frequencies are compared with the expected or theoretical frequencies.
5. If the calculated value of χ^2 is less than the table value at a certain level of significance (generally 5 percent level) and for a certain degree of freedom, the fit is considered to be good, the divergence between actual and expected frequencies is attributed to fluctuations of simple sampling. On the other hand if the calculated value of χ^2 is greater than the table value, the fit is considered to be poor i.e. it cannot be attributed to fluctuations of simple sampling rather it is due to the inadequacy of the theory to fit the observed facts.

For determining the degrees of freedom for the chi-square goodness-of-fit test, we should first count the number of classes (symbolized by K) for which comparison between observed and the expected frequencies is going to be made. As a general rule the degrees of freedom would be (k–1).

However, if in addition to the total, we have to impose further restrictions, the degrees of freedom would be reduced by the number of restrictions imposed. For example, for normal distribution we have seven classes of observed frequencies k = 7, and v = 7 – 1 = 6. If we have to use the sample mean as an estimate of the population mean, we will have to subtract an additional degree of freedom which leaves us with only 5, and if we have to use the sample standard deviation to estimate the population standard deviation, we will have to subtract one more degree of freedom leaving us with 4. Hence, as a general rule, we should first employ the (k – 1) rule and then subtract the additional degree of freedom for each population parameter, that has to be estimated from the sample data.

χ^2 *test as a test of homogeneity:* The χ^2 test of homogeneity is an extension of the Chi-square test of independence. Test of homogeneity are designed to determine whether two or more independent random samples are drawn from the same population or from different populations. Instead of one sample we use with independence problem, we shall now have 2 or more samples. For example, we may be interested in finding out whether or not the university students of various levels, i.e. undergraduate, post-graduate, and Ph.D. feel the same in regard to the amount of work required by their professors, i.e. too much work, right amount of work or too little work. We shall take the hypothesis that the three samples come from the same population; that is, the three classifications are homogeneous in so far as the opinion of three different groups of students about the amount of work required by their professors is concerned. This also means that there exists no difference in opinion among the three classes of people on the issue.

In an anti-malarial campaign in a certain area, quinine was administered to 812 persons out of a total population of 3,248. The number of fever cases is shown below.

Treatment	Fever	No Fever	Total

Quinine	20	792	812
No quinine	220	2216	2436
Total	240	3008	3248

Discuss the usefulness of Quinine in checking malaria.

Expectation of (AB)

$$= \frac{(A)\times(B)}{N} = \frac{240\times 812}{3248} = 60$$

or

E_1 i.e., expected frequency corresponding to first row and first column is 60.

The table of expected frequencies shall be.

60	752	812
180	2256	2436
240	3008	3248

O	E	$(O-E)^2$	$(O-E)^2/E$
20	60	1600	26.667
220	180	1600	8.889
792	752	1600	2.128
2216	2256	1600	0.709

$[\ (O\text{-}E)^2/E] = 38.393$

$^2 = [\ (O\text{-}E)^2/E] = 38.393$

$V = (r\text{-}1)\ (c\text{-}1) = (2\text{-}1)\ (2\text{-}1) = 1$

For $V = 1$, $^2 0.05 = 3.84$.

The calculated value of ^{2} is greater than the table value. The hypothesis is rejected. Hence, quinine is useful in checking malaria.

Based on information on 1000 randomly selected fields about the tenancy status of the cultivators of these fields and use of fertilizers, collected in an agro-economic survey, the following classification was noted.

	Owned	Rented	Total
Using Fertilizers	416	184	600

Not using Fertilizers	64	336	400
Total	480	520	1000

Would you conclude that owner cultivators are more inclined towards the use of fertilizers at 5 percent level?

Carry out Chi-square test as per the testing procedure.

Expectation of (AB)

$$= \frac{(A) \times (B)}{N}$$

$$= \frac{480 \times 600}{1000} = 288$$

The table of expected frequencies shall be:

288	312	600
192	208	400
480	520	1000

Applying ^{2} test:

O	E	$(O-E)^2$	$(O-E)^2/E$
416	288	16384	56.889
64	192	16384	85.333
184	312	16384	52.513
336	208	16384	78.769

$[\ (O-E)^2/E] = 273.504$

$^2 = [\ (O-E)^2/E] = 273.504$

$V = (r-1)(c-1) = (2-1)(2-1) = 1$

For $V = 1$, $^2_{0.05} = 3.84$.

The calculated value of ^{2} is much more than the table value. The hypothesis is rejected. Hence, it can be concluded that owners cultivation are more inclined towards the use of fertilizers.

In an experiment on immunization of cattle from tuberculosis the following results are obtained.

	Affected	Not Affected

Inoculated	12	26
Not Inoculated	16	6

Calculated ^{2} and discuss the effect of vaccine in controlling susceptibility to tuberculosis (5 percent value of ^{2} for one degree of freedom = 3.84).

Let us take the hypothesis that the vaccine is not effective in controlling susceptibility to tuberculosis. Applying ^{2} test:

Expectation of (AB)

$$= \frac{(A)\times(B)}{N} = \frac{38\times 28}{60} = 17.7$$

The table of expected frequencies will be as follows:

17.7	20.3	38
10.3	11.7	22
28	32	60

Since one of the observed frequencies is less than 10 we will use Yates correction and then apply ^{2} test.

O	E	$(O-E)^2$	$(O-E)^2/E$
12.5	17.7	27.04	1.528
15.5	10.3	27.04	2.625
25.5	20.3	27.04	1.332
6.5	11.7	27.04	2.311

$[\ (O\text{-}E)^2/E] = 7.796$

$^2 = [\ (O\text{-}E)^2/E] = 7.796$

$V = (r\text{-}1)\ (c\text{-}1) = (2\text{-}1)\ (2\text{-}1) = 1$

For $V = 1$, $^2_{0.05} = 3.84$.

Since the calculated value of ^{2} is greater than the table value the hypothesis is not true. We, therefore, conclude that vaccine is effective in controlling susceptibility to tuberculosis.

14

Measurement and Scaling Techniques

Objective

After reading this unit the scholars should be able to understand various types of measurement and scaling techniques and apply them in their research work.

Measurement

Concept of Measurement: Measurement may be defined as the assignment of numerals to characteristics of object, person, state, or events, according to rules. What is measured is not the object, person, state, or events, itself but some characteristic of it. For example, we do not measure the object itself but only its characteristic of being present. We never measure people, only their age, height, weight, or some other characteristic.

Levels of measurement

There are four levels of measurement: *Nominal, Ordinal, Interval and Ratio.* We describe below the characteristics of each of these levels.

Nominal Measurement: Nominal measurement is the most elementary method of measurement which classifies persons, objects or events into a number of mutually exclusive categories on the basis of the simple presence or absence, applicability or inapplicability, possession or non-possession of certain property. That is 'have' vs. 'have not' measurement which assigns mutually exclusive labels to identify objects. Thus, the population of town may be classified according to sex—into 'males' and 'females' or according to religion—into Hindus, Muslims, Sikhs and Christians and each category of persons given certain labels either in the from of numerals (0,1,2,3) or in the form of letters (A,B,C,D).

Ordinal Measurement: In ordinal measurement, numerals, letters or other symbols are used to rank objects. This is essentially an advanced form of categorization. Objects in this measurement are classified not only as to whether they share some characteristic with another object but also whether they have more or less of this characteristic than some other object. Thus, ordinal data indicates the relative position of two or more objects of some characteristic. A significant amount of marketing research, particularly consumer-oriented research, relies on this type of data. Their most common use is in obtaining preference measurements. For example, a consumer or a sample of experts may be asked to rank preferences for several brands, flavours, or package designs. Attitude measures are also often ordinal in nature.

Interval Measurement: Interval measurements represent numerals used to rank objects such that numerically equal distance on the scale represents equal distance in the property being measured. The distances between numerals are thus very meaningful because, by comparing these distances we can know how far apart the objects are with respect to the property in question. For example, if we are measuring the achievements of 4 students A, B, C, and D on an interval scale and obtain the values 1, 4, 5,and 8 respectively (as shown on next page) then by comparing the intervals, we can legitimately say that the difference between A and C in their achievements is the same as the difference between B and D and that the difference between B and D is four times the difference between B and C.

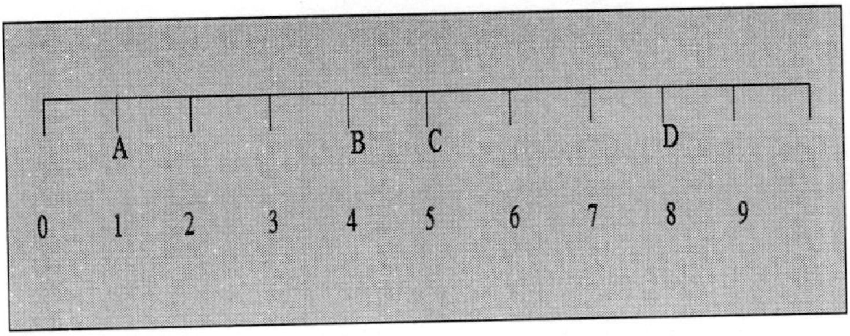

Ratio Measurement: This measurement besides possessing the property of the interval measurement, possesses one additional property, viz. it has a true, natural or absolute zero point, one for which there is universal agreement as to its location. A true zero means that the object measuring zero possesses none of the property in question. Height and weight are obvious examples. In general, wherever the objects are being 'counted' for possessing or not possessing a certain characteristic, ratio measurement is being done. In all such cases, the number 0 measured. Other common examples of this type of measurement are sales, costs, number of purchasers, length, time, etc.

The following table summarizes the above discussion about four types of measurements:

Type	Basic empirical operation	Typical usage	Typical statistics	
			Descriptive	Inferential
Nominal	Determination of equality	Classification male – female, purchase non – purchaser, team-A; team-B	Percentage mode	Chi-square, binomial test
Ordinal	Determination of greater or less	Rankings: Preference data, market position, attitude	Median	Rank-order correlation

		measures, many psycho –logical measures		
Interval	Determination of equality of intervals	Index numbers, attitude measures	Mean, range, standard deviation	Product-moment correlation, T-test, factor analysis
Ratio	Determination of equality of ratios	Sales, units produced, number of customers, costs, age	Geometric mean	Coefficient of variation

Characteristics of Research Tools

Overview: There are three major characteristics expected of a research tool viz. reliability, validity and objectivity. Each characteristic is examined in detail. The concept of reliability is examined for its two major components viz. internal consistency and temporal stability.

The different components of validity viz. content validity, construct validity and criterion related validity are discussed. Then a discussion of the concept of objectivity is attempted. This is followed by a discussion of the different procedures used for estimating the reliability of tests. The unit concludes with a discussion of the relation between reliability and validity.

The Importance of Selecting the Right Type of Tool

A very important problem that has to be faced by a researcher concerns the selection of appropriate tools for measuring the different variables included in the study. The research instruments are to be selected very carefully to see that dependable data is made available for the study. If this is not so, the findings which are evolved from the study will not be valid. Let us assume that an investigator is trying to investigate the relation between the height and weight of the college students. The measurement of height being direct, will not present any difficulty. But suppose the weighing machine is defective and hence gives wrong measures of the weights, the study using this data will not indicate the actual relationship which exists between height and weight. We cannot place any reliance on the finding so obtained. Hence, it is very important that the researcher selects the ideal instruments available for measuring the variables. When tests are not available, the investigator will have to construct the most dependable instruments for measurement. We have to examine in detail the criteria in terms of which the selection of tests is made—for any good research tool must possess the following three characteristics.

Reliability: Reliability of a tool refers to the dependability of consistency of the measures provided by it. It refers to "the accuracy of the data in the sense of their stability, repeatability, or precision" (Fox). There are two ways of looking at dependability. One is comparability of measures provided by different parts of the same test. Second is comparability of measures provided by the test on different occasions. In both the procedures, we produce two sets of measures which can be correlated to provide an estimate of reliability.

Comparability of Measures Provided by Different Parts of a Test: This procedure is based on the rationale that different parts of the test (different items) should make comparable estimates of the trait measured in an individual. Let us illustrate this with respect of an achievement test. Suppose 'item 1" shows that the individual is a very superior achiever. Normally 'item 2' should make the same assessment of the person, if the test is a satisfactory measure of achievement. If for some reason 'item 2 'makes a different estimate of the person's ability (suppose 'item 2' assesses the person as one of inferior achievement), then both the items will be looked upon with disbelief.

This aspect of reliability is usually assessed by comparing the scores obtained by different parts of the same test. The measures provided by different parts of a test should be comparable. The method used for estimating reliability using this argument is called the 'split-half method'. A narration of this method is called "odd-even method". This form of reliability is called the internal consistency. These methods are descried in detail in another section of this chapter.

Comparability of Measures Provided by the Test on Different Occasions: This method of assessing reliability is based on the rationale that a good test must give almost the same measurement when applied on the same person on different occasions. Suppose a test of intelligence is administered on a student today and is IQ as per the test is 100 (which stands for superior intelligence). But suppose we use the test on the same person after one month and find that his IQ has been reversed by the test at 90 (which indicates below average intelligence)—we conclude that the measures proved by the test are not dependable. Ideally, the two scores must be the same. But when we take into consideration the inaccuracies which enter into mental measurement (factors like maturation, forgetting, varying test conditions etc.) we are willing to admit small differences. Anyway we will be satisfied with the test only if the test provides comparable measures from time to time. This form of reliability is also called temporal stability.

The efficiency of the test, assessed from this point of view forms another component of reliability. This component of reliability is assessed using 'test-rest method' and 'parallel forms method'. These methods are described in another section of this chapter.

Validity: We know that every test is constructed with a purpose viz. to provide measures of a defined variable. We may define validity as the degree to which this purpose is attained. In other words, "validity refers to the ability of a test to measure what seeks to measure" (Fox).

Although a test is developed to serve a defined purpose, often it is used for other purposes also. For example, a test of intelligence developed to measure the mental ability of children can serve other useful purposes: predict school performance, serve as a basis of classification in vocational selection, identify learning difficulties, etc. It is usual to speak of 'validities' for a test, because it is used for different purposes. The different purpose for which a test is used implies the existence of different types of validities. Validity has been classified mainly into three forms as described below:

Content Validity: This form of validity is usually meaningful when we speak about achievement tests. When an achievement test adequately covers the course content and objectives specified for the test, it is said to possess content validity. A close examination of the items would reveal whether this form of validity is present in the test. Usually, content validity is established by a logical examination of content of the test.

Construct Validity: This form of validity is based on the argument that a test is developed using a psychological or logical construct (idea) and as such the test should provide evidence of measuring this construct. For example, a test for measuring study habits must correlate with school achievements. On this evidence, we may conclude that the test measures the construct (study-habit) which is supposed to be measured by it.

Alternatively, we can establish this type of validity by logically analyzing the test content. We can examine the items and satisfy ourselves that what we usually mean by good study-habits that is reflected in the test items.

Construct validity can be established using both statistical procedures (correlation with some suitable measure) or through logical examination of the test content.

Criterion Related Validity: This method of validity makes use of the statistical comparison of the statistical comparison of the scores of a test with some independent criterion. Reasonable agreement between the two measures is interpreted as evidence of this type of validity. The external measure for comparison is termed the criterion for validation. The external criterion is justified on the basis of some logical connection which should exist between the test and the criterion.

Any newly constructed test of intelligence is validated with the help of other existing tests of intelligence. The new test and the existing test are administered on a common group and the agreement between the two measures is expressed as a coefficient of correlation. When the correlation is reasonably high we say that the test is valid. Other forms of criteria are also an external criterion for the purpose.

There are other terms like validity, empirical, face validity, factorial validity, etc. to describe different concepts of validity. All these terms are basically covered by the three major classifications attempted above.

Another important term that is used in test literature is item validity or internal validity of a test. This refers to the inter-connectedness of different items in the same test. Ideally, a good test must have items which measure the main traits to be measured. If this condition is satisfied, the measures provided by different items will correlate with each other. This property is ensured using items analysis.

Validity and reliability are closely related concepts: this is so because when a test is said to be valid (a test measures what it is supposed to measure),it follows that it is reliable, because measurements provided by a test cannot be taken as useful measurements if they are not dependable or reliable. Hence, reliability is a pre-condition to validity.

Objectivity: The extent to which a measure is a function of the trait measured, is referred to as the objectivity. This is exact opposite of the term called subjectivity. A subjective measure is one in which the human being who makes the measurement permits his own values, judgments and prejudices to enter into the measurement. Examples of subjective judgments are many. When valuing a theory paper, suppose one teacher decides to give top scores for those who write maximum number of historical facts. In this case, he may ignore other aspects like handwriting, method of presentation etc. Another teacher may decide to combine facts with presentation in assigning scores.

The two teachers differ in their judgment of what is expected in a theory paper test. Still, others go in terms of their previous assessment of the individuals taking the test, their appearance and such extraneous factors. These are examples of subjective methods of assessment. The opposite of this concept is evident in the measurement provided by a weighing machine or a thermometer. These instruments provide measures which are independent of the people who are measured by them. These are examples of objective measurements. Ideally, a research instrument has to prove objective measures of the concepts to be measured.

Some techniques of measurement are more likely to be subjective. Interviews, for example, can yield results which are not completely objective, unless very adequate precautions are taken to make them objective. The behavior of the researcher in an interview itself can disturb the objectivity. The appearance and behavior of the person, of administration of the test etc. can all cause subjectivity. Essay type questions included in achievement tests often lead to subjectivity.

In psychological testing, it is usual to include objective type questions only. The scoring for such items can be done using mechanical methods. This is possible because each question has only one correct choice as answer. Valuing an essay question in constant is very often subjective. Most of the good research instruments have been specially developed to ensure objectivity, or to decrease the possibility of subjective scoring.

Besides specifying objective scoring procedures, many other precautions are usually taken to ensure objectivity in measurements. Examples of such procedures are providing standardized conditions for testing, standardized conditions for scoring and interpreting test scores and specific directions using the test scores (classification, prediction, diagnosis etc).

Many of the precautions taken for attaining reliability for a test will very often be of help in ensuring objectivity.

Procedures for Estimating the Reliability Tests

The following procedures are available for estimating the reliability of test:

1. Split-half or parallel-form method for estimating the comparability of measures provided by different parts of a test (internal consistency).
2. Test-retest method for estimating the comparability of measures provided by the test from time to time (temporal stability).
3. Kuder-Richardson technique for estimating the homogeneity of items (internal consistency).

Split and Parallel-Form Methods: The basic idea implied in this method is that the test must be capable of being split into two identical parts, both of which should provide comparable measures. Theoretically, we can think of the test as two test (split into two using some scores in the procedure). The test is administered on a representative group and the two are compared by working out a coefficient of correlation. If the two scores are comparable, there will be considerable agreement between the measures. This agreement will be indicated by a high coefficient of correlation. This agreement will be indicated by a high coefficient of correlation. This coefficient is taken as an index of reliability. It is referred to as split-half reliability coefficient.

A variation of this method is called the odd-even reliability estimate. In this procedure, we do not divide a test arbitrarily into two groups. But all the odd numbered items are treated as one half, whereas the even numbered items forms the second half of the test. The scores of an individual will be separated into two. The agreement between the scores provided by the two have's will be compared as before using a coefficient of correlation. This coefficient is referred to as odd-even reliability coefficient or "coefficient of internal consistency".

Correction for Shortening: This method will not give a correct estimate of the whole test because our calculation was based on the measures provided by half the test. It is known that when other factors remain the same, reliability of test the greater will be its reliability. Hence, when we estimate reliability using the split-half or odd-even method, the reliability coefficient indicated will be less than the actual value (split-half method underestimates the reliability of a test). There are mathematical procedures which help us to estimate the reliability of the whole test using reliability of half the test. This correction formula (developed by two psychometricians, Spearman and Brown) is referred to as the Spearman-Brown correction formula. If 'r' is the reliability coefficient estimated using half the test, 'r' is the reliability of the whole test, we can calculate 'R' from 'r' the formula is:

$$R = \frac{2r}{1+r}$$

Let us assume that the reliability of the half test is 0.8, then the reliability of the whole test can be estimated by substituting r = .8, in the above formula. Then,

$$R = \frac{2r}{1+r} = \frac{2 \times .8}{1+.8} = \frac{1.6}{1.8} = .89$$

approximately

The Parallel Form Method: This method is an improvement over the split-half method? Here, instead of splitting a test into two halves, two identical tests are constructed and used interchangeably. These tests are referred to as parallel forms. The two tests are considered parallel (or identical) if the two tests are identical with respect to number of items, content of items, format of items, scoring procedures and difficulty level of items. Thus, for every item in the first test, there must be equivalent in the second test. We can administer any one the forms for measurement. For assessing the reliability using this method, both the tests are administered on the same group almost simultaneously (or within a short interval) and the scores for the two tests are correlated. This correlation is referred to as the parallel form reliability coefficient. This is also referred to as the coefficient of equivalence.

Test-retest Method: This method uses the agreement between the scores obtained in a test, when the test is administered on a common group on two occasions. Usually, the two tests are given within a short interval (a few days to a few months). The two scores obtained by one individual are treated as two variables, and the correlation is taken as an index of this form of reliability. The coefficient is referred to as the test-retest coefficient of reliability. It is also referred to as the coefficient of stability.

Kuder-Richardson Technique: This method is based on the reasoning used in the split-self technique. That is, it is basically a measure of the internal consistency of the rest. The technique uses the difficulty values of individual items for estimating reliability. The difficulty of an item is expressed using the proportion of people getting an item correct. Then the item is administered on a group. Thus, if an item is answered correctly by 75 percent of the people in a group, its difficulty value is indicated as 75 percent or as 75 (as a proportion). The difficulty value of an item is represented by letter 'p' (as a proportion). We can work out a related quantity 'q' for the item which is (I-p). The value of 'q' for an item of 75 percent difficulty is (1-.75) = .25. If we know the values of p and q for all the items of a test (obtained through actual administration on a group), 'the number of items in a test (K), and also the variance (s^h which is the square of the standard deviation of the scores in the whole test when administered), then the reliability 'r' of the test can be calculated using the following formula;

$$r = \frac{k}{k-1}\left(1 - \frac{\Sigma pq}{s^2}\right)$$

Assessing Validity and Objectivity: Estimation of validity was discussed along with the theoretical discussions, presented earlier. Objectivity will have to be assessed by looking at the format procedures for administration, scoring etc.

Acceptable Levels of Reliability and Validity: Usually, high reliability coefficients are expected in tests, in order to classify then as reliable measuring instruments. Usually, reliability coefficients around 0.8 and above are required before a test and can be classified as a reliable instrument. But with respect to validity, we have to accept a lower co-efficiency. We have to interpret them meaningfully before they are selected. Even low coefficients will have to be treated as low when a test of intelligence is correlated with another test of indigence. In this case, we may look for higher coefficients of say 0.4 to 0.6. But if the intelligence test is validated against teacher rating, we must be willing to accept a smaller coefficient of say 0.3.

Every standardized test will usually have a 'manual of instructions' which contains all the details regarding scoring, validity, reliability etc.

The instructions and data given in the test manuals are used for deciding the reliability of a research instrument.

Scales

The instrument with the help of which a concept is measured is called a scale. A scale has a wide range of application in social science research. It is used in all types of data collection techniques such as observation, interview, projective techniques, etc. Broadly, there are two types of scales—rating scales and attitude scales.

Rating Scale

In rating scale, the rater makes a judgment about some characteristic of a subject and places him directly on some point on the scale. These scales can be either discrete or continuous.

Discrete Scales: These scales are used for raising ordinal data about an object. In these scales, two or more categories are provided representing discrete amounts of some characteristic. The rater can tick the category which he feels best describes the person of object being rated. Thus, for example, the characteristic 'job knowledge' may be divided into five categories on a discrete scale, as follows:

Exceptionally good,
Above average,
Average,
Below average, and
Poor.

Continuous of Graphic Scales: These scales are used for raising interval data about an object. In these scales just above the category nation, an uninterrupted line is provided and the rater can tick anywhere along its length.

Both types of rating scales can use three kinds of standards for measuring a characteristic: numerical or alphabetical, descriptive and behavior-sample.

In numerical standards, a series of numbers is provided which is supposed to indicate varying amounts of the characteristic being rated. For example, on a scale ranging from zero to ten, sometimes zero is the value assigned to an average ability with a series of positive numbers indicating superior degrees of the characteristic and a series of negative numbers indicating inferior degrees. Similar to numerical standards are those in which letters are used as standards. In a five category scale, the highest category might be A and the lowest E.

In descriptive-adjective standards, a series of descriptive adjectives such as exceptional, superior, good, competent, satisfactory, adequate, average, ordinary, fair, weak, poor, etc. are used to indicate varying amounts of the characteristics being rated.

Attitude Scales

Attitude scales are a carefully constructed sets of rating scales designed to measure one or more aspects of an individual's or group's attitude towards some object. The individual's responses to the various scales may be aggregated or summed to prove a single attitude for the individual. Or, more commonly, the responses to each scale item or sub-group of scale items may be examined independently of the other scale items.

We hereby describe below four types of these scales:

1. Likert's Summarted Scale;
2. Thurstone's Equal Appearing Intervals Scale;
3. Guttman's Cumulative Scale; and
4. Osgood's Semantic Differential Scale.

Summated Rating Scale: A summated rating scale is a set of attitude statements all of which are considered of approximately equal 'attitude value' and to each of which subjects respond with degrees of agreement or disagreement (intensity) carrying different scores. These scores are summed or summed and averaged to yield an individual's attitude score. We can understand the procedure for the construction of this scale with the help of an example. Let us suppose that we desire to rank individuals with respect to their attitude towards the authorities. For this purpose, we choose the following five statements each for which has only two answers—agree and disagree. The respondents have to say either agree or disagree in their answers to each statement. We may score the answer by giving one for each agree and zero for each disagree as illustrated below.

Statement	Agree	Disagree
1. Obedience and respect for authority are most important virtues children should learn.	1	0
2. An insult to our honour should always be punished.	1	0
3. Familiarity breeds contempt.	1	0
4. What the youth needs most is strict discipline, rugged determination and the will to work and fight for the family and the country.	1	0
5. A person who has bad manners, habits and breeding can hardly expect to get along with decent people	1	0

Each respondent's ranking relation to one another is found out by totaling his seconds on all the five statements. Thus, an individual who disagrees on all statements will have a score of zero.

The most frequently used form of summated scale is the Likert scale. This scale usually has 15 statements. The respondent is asked to respond to each statement in terms of 5 degrees of agreement or disagreement, for example, "strongly agree", "agree", "undecided", "disagree" and "strongly disagree". Each statement thus becomes a scale in itself having five points on it. At one end of this scale is strong disapproval and between them lies the intermediate points. The subject indicates with references to each statement where he stands on this scale. The total of this score on all statements is taken as the measurement of his attitude.

Of the total number of statements included in the questionnaire nearly half are those which are favourable and the other half those which are unfavourable. For the favourable statements the value given to "strongly agree", "agree", "undecided", "disagree" and "strongly disagree" are 5, 4, 3, 2, and 1 respectively. For unfavorable statements, the values are 1, 2, 3, 4, and 5 respectively. Thus, agreement with favourable statements and disagreement with unfavorable statements are treated as equivalent. The following example will make it clear:

Statement	Strongly Agree	Agree	Undecided	Disagree	Strongly Disagree
Religion is an enemy of science and truth.	5	4	3	2	1
Religion is needed to overcome the	1	2	3	4	5

tendency to individualism and selfishness.					

This scale is not cluttered up with irrelevant statements. It includes only those statements which have the ability to discriminate among persons with favorable and unfavorable attitudes. Knowledge about the discriminate ability of each statement is gathered by first administering a large number of statements (usually at least 0) to all small sample of subjects (at least 100) representative of those to whom the questionnaire is to be finally administered. Statements to what types of persons—those with favorable attitude and those with better discriminative power are retained. This procedure, known as item analysis, rests on the proposition that there should be consistency in the response pattern of any individual. If the individual has a very favorable attitude towards the object, he should basically agree with the favorable statements and disagree with the unfavorable ones and vice-versa. If we happen to have a statement that generates a very mixed response, we would tend to question it on the grounds that it must be ambiguous or at the very best not discriminatory of the attitude.

One very common way of performing an item analysis to ascertain which statement is discriminatory and which is not, is to proceed as follows:

First of all, subjects are divided into two arbitrarily defined groups. For example, those subjects with the top 25 percent of all total scores may be considered to have the most favorable attitudes and those with the lowest 25 percent of all total scores may be considered to have the least favorable attitudes.

Next, the mean score for each statement is calculated separately in the two groups. The following table illustrates this on the basis of assumed responses of 50 subjects from each group.

Calculation of Means for One Statement for the Two Groups with the Most Favorable and the Least Favorable Attitudes

Response category	Scale Value X	High F	Group GX	Low F	Group FX
Strongly Agree	5	28	140	2	10
Agree	4	14	56	6	24
Neither Agree nor Disagree	3	6	18	18	54
Disagree	2	2	4	20	40
Strongly Disagree	1	0	0	4	4
Sums		50	218	50	132

Next, the difference of the two mean scores is calculated in respect of each statement. For example, it is 1.72 in the table above.

Finally, all statements are ranked according to their difference in the mean scores. Those with mean differences near zero are considered poor and therefore eliminated. The statement in the above example is a discriminating one since the difference in its case is a positive one.

Equal-Appearing Interval Scale: Known after the name of its inventor (L. L. Thurstone), this scale consists of 15 to 20 statements which form a continuum of attitudes towards a subject ranging from the most favorable to the least favorable. The steps involved in the construction of this scale are as follows:

1. First of all the researcher is required to generate a large number of statements (Thurstone used 130 statements) expressing attitudes about a particular issue from search of the literature, discussions with knowledgeable people, personal experience or in any of the other ways one uses to develop insight in to a phenomenon.

   The important thing is at this stage is that the statements be as exhaustive as possible; that is they reflect all the attributes of the object which may lead to formation of attitudes about it. Further, they should be in such a form that they can be endorsed or rejected in terms of a definitely expressed attitude. Thus, a bank interested in knowing about its image in the public may develop a number of statements relating to its service, location, timings, interest rates, etc.

Next, two types of slips are prepared:

–slips bearing each statement, and

-slips bearing letters a to k (11 in all).

2. Some individuals are selected as judges. Each judge is given one set of each type of slips. He is not asked to arrange the 11 alphabet slips before him in sequence and sort the statement slips into 11 piles represented by these alphabet slips. On slip A, he must put those statement slips which express the most unfavourable attitude towards the concept being measured. On slip F (the middle on) he must put those slips which express neutral statement and on slip K he must put those which express most favourable attitude towards the concept. On the rest of the alphabet slips, he must arrange statement slips according to the degree of favour and disfavor expressed in them. Note that the judges are not asked whether they agree or disagree with a statement, but rather they are asked to evaluate the statement on its own merits. The presumption is that each will perceive the categories as representing equal increments of favourableness, and thus, the name equal appearing intervals.
3. The researcher is now to find out a scale value for each statement. This is done by finding out for each statement the median of different values which the group of judges has assigned to it. For this purpose, each pile is considered a part of the continuous scale with values as shown below.

Pile	A	B	C	D	E	F	G
Assigned value	1	2	3	4	5	6	7

Continuous value	0.5-1.5	1.5-2.5	2.5-3.5	3.5-4.5	4.5-5.5	5.5-6.5	6.5-7.5

Take for example pile B. Although 2 is assigned to this category, the categories is assumed to reflect all values from 1.5-2.5. Thus, if there are 50 ratings of the 25th judge) it would lie in the group 1.5-2.5.

Pile	Value	No. of Judges (f)
A	0.5 -0.5	9
B	1.5 – 2.5	18
C	2.5 – 3.5	13
D	3.5 – 4.5	6
E	4.5 – 5.5	4

By interpolation one can arrive at the median value. It is 2.4. Thus, 2.4 becomes the scale value of the statement in question.

In this way, the median values will be calculated for all the statements and they will cover the full range of positions from 1 to 11.

1. It is now necessary to select from the total number of statements some 15 to 20 statements for inclusion in the final scale. The researcher selects only those statements in respect of whose placement there is least disagreement among the judges. This is known by calculating the interquartile range (Q_3–Q_1) for every statement. The smaller the value of interquartile range, the more worthy is the statement of inclusion in the final scale because greater is the consistency in the opinion of the judges with regard to the statement. The researcher finally selects 15 to 20 statements which span the whole scale and also have the smallest interquartile range.
2. The scale thus prepared can be administered to the subjects to measure their attitude. The subjects are asked to check only those statements with which they agree. The scale values are not shown on the schedule and the statements

are usually arranged in random order. A subject's score is equal to the average of the scale values attached to the items he endorses. This average may be either be median or the mean, though the latter is more generally employed. Thus, if the subjects agree with three statements with the scale score of 8.2, 8.7, and 9.8, the person's attitude score would be 8.9 since the value 6 represents the neutral attitude. The conclusion would be that the subject added a favorable attitude towards the issue in the questions.

Cumulative Scale

After the name of its inventor Louis Guttmann, this scale is also known as Guttmann's scale. It is made up of relatively small number of statements which have been tested for their unidimensionality. A one-dimensional scale measures one variable and one variable only. The scale gets its name from the cumulative relation between statements in which persons agreeing with most favorable statement are theoretically presumed to agree with all other statements expressing 'lesser' degrees of favorability. This can be made clear with the help of an example taken from a broader social distance scale which is also a cumulative scale. Suppose in a study of attitudes towards English people, subjects are asked to tick those of the following relationships which they would like the English people to be admitted to:

Close kinship by marriage,
Club membership,
Next door neighbourhood,
Employment in the same occupation,
Citizenship of country,
Entry as tourist only, and
Would exclude from my country.

In the above scale, it is reasonable to expect the respondent who ticks off C (i.e. who indicates his willingness to have English people as his neighbours) would ordinarily tick off D and E i.e. he would also accept them as employees in his occupation and as citizens in his country. But he would not tick off F and G because these are statements denoting exclusion. If an individual does not tick off C then it is reasonable to expect that he will not tick off A and B since these are statements indicating even closer relationship (marriage or friendship) compared to C (neighborhood).

Semantic Differential Scale

This scale has been developed by Osgood and his colleagues. In this scale, a series of bipolar 3 to 7 point rating scales are used. The ends of each scale are described by adjectives which are a polar opposite. Respondents are asked to place a check mark in one of the spaces on each scale to indicate their rating. To counter attack the bias due to response set, the position of the poles is changed between scales. Thus, for instance, one scale may run 'good' to 'bad' from left to right while another may run from 'dishonest' to 'honest'. A respondent's total score is the measure of his attitude. Thus, the semantic differential scale, like a Likert scale is a summated rating scale; however, while with Likert scaling there is a range of statements but typically only one standard form of response (strongly agree, agree, etc.), with the Semantic Differential there is a range of areas of response but only one issue to evaluate a common application of this scale is to develop comparative profiles of various competitive brands of a good in a market research enquiry. Thus, for comparing the images of different car models one might for instance employ scales such as 'comfortable-uncomfortable', 'safe-unsafe', 'expensive-cheap', and so on.

Self-assessment Questions

1. What is meant by measurement? What measurement components can exist in any specific measurement?
2. What is nominal, ordinal, interval and ratio measurement? How statistics can be used with each type of measurement?

3. What is meant by the reliability and validity of a measurement? Describe the various techniques available to assess each.
4. As a researcher, what are the indicators of a measurement? Describe the various techniques available?
5. Describe the advantage and imitations of the following scale:
   Summated Tings Scale.
   Equal Appearing Interval Scale.
   Cumulative Scale.
6. Describe how the following scales are constructed:
   Likert Scale.
   Thurstone's Scale.
7. Suggest a suitable scale for measuring the attitude of workers towards their job and work environment.

Bibliography

Bibliography

Ackoff, Russell L., The Design of Social Research, Chicago: University of Chicago Press, 1961.

Ackoff, Russell L., Scientific Method, New York: John Wiley and Sons, 1962.

Allen, T. Harrell, New Methods in Social Science Research, New York: Praeger Publishers, 1978.

Anderson, H. H., and Anderson, G. L., An Introduction to Projective Techniques and Other Devices for Understanding the Dynamics of Human Behaviour, New York: Prentice Hall, 1951.

Anderson, T.W., An Introduction to Multivariate Analysis, New York: John Wiley and Sons, 1958.

Bailey, Kenneth D., Methods of Social Research, New York, 1978.

Baker, R.P., and Howell, A.C., The Preparation of Reports, New York: Ronald Press, 1938.

Bartee, T.C., Digital Computer Fundamentals, 5th ed., McGraw-Hill, International Book Co., 1981.

Barzun, Jacques, and Graff, H. R., The Modern Researcher, rev. ed., New York: Harcourt, Brace and World, Inc., 1970.

Bell, J.E., Projective Techniques: A. Dynamic Approach to the Study of Personality, New York: Longmans Green, 1948.

Bellenger, Danny N., and Greenberg, Barnett A., Marketing Research - A Management Information Approach, Homewood, Illinois: Richard D. Irwin, Inc., 1978.

Berdie, Douglas R., and Anderson, John F., Questionnaires: Design and Use, Metuchen N.J.: The Scarecrow Press, Inc., 1974.

Berelson, Bernard, Content Analysis in Communication Research, New York: Free Press, 1952.

Berenson, Conard, and Colton, Raymond, Research and Report Writing for Business and Economics, New York: Random House, 1971.

Best, John W., and Kahn, James V., Research in Education, 5th ed., New Delhi: Prentice-Hall of India Pvt. Ltd., 1986.

Bhattacharya, Srinibas, Psychdmetrics and Behavioural Research, New Delhi: Sterling Publishers Pvt. Ltd., 1972.

Boot, John C.G., and Cox, Edwin B., Statistical Analysis for Managerial Decisions, 2nd ed., New Delhi: McGraw-Hill Publishing Co. Ltd., (International Student Edition), 1979.

Bowley, A.L., Elements of Statistics, 6th ed. London: P.S. King and Staples Ltd., 1937.

Burgess, Ernest W., "Research Methods in Sociology", in Georges Gurvitch and W.E. Moore (ed.), Twentieth Century Sociology, New York: New York Philosophical Library, 1949.

Chance, William A., Statistical Methods for Decision Making, Bombay; D.B. Taraporevala Sons and Co Pvt. Ltd., 1975.

Chaturvedi, J.C., Mathematical Statistics, Agra: Nok Jhonk Karyalaya, 1953.

Chou, Ya-Lun, Statistical Analysis with Business, and Economic Applications, 2nd ed. New York: Holt, Rinehart and Winston, 1974.

Clover, Vernon T., and Balsley, Howard L., Business Research Methods, Columbus, O.: Grid, Inc., 1974.

Cochran, W.G, Sampling Techniques, 2nd ed. New York: John Wiley and Sons, 1963.

Cooley, William W, and Lohnes, Paul R., Multivariate Data Analysis, New York: John Wiley and Sons, 1971.

Croxton, F.E., Cowden, D.J., and Klein, S., Applied General Statistics, 3rd ed., New Delhi: Prentice-Hall of India Pvt. Ltd., 1975.

Dass, S.L., Personality Assessment through Projective Movie Pictures, New Delhi: S. Chand and Co. Pvt. Ltd., 1974.

Davis, G.B., Introduction to Computers, 3rd ed., McGraw-Hill International Book Co., 1981.

Deming, W. Edwards, Sample Design in Business Research, New York: John Wiley and Sons, 1960.

Dennis, Child, The Essentials of Factor Analysis, New York: Holt, Rinehart and Winston, 1973.

Denzin, Norman, The Research Act, Chicago: Aldine, 1973.

Edwards, Allen, Statistical Methods, 2nd ed., New York: Holt, Rinehart and Winston, 1967.

Edwards, Allen L., Techniques of Attitude Scale Construction, New York: Appleton-Century-Crofts, 1957.

Emory, C. William, Business Research Methods, Illinois: Richard D. Irwin, Inc., Homewood, 1976.

Ferber, Robert (ed.), Handbook of Marketing Research, New York: McGraw-Hill, Inc., 1948.

Ferber, R., and Verdoorn, P.J., Research Methods in Economics and Business, New York: The Macmillan Company, 1962.

Ferguson, George A., Statistical Analysis in Psychology and Education, 4th ed., New York: McGraw-Hill Book Co., Inc., 1959.

Festinger, Leon and Katz, Daniel (eds.), Research Methods in Behavioral Sciences, New Delhi: Amerind Publishing Co. Pvt. Ltd., Fourth Indian Reprint, 1976.

Fiebleman, J.K., Scientific Methods, Netherlands: Martinus Nijhoff, The Hague, 1972.

Fisher, R.A., Statistical Methods for Research Workers, 13th ed., New York: Hafner Publishing Co., 1958.

Fisher, R.A., The Design of Experiments, 7th rev. ed., New York: Hafner Publishing Co., 1960.

Fox, James Harold, Criteria of Good Research, Phi Delta Kappa, Vol. 39 (March 1958).

Freedman,P, The Principles of Scientific Research, 2nd ed., New York: Pergamon Press, 1960.

Fruchter, Benjamin, Introduction to Factor Analysis, Princeton, N.J.: D. Van Nostrand, 1954.

Gatner, Elliot S.M., and Cordasco, Francesco, Research and Report Writing, New York: Barnes and Noble Inc., 1956.

Gaum, Carl G., Graves, Harod F., and Hoffman, Lyne, S.S., Report Writing, 3rd ed., New York: Prentice-Hall, 1950.

Ghosh, B.N., Scientific Methods and Social Research, New Delhi: Sterling Publishers Pvt. Ltd., 1982.

Gibbons, J.D., Nonparametric Statistical Inference, Tokyo: McGraw-Hill Kogakusha Ltd., (International Student Edition), 1971.

Giles, G.B., Marketing, 2nd ed., London: Macdonald and Evans Ltd., 1974.

Glock, Charles Y., Survey Research in the Social Sciences, New York: Russell Sage Foundation, 1967.

Godfrey, Arthur, Quantitative Methods for Managers, London: Edward Arnold (Publishers) Ltd., 1977.

Good, Carter V., and Douglas, E. Scates, Methods of Research-Educational, Psychological, Sociological, New York: Appleton-Century-Crofts, Inc., 1954.

Goode, William J., and Hatt, Paul K., Methods in Social Research, New York: McGraw-Hill, 1952.

Gopal, M. H., An Introduction to Research Procedure in Social Sciences, Bombay: Asia Publishing House, 1964.

Gopal, M. H., Research Reporting in Social Sciences, Dharwad: Karnatak University, 1965.

Gorden, Raymond L., Interviewing: Strategy, Techniques and Tactics, rev. ed., Homewood, 111: Dorsey Press, 1975.

Green, Paul E., Analyzing Multivariate Data, Hinsdale, 111: Dryden Press, 1978.

Green, Paul E., and Carmone, F.J., Multidimensional Scaling in Marketing Analysis, Boston: Allyn and Bacon, Inc., 1970.

Guilford, J.P., Psychometric Methods, New York: McGraw-Hill, Inc., 1954.

Harnett, Donald L., and Murphy, James L., Introductory Statistical Analysis, Philippines: Addison-Wesley Publishing Co., Inc., 1975.

Hillway, T., Introduction to Research, 2nd ed., Boston: Houghton Mifflin, 1964.

Hollander, Myles, and Wolfe, Douglas A., Nonparametric Statistical Methods, New York: John Wiley, 1973.

Hunt, R., and Shelley, J., Computers and Common Sense, 3rd ed., New Delhi: Prentice-Hall of India Ltd., 1984.

Hyman, Herbert H., et al., Interviewing in Social Research, Chicago: University of Chicago Press, 1975.

John, Peter W. M., Statistical Design and Analysis of Experiments, New York: The Macmillan Co., 1971.

Johnson, Ellen, The Research Report: A Guide for the Beginner, New York: Ronald Press, 1951.

Johnson, Rodney D., and Siskin, Bernard R., Quantitative Techniques for Business Decisions, New Delhi: Prentice-Hall of India Pvt. Ltd., 1977.

Kahn, Robert L. and Cannell, Charles F, The Dynamics of Interviewing, New York: John Wiley and Sons, 1957.

Karson, Marvin J., Multivariate Statistical Methods, Ames, Iowa: The Iowa State University Press, 1982.

Kendall, M.G., A Course in Multivariate Analysis, London, Griffin, 1961.

Kerlinger, Fred N. and Pedhazur, Elazar J., Multiple Regression in Behavioral Research, New York: Holt, Rinehart and Winston, 1973.

Kerlinger, Fred N., Foundations of Behavioral Research, 2nd ed., New York: Holt, Reinhart and Winston, 1973.

Kish, Leslie, Survey Sampling, New York: John Wiley and Sons, Inc., 1965.

Kothari, C.R., Quantitative Techniques, 2nd ed., New Delhi: Vikas Publishing House Pvt. Ltd., 1984.

Lastrucci, Carles L., The Scientific Approach: Basic Principles of the Scientific Method, Cambridge, Mass.: Schenkman Publishing Co., Inc., 1967.

Lazersfeld, Paul F, Evidence and Inference in Social Research, in David Lerher, Evidence and Inference, Glencoe: The Free Press, 1950.

Leonard Schatzman, and Anselm L. Strauss, Field Research, New Jersey: Prentice-Hall Inc., 1973.

Levin, Richard I., Statistics for Management, New Delhi: Prentice-Hall of India Pvt. Ltd., 1979.

Levine, S. and Elzey, Freeman F., A Programmed Introduction to Research, California: Woods Worth Publishing Co., 1968.

Maranell, Gary M. (ed.), Scaling: A Source Book for Behavioral Scientists, Chicago: Aldine, 1974.

Maxwell, Albert E., Analyzing Qualitative Data, New York: John Wiley and Sons, 1961.

Meir, Robert C, Newell, William T., and Dazier, Harold L., Simulation in Business and Economics, Englewood Cliffs, N.J: Prentice Hall, Inc., 1969.

Miller, Delbert C, Handbook of Research Design and Social Measurement, 3rd ed., New York: David Mckay Company, Inc., 1977.

Moroney, M., Facts from Figures, Baltimore: Penguin Books, 1956.

Morrison, Donald F, Multivariate Statistical Methods, New York: McGraw-Hill, 1967.

Nagel, Stuart S., and Neef, Marian, Policy Analysis in Social Science Research, London: Sage Publications, 1979.

Nie, N. H., Bent, D. H., and Hull, C. H., Statistical Package for the Social Sciences, New York: McGraw-Hill, 1970.

Noether, G.E., Elements of Nonparametric Statistics, New York: John Wiley and Sons, Inc., 1967.

Nunnally, Jum C., Psychometric Theory, 2nd ed., New York: McGraw-Hill, 1978.

Odum, H.W., and Jocher, Katharine, An Introduction to Social Research, New York: Henry Holt and Co., 1929.

Oppenheim, A. N., Questionnaire Design and Attitude Measurement, New York: Basic Books, 1966.

Ostle, Bernard, and Mensing, Richard W., Statistics in Research, 3rd ed., Ames Iowa: The Iowa State University Press, 1975.

Payne, Stanley, The Art of Asking Questions, Princeton: Princeton University Press, 1951.

Pearson, Karl, The Grammar of Science, New York: Meridian Books, Inc., 1957.

Phillips, Bernard S., Social Research, Strategy and Tactics, 2nd ed., New York: The Macmillan Company, 1971.

Piaget, Jean, Main Trends in Interdisciplinary Research, London: George Allen and Unwin Ltd., 1973.

Popper, Karl R., The Logic of Scientific Discovery, New York: Basic Books, 1959.

Rajaraman, V., Fundamentals of Computers, New Delhi: Prentice-Hall of India Pvt. Ltd., 1985.

Ramchandran, P., Training in Research Methodology in Social Sciences in India, New Delhi: ICSSR 1971.

Redman, L.V., and Mory, A. V. H., The Romance of Research, 1923.

Roscoe, John T, Fundamental Research Statistics for the Behavioral Sciences, New York: Holt, Rinehart and Winston, Inc., 1969.

Runyon, Richard P., Inferential Statistics, Philippines: Addison-Wesley Publishing Company, Inc., 1977.

Sadhu, A. N., and Singh, Amarjit, Research Methodology in Social Sciences, Bombay: Himalaya Publishing House, 1980.

Seboyar, G.E., Manual for Report and Thesis Writing, New York: F.S. Crofts and Co., 1929.

Selltiz, Claire: Jahoda, Marie, Deutsch, Morton, and Cook, Stuart W., Research Methods in Social Relations, rev. ed. New York: Holt, Rinehart and Winston, Inc., 1959.

Sharma, B.A.V., et al., Research Methods in Social Sciences, New Delhi: Sterling Publishers Pvt. Ltd., 1983.

Sharma, H.D., and Mukherji, S.P., Research in Economics and Commerce, Methodology and Surveys, Varanasi: Indian Biographic Centre, 1976.

Siegel, S., Nonparametric Statistics for the Behavioral Sciences, New York: McGraw-Hill Publishing Co. Inc., 1956.

Subramanian, N., Introduction to Computers, New Delhi: Tata McGraw-Hill Publishing Co. Ltd., 1986.

Summers, Gene R, (ed.), Attitude Measurement, Chicago: Rand McNally and Co., 1970.

Takeuchi, K., Yanai, H. and Mukherjee, B.N., The Foundations of Multivariate Analysis, New Delhi: Wiley Eastern Ltd., 1982.

Tandon, B.C., Research Methodology in Social Sciences, Allahabad: Chaitanya Publishing House, 1979.

Thorndike, Robert L. and Hagen, Elizabeth P., Measurement and Evaluation in Psychology and Education, 4th ed., New York: John Wiley and Sons, 1977.

Thurstone, L.L., The Measurement of Values, Chicago: University of Chicago Press, 1959.

Torgerson, W, Theory and Methods of Scaling, New York: John Wiley and Sons, 1958.

Travers, Robert M. W, An Introduction to Educational Research, 4th ed., New York: Macmillan Publishing Co., Inc., 1978.

Tryon, R.C., and Bailey, D.E., Cluster Analysis, New York: McGraw-Hill, 1970.

Ullman, Neil R., Elementary Statistics, New York: John Wiley and Sons Inc., 1978. .

Whitney, F.L., The Elements of Research, 3rd ed., New York: Prentice-Hall, 1950.

Wilkinson, T.S. and Bhandarkar, P.L., Methodology and Techniques of Social Research, Bombay: Himalaya Publishing House, 1979.

Willemsen, Eleanor Walker, Understanding Statistical Reasoning, San Francisco: W.H. Freeman and Company, 1974.

Yamane, T, Statistics: An Introductory Analysis, 3rd ed., New York: Harper and Row, 1973.

Young, Pauline V., Scientific Social Surveys and Research, 3rd ed., New York: Prentice-Hall, 1960.

Index

Index